Contents

G

H

I

Q

R

S

T

Introduction

In the previous volume, The Serious Joke Book, we banned the rude, the racist and the blasphemous due to a false notion of sensitivity. In a blow for free speech they are resurrected in this volume.

You have heard the stories about the Englishman, the Scotsman and the Irishman; and you always will, for these jokes are as old as the language itself. Now we have listed the best to include the Greeks, Germans, French, Italians, Turks, Russians, Chinese, Japanese, Vietnamese, New Zealanders, English and the Australians.

It seems all nations have their fall guys, and usually the butt of their jokes is the inhabitants of the country next door. In the United States a few years ago a Pole gained notoriety by entering bookshops and ripping out pages of Polish jokes from a magazine. He left the Jewish, Irish and Italian sections because they didnt offend him; a statement in itself. This author takes the view that nationalism, like patriotism, is the last refuge of scoundrels and therefore should not be protected. The best way to break down ethnic barriers is to laugh at ourselves and anyone else who takes jingoistic nationalism too far. So read them while you can. And if you are a Scot then you are quite at liberty to re-tell the joke and call Jock an Irishman.

Jokes can heal as well as wound. In Australia Greek and Italian migrants are accepted. The last wave of arrivals to bear the brunt of discrimination are Vietnamese boat people. A Vietnamese comedian, Hung Le, is smashing through this prejudice by telling jokes and is the most unlikely comedian for the pub circuit. He tells his audience he was excited to find a hot dog stand when he arrived in Australia, but his elation turned to disgust when he took a closer look.

"Thats the only bit of the dog we dont eat," he said.

Religion gets a belting in this edition too. In earlier times when blasphemy was a capital offence, most of the jokes in this volume would have had the authors balls burned at the stake. Today one can get away with it. Thanks to the English church and its notorious proclivity for extra-mural activities such as bishops dropping their breeches, deans dressing in drag, transvestite vicars and other eccentric ecclesiastics, the church has become a legitimate butt of ridicule.

"I'll be buggered if I'll be a bishop," said the curate.

The Roman Catholic church is also in disarray with a legion of priests and brothers following their carnal calling. Meanwhile the succession of American television evangelists and fundamentalists who have embezzled profits to pursue sins of the flesh have evidently checked the dictionary to learn that fundament means buttocks. It is hoped that the ribald jokes deflate the pompous and cause the Church to suffer in dignified silence.'

As for the ribald jokes that are just plain rude, the Kama Sutra has been around for centuries, proving that sex is here to stay, and while there are many ways of doing it, there are also many ways of laughing at it.

A

ACCIDENTS

FRED pulled out to avoid a child, fell off the sofa and strained his ankle.

* * *

REMEMBER, ninety per cent of the population was caused by accident.

* * *

SIGN in the Family Planning Agency's car park: "Be Careful when Pulling Out."

* * *

THE inspector at the bus terminal was checking schedules with the drivers: "What time did you pull out this morning?"

Murphy: "I didn't. And I'm worried about it."

* * *

THE Hare Krishna rushed in to tell the priest:

"My karma has run over your dogma."

* * *

ONE car had stopped at the lights, the second ran into its rear with the tinkle of broken headlights. The odd thing was that the first car was driven by a vicar and the second by a priest. They were arguing about the blame when the police arrived on the scene.

"How fast would you say he was going," interjected Sergeant O'Flaherty, "when he backed into you, Father?"

THE truck driver couldn't believe his eyes. When he rounded the bend there, at the bottom of the hill, was a couple making love in the middle of the road.

He blew the horn. They didn't stop screwing.

The truck finally screeched to a halt barely a hair's breadth from the humping couple.

The driver got out and demanded an explanation: "What the bloody hell is going on?"

When the young man recovered he stood up. "I was coming. She was coming. You were coming," he said, "and you were the only one that had brakes."

*   *   *

FARMER Brown lost control of his jalopy on the bend and ended up in the river. He managed to climb out and scramble on top of the car to await rescue.

He heard one car stop. It was his neighbours, Mr and Mrs Jones. Then a second car arrived with more neighbours, Mr and Mrs Ball.

As Bill Jones pulled him to safety Farmer Brown said: "I'm glad you got here first Bill. I'd hate to be pulled out by the balls."

*   *   *

IN a factory accident a worker lost two fingers. But he didn't notice the loss until he was saying goodnight to the boss.

*   *   *

A SCOT bought a round of drinks at the pub the other night. He has asked police to appeal for witnesses to the accident.

*   *   *

THE cop arrived at the scene of the accident to find a couple bonking their heart out on the nature strip.

"My fault," said the blonde when the cop pulled her off the recovering victim.

"I was giving him mouth to mouth resuscitation when we both got carried away."

AFTER the car skidded into the tree the first man on the scene found the driver still behind the wheel, dazed and bleeding.

"How badly are you hurt?" he enquired.

"How the hell should I know," muttered the driver. "I'm a doctor not a lawyer."

* * *

TEN per cent of all accidents are caused by drivers affected by alcohol.

Which is another way of saying 90 per cent of accidents are caused by non-drinkers.

* * *

A BUSINESSMAN returned to his parked car to find the headlights broken and damage to the front end. Stuck under the windscreen wiper he found a note which read:

"Hey, man. I just backed into your car. The folks that saw the accident are nodding in approval because they think I am writing down my name and other particulars, but I aint."

* * *

IT was a nasty accident. A woman who swallowed a razor blade was rushed to the emergency ward. After an X-ray the doctors decided to let it take its natural course.

A few months later she eventually passed the razor blade, but in the meantime she had not only given herself a tonsillectomy, an appendectomy and a hysterectomy but had also castrated her husband, circumcised his best friend, given the vicar a hare lip and cut the finger of a passing acquaintance.

* * *

THE woman at the cocktail party was intent on making the acquaintance of the young medical officer.

"Do you deal with many accidents?" she asked.

"I really don't know," he replied.

"But you are a doctor, what do you mean you don't know?"

3

"How could I," he said. "My field is obstetrics."

ADVERTISEMENTS

BY-SEXUAL man aged 40 seeks young married couple.

* * *

LOST. Antique cameo brooch depicting Adam and Eve in St Killed Saturday night.

* * *

ADVERTISEMENT in a tourist guide: Accommodation, Bed & Breakfast, $60. Mrs Frampton, $80.

* * *

FOR Sale: Complete set of Encyclopaedia Britannica. Never been opened. Wife knows everything.

* * *

LOST dog. Has three legs, blind in left eye, right ear missing, broken tail, no teeth, recently castrated. Answers to Lucky.

* * *

GIRL wanted for petrol pump attendant.

* * *

IT pays to advertise. A salesman found himself in a country town overnight where the only excitement appeared to be watching the clothes go round in the laundromat.

Out of sheer boredom he opened the Gideon Bible supplied in all motel rooms.

On the flyleaf was the message: "If thou art bored and lonely and desireth some warm comfort, ring Lulu, 580-6683.

ADVICE

THE doctor told the young man the reason for his depression was stress. "Take life easier," was the doc's advice. "Do you drink?"

"No," said the young man, "never have."

"There is no harm in a quiet drink," said the doctor, "even

4

a smoke to relax, and sex at least once a week. In fact, in your case it is essential."

Two months later the patient returned and was evidently in much better health. He told the doctor he enjoyed a glass of beer each night and had taken up the pipe.

"And sex?" asked the doctor.

"Hard to find it every week," admitted the patient, "especially for a parish priest in a small country town like this."

*   *   *

MURIEL was in a serious mood and asked her mother for advice. She was about to be married and the groom had come to stay with the family for the weekend during which time she had blundered into the bathroom and saw him naked.

"Mother," she said, "what was that thing hanging down between his legs?"

"They call it a penis my dear, nothing to worry about."

"And the knob on the end, like a fireman's helmet."

"Just the glans," said Mother.

"And there are two round things about 13 inches back from this glans. What are they?"

"For your sake, my dear," said Mum, "I hope they are the cheeks of his arse."

*   *   *

FRED had a problem and he confided in Jed because he was a little older.

"Problem is," said Fred, "I have a choice of two women. One is young and beautiful and I love her dearly. But she is broke. The other is an older woman, a widow and quite plain, but she is a millionaire. What should I do?"

It was no problem for Jed.

"Follow your heart," he said. "Marry the young girl you love. And give me the address of the widow."

ALCOHOLICS

AN alcoholic is a man who goes in to a topless bar for a drink.

*   *   *

THE difference between being a drunk and being an alcoholic is that the drunk doesn't have to bother attending all those boring meetings.

*   *   *

"WHY was alcohol invented?" asked one wino of another.

"So that ugly women could get laid too," said his mate.

ANIMALS

"ARE you an animal lover?"

"Well, my wife thinks so."

*   *   *

THE tortoise told the police she had been raped by two snails.

"Can you describe them?" asked the cop.

"No," she said, "it all happened so fast."

*   *   *

THE bi-sexual donkey had a hee in the morning and a haw at night.

*   *   *

A BEAR and a rabbit were sitting side by side having a crap in the woods.

The bear said, "Do you have any trouble with shit sticking to your fur?"

"No," said the rabbit.

With that the bear promptly picked up the rabbit and wiped his arse with him.

*   *   *

MIKE the Monk was having a quiet drink in the Animals

Bar when Mick the Mouse climbed up on the stool beside him.

"How did you go with that giraffe last night?" enquired the monk.

"What a night!" said the mouse, "I'll never take her out again. She's a nymphomaniac, and what with kissing her and screwing her I must have run a hundred miles last night."

* * *

LEO the lion was drinking from a stream with his bum in the air, just as a big chimp was passing. From the chimp's viewpoint it looked like Lily the lion so he crept up quietly and planted the sausage with a wallop.

The lion let out a mighty roar and the chimp took off like greased lightning. He sped through the jungle with the outraged lion in hot pursuit.

The chimp dashed into a hunter's camp, quickly donned a safari suit, snatched on a pith helmet, dived into a chair, grabbed a copy of The Times and hid behind it as if were reading.

The lion screeched into the clearing and as soon as the dust settled asked the "hunter."

"Have you seen a chimp dash past here?"

"Not the chimp that rooted the lion down by the stream?"

"Hell," said the lion, "don't tell me it's in the papers already."

ANNIVERSARIES

"I'M afraid I can't make the darts match tomorrow night, Fred. I promised to take Thingummy out for our silver anniversary."

* * *

ANNIVERSARIES are like toilet seats.

Men usually miss both.

7

ARMY

THE colonel was a rare drinker, but at the annual regimental dinner he ate too much food, drank too much wine and got the fright of his life when he was challenged to a duel.

His colleagues were quickly to the rescue and sent him home in a cab.

Next morning he had to explain to his batman why there was such a mess on his jacket. "Some bounder bumped into me and was sick all over my tunic. I'll give him a month's detention when I find him," he said.

The batman gathered up the clothes. "I'd make it two months, sir. The bastard has shit in your trousers, too,"

* * *

THE seat-belt sign switched off and the three men seated together settled down for a long flight.

The distinguished man in the middle began the introductions with himself: "General, Australian Army, married, two sons, both lawyers."

The second took the cue: "General, Artillery, married, two sons, one a surgeon the other a judge."

There was an embarrassing silence until the third responded, "Petty Officer, Australian Navy, never married, two sons, both generals."

* * *

A POSTING to the Far East was a plum reward for officers during the height of the British Empire so when Ponsonby won such a posting and had been established there for several months his wife eventually came out to join him.

With servants on hand the wife decided to sleep in on her very first morning, but around 9-30 the Chinese valet came in, whipped off the bedclothes, slapped her on the bum and said: "All light Missy, get your bleakfast then go home."

PRIVATE Murphy was on patrol in the jungle when he discovered a quiet pool by the edge of the river. He stripped off for a swim and was standing by the bank when a shot rang out.

He woke up in hospital.

"What happened?" he said to the medical team around him.

"Actually, to come to the point old man," said the chief medic, "a sniper's bullet has shot your balls off. Neatly off I might add. We just had to sew up the wound."

Murphy surveyed the damage.

"Could of been worse," he said. "Lucky I was thinking of me wife's younger sister when it happened."

* * *

IN the same hospital one of the soldiers had his head so swathed in bandages he could only be fed rectally, through a tube.

The nurse had just served his morning coffee when he began waving his arms around.

"What's up?" she said, "too hot?"

She bent down to hear his muffled response: "Too much sugar."

* * *

NEXT day the wife of the soldier with his head in bandages called to see how he was recovering.

"How is his appetite?" she asked.

"Terrific," said the orderly. "It would have done your heart good, ma'am, to see his arse snap at a piece of toast this morning."

* * *

THE young officer arrived at the India regiment and reported that he was eager for active service to defend the empire.

"Oh no, all that skirmishing stuff is over," said the colonel, "we have a different program now, old chap. Tomorrow is Tuesday, which means we play tennis."

9

"Oh, I don't play tennis," said the officer.

"Well then, Wednesday we play polo. You do play polo?"

"No sir."

"Hmmm," said the colonel, "Then Thursday we enjoy the regimental dance."

"I'm afraid I don't dance at all, sir."

"Then you will enjoy Fridays," said the colonel. "That's wife-swapping night. Lot's of sex and fun."

"Sir, I'm afraid I couldn't be part of anything like that," said the officer.

"Good gracious man," said the colonel. "You must be some kind of homosexual?"

"No, I certainly am not," replied the officer.

"Then you probably won't like Saturday nights either," said the colonel.

* * *

"DEAR Dad," said the letter from his soldier son, "I can't tell you where I am, but yesterday I shot a polar bear."

Two months later another letter arrived: "Dear Dad," it began. "I can't tell you where I am but yesterday I danced with a native girl."

Another month passed before the third letter: "Dear Dad. The doctor tells me I should have danced with the polar bear and shot the native girl."

* * *

FRED decided to dodge the call-up by being medically unfit. The easiest way, he decided, was to pull the last of his remaining teeth out. They wouldn't take a bloke with a completely gummy mouth.

Fred was third in line when a tough sergeant major began the examination.

"What's wrong with you?" he demanded of the first man.

"No teeth at all," was the reply.

The sergeant stuck his finger in the man's mouth and felt around. "You're right. You are no good to us."

Fred's spirits brightened when he heard that decision.

10

"And what's wrong with you?" said the sergeant to the second man.

"Piles, sir."

The sergeant stuck his finger up the man's bum, felt around and said: "Yes. You are no bloody good to us."

Turning to Fred he said: "And what's wrong with you?"

"Nothing at all," said Fred.

ARTS

A RENOWNED art critic named Flo
Was accosted a fortnight ago
When the flasher unzipped
She allegedly quipped
"An exhibit well hung sir, Good show."

*   *   *

THE celebrated eye surgeon had operated on the eyes of the ageing artist and fully restored his sight. In his everlasting gratitude the artist insisted on painting a large mural across the front of the hospital to honour the doctor.

When the surgeon saw the massive work depicting a large eyeball and massive lashes he was asked for his opinion of the work.

"I'd just like to say thank God I decided against being a gynaecologist," he said.

*   *   *

CURLY had a way with words which made him a winner with women. So when he scored the loveliest girl at the party his two mates followed and pressed their ears to the bedroom door.

"You've got a magnificent body," they heard him say. "It is so lovely that it should be captured on canvas and painted by a master."

Just then there was a knock on the door.

"Who's there?" asked Curly.

"Rembrandt and Reubens," came the reply.

11

"GOOD news," said the promotor to the artist. "I told a guy that paintings appreciate in value after the artist's death and he bought all your works."

"Who was it?" asked the artist.

"Your doctor," replied the promotor.

ASTRONAUTS

THE first Jewish astronaut was Nose Cohen.

* * *

THE first male and female astronauts landed on Mars and made scientific contact with the locals. The Martians showed how they made little Martians, by shaping little boys and girls out of plastic, putting them on a conveyor belt which went through an oven and produced little children at the other end.

"How do you make humans?" asked the Martian.

The astronauts removed their clothes and gave a perfect performance of sexual intercourse.

When they had finished the Martian said: "Well, where are the babies?"

"Oh, it takes nine months," said the Earthlings.

"Well why were you in such a hurry at the end?"

ATHEISTS

THE Atheists organised a dial-a-prayer service.

When you phone up, nobody answers.

* * *

A SINCERE Atheist is one who eats pork on Good Friday and wipes his bum with his right hand.

It's the only way he can insult three religions at once.

AUSTRALIANS

HE couldn't believe it himself, but there he was, shipwrecked with Miss Australia.

There would be no hanky-panky of course because he was a married man and she was too famous to have her reputation damaged. So they made a pact.

He said: "You stay this side of the island and I will keep to the other. We will meet in a week to check on provisions and rescue prospects." She agreed. But of course when they met a week later they were as horny as hell.

"We might never be rescued," he said, "so why don't we do it?"

They virtually tore each others clothes off and went at it hammer and tongs. In fact it was so good they promised each other to meet the next night, same time, same place.

"But could you do me a favour," said the Aussie.

"What's that?"

"Could you dress up as a man?" he said. "I have salvaged some shirts and trousers."

Miss Australia looked at him askance. "You're not kinky are you?"

"No. Nothing like that."

She reluctantly agreed. And next evening she was walking along the beach looking for all the world like a bloke when he fell into step beside her.

"G'day mate," he said slapping an arm around her shoulder. "You'll never guess who I fucked last night!"

*   *   *

A LION in the London Zoo was lazing in the sun and licking its arse when a visitor turned to the keeper and said, "that's a docile old thing isn't it?"

"No way," said the keeper, "it is the most ferocious beast in the zoo. Why just an hour ago it dragged an Australian tourist into the cage and completely devoured him."

"Hardly seems possible," said the astonished visitor, "but why is he lying there licking his arse?"

"The poor thing is trying to get the taste out of his mouth," said the keeper.

AN Englishman, a Scotsman and an Australian went for a job. The boss asked them all the same question: What is the capital of Ireland?"

"New York," said the Scot.

"No. It's Vancouver," said the Englishman.

"Fools," said the Australian, "anybody knows the capital of Ireland is Brussels."

The Australian got the job because he was closest.

* * *

WHEN their car broke down a Jew, an Indian and an Australian knocked on a farmer's door to ask for accommodation for the night.

"One will have to sleep in the barn," said the farmer.

"I will," said the Jew.

But five minutes later there was a knock on the door.

"There's a pig in the barn," said the Jew.

"Okay, I'll go," said the Indian.

Five minutes later there was a knock on the door.

"There is an un-sacred cow in the barn," he said.

"I'll go," said the Australian.

Five minutes later there was yet another knock on the door. It was the pig and the cow.

* * *

THERE was a young man from Australia
Who painted his arse like a dahlia
The drawing was fine, the colour divine
But the scent? Ar, that was a failure.

* * *

IN Sydney she was Rhonda
She was Patsy out in Perth
In Brisbane she was Brenda,
The sweetest girl on earth.
In Wagga she was Wendy
The pick of all the bunch,
But down on his expenses
She was petrol, oil and lunch.

14

THREE men and a woman were in the lift of Australias tallest building when the cable broke and they began plummeting towards certain death. The woman was a quick thinker . She looked at the three men and said: "Is there one more chance of being a woman?"

Only one had the presence of mind to whip his trousers off. He flung them at her and said:

"Here, iron these."

AVIATION

THE pilot's girlfriend hung on every word he said, and when he spotted an aircraft flying high overhead, he made the idle comment, "thats the mailplane."

She said: "Marvellous how you can tell from this distance."

* * *

IT had been an all-night flight and with the sun beginning to rise the crew switched on the cabin lights for breakfast.

"Who switched on those fucking lights?" said a male passenger who had made a constant nuisance of himself.

The hostess had had enough.

"These are the breakfast lights, sir," she said. "The fucking lights are much dimmer and you snored right through them."

* * *

THE aircraft was just about to take off when the door of the flight deck opened and the stark naked pilot dashed down the aisle with a microphone in his hand.

"This is your captian streaking," he said.

* * *

THE aircraft was on its final approach and the captain had announced landing time. However he left the PA system on and the next statement surprised the passengers.

"As soon as I clock off I'm going to have a nice cool beer and then screw the arse off that red-headed hostess."

The hostess was shocked and began a hurried dash to the flight deck but tripped over a suitcase.

A little old lady leant down. "No need to hurry dear," she advised, "he said he was going to have a beer first."

*   *   *

IT was the first time Harry had flown the modern wide-bodied jets equipped with the latest facilities. Even separate ladies' and gents' loos.

Finding the men's room occupied during a quiet section of the flight he thought he would slip into the Ladies. While sitting on the seat he noticed the array of buttons and pushed the one marked "WW". Immediately warm water was squirted on his bum. He pushed "PP" and was delighted to feel a powder puff gently tapping him dry.

Thrilled at the service he pushed the button marked "ATR". And and that's the last thing he remembered.

He woke up back in his seat looking up at the smiling faces of the hostesses.

"Christ, what happened?" he said.

"You pressed the Automatic Tampon Remover," said the hostess, "when you are able to walk you will find your penis waiting for you with the purser."

B

BACHELORS

EVERY man should have a girl for love, companionship and sympathy, said a wise and mature bachelor, "and preferably at three different addresses," he added.

BAKERS

PETE the Pastrycook was preparing apple pies and crimping the edges down a set of false teeth when the health inspector made a visit.

"Hey, haven't you a tool for that?"

"Yes," said Pete, "but I use it for putting the holes in the doughnuts."

*   *   *

THE sign out front declared it was the Hygiene Bakery, and indeed, Mrs Grump was delighted to be offered her loaf of bread on a long toasting fork.

"Untouched by human hands," said the baker.

Mrs Grump was impressed, but she noticed a piece of string hanging from the baker's trouser fly.

"What's that?" she asked.

"Part of the hygiene program," said the baker, "when I go for a leak I pull it out with the string, untouched by human hands."

"But how do you get it back?" asked Mrs Grump.

17

"With the fork," said the baker.

BALLS
THERE was a young Scot named McIvers
  Whose knackers were two different sizes
  One was so small
  'Twas no ball at all
  But the other won several first prizes.

* * *

TWO inquisistive old maids approached the giraffe enclosure at the zoo and were intrigued to find a pair of balls at eye-level.

"They're testicles alright," said one "and I reckon I could touch them from here." She reached through and squeezed one of the giraffe's coconuts.

The animal reacted in the normal manner, by jumping 20 metres into the air, clearing the enclosure fence and galloping out of the zoo.

The keeper dashed out and asked the startled old maids what had happened. When they explained he dropped his dacks.

"Here," he said, "you'd better squeeze mine because I have to catch the bastard."

* * *

A TOURIST went into a Madrid restaurant and asked for the speciality of the house. He was served a magnificent plate bearing two king-sized rissoles.

The tourist tucked in, found them to be delicious and called the waiter to express his appreciation.

"What do you call that dish?" asked the tourist wiping his lips with the napkin.

"They are gonads," said the Spanish waiter. He went on to explain that the gonads were the testicles of the bull killed in the adjoining bull ring that very day.

"Always fresh, senor," said the waiter.

It was quite a shock for the tourist, but he had to admit they were tasty, satisfying and cheap.

In fact, the very next evening he returned and asked for the same dish. When they were served he called the waiter back to complain about the size of the two miserable rissoles which sat forlorn and lonely in the centre of the plate.

"Yes, senor," agreed the waiter, "they are much smaller than yesterday, but today, the bull wins."

*　　*　　*

THERE are fancy dressed balls too, and dusky Rita went to such an event stark naked. But the doorman refused to let her in.

"You have to represent something," he said.

Rita returned wearing black gloves and shoes.

"I'm the five of spades," she said.

*　　*　　*

IT was a fancy dress ball with scores of lavish costumes but Lulu arrived stark naked.

"What do you represent?" asked the host.

"I'm Adam," she said.

He took a close look and said, "But you don't have a cock."

"I'll soon find one," she said.

*　　*　　*

NEXT to be admitted to the fancy dress ball was a stunning brunette in red stockings, thigh length boots, red suspenders and matching bra and panties.

"And what are you?" asked the host.

"I am Dying Embers," she said, "and if I don't get a poke soon I'm going out."

*　　*　　*

FRED got up to join the parade at the fancy dress ball wearing nothing but his underpants.

"What's this?" said the MC with his notebook, "You've got to represent something."

19

Fred insisted he did. He was Premature Ejaculation. After several attempts the MC admitted he was unable to spell it.

"Just say I came in my underpants," said Fred.

*   *   *

IF you have a green ball in your right hand and a green ball in your left, then you have Kermit the Frog's undivided attention.

*   *   *

WHY do dogs lick their balls?

Because they can.

BANANAS

DOCTOR Watson was amazed to be told by Sherlock Holmes that the three women eating bananas in the park were a spinster, a hooker and a newly-wed.

"Amazing," said Watson, "but how can you tell?"

"Elementary, my dear Watson," replied Holmes. "You see how the spinster breaks the banana into little pieces before delicately popping them into her mouth, while the prostitute, the one in the middle, holds the banana in both hands."

"Yes, Holmes, but how can you tell the third is a bride?"

"See how she holds the banana in one hand and thumps herself on the back of the head with the other?" explained the detective.

*   *   *

"WHAT are you shaking for?" said the banana to the vibrator, "I'm the one she's going to eat."

BARBERS

BOB the barber broke his leg in a skiing accident.

Now he can only cut hair on crutches.

SUPPORT your local barber and help get rid of the lunatic fringe.

* * *

A CASANOVA type entered the barber shop. " How many before me?" he asked.

"Three haircuts and two shaves, sir," replied the barber.

The young man left and didn't come back.

Next day he reappeared. "How many before me today, barber?"

"Two haircuts, one shave and one trim."

The young man left and didn't return until the following day for the same routine.

Finally the barber sought an explanation of such behaviour and sent his apprentice to follow him.

"I'm none the wiser," said the lad. "He just goes round to your place, Boss."

* * *

IT was an Italian barber shop and Guiseppe had always promised his son Luigi that he would teach him the trade.

So on the boy's 21st birthday Guiseppe took him to the shop for the first time and presented him with a white coat and a brand new razor.

"Here comes a man for a shave Dad, please let me practise on him."

"Okay," said Guiseppe, "but be careful and don't cut yourself."

* * *

BOB the barber had a secret formula for hair restorer and used to pass it on to special customers. One day a completely bald man pressed $500 in his hand for the remedy.

Bob relented. "It's simple. All you do is apply female secretions to the bald patch. It stimulates hair," he said.

"How do I know it works?" said the punter. "I notice you have a bald spot yourself."

"Yes," said Bob, "and did you notice my one hell of a moustache?"

THE customer was complaining about the price of the haircut. "I've just been to Italy," he said. "Over there you can get a haircut for five dollars."

"Maybe," said the barber, "but what about the bloody fare!"

* * *

JAKE and Fred were getting their hair cut and when the barber started to sprinkle Eau de Cologne on his hair Jake protested. "Don't put that stinky stuff on me. My wife will think I smell like a whore-house."

In the next chair Fred chirped up. "You can sprinkle it on me. My wife doesn't know what a whore-house smells like."

BARS

IT is the ultimate in singles bars.

Girls have to show their IUDs to be admitted.

* * *

EVERY night the bloke in the corner was attracting all the girls.

The rest of the fellows couldn't understand it. The barman couldn't explain it. "He's not that handsome," he said, "he's not a flashy dresser and he hardly says a word. Just sits there licking his eyebrows."

* * *

A BLOKE sidles up to a long-legged blonde in the singles bar and says: "Would you like a Harvey Wallbanger?"

"Yes," she says, "but can we have a drink first?"

* * *

A CAR salesman appeared dejected as he leant on the bar.

"What's the trouble?" asked a blonde who sat beside him.

"If I don't sell more cars this month I'll lose my arse."

"I know the feeling," she said. "If I don't sell more arse this month I'll lose my car."

A BLOKE went in to a bar with a chequered flag.

The barman said: "I hope you're not going to start anything."

* * *

TWO middle-aged blokes were leaning on the bar.

"Ya know Kev, we should be grateful we are not young anymore. Sex is such an accepted thing to the younger generation today that it has almost become meaningless to the lucky bastards."

BIKIES

IT was after closing time at the country pub yet the local cop noticed two motorbikes still parked out front.

He walked round the back of the hotel and found the two bikies, one with his pants down, the other with his finger up his friend's bum.

"Hullo, hullo, hullo," said the cop. "What's going on?"

"My mate's had too much to drink, I'm trying to make him sick."

"Well you don't put your finger in there. You put it down his throat," said the cop.

"Yeah, I'm just about to."

* * *

FLASH the bikie told his gang that he was divorcing his wife because of her disgusting habits.

"I went to piss in the sink this morning, only to find it was full of dirty dishes," he said.

BIRDS

A SMALL boy told his mother that he was surprised to learn that birds had spare parts.

"What do you mean, son?"

"Well, I just heard Dad tell Uncle Ron that he would like to screw the arse off the bird next door."

23

"SEEN any unusual birds lately," said the ornithologist to Fred at the bar.

"Well, apart from a double-breasted seersucker, a morning pee-wee, an extramarital lark and a pink-titted bed-thrasher, no. Nothing to crow about."

* * *

NEVER cross a disobedient dog with a rooster.

You will only get a cock that doesn't come.

* * *

WHILE on the long migratory flight one crow said to the other: "Have you bred any good rooks lately?"

* * *

MY wife does bird imitations. She watches me like a hawk.

* * *

WHAT'S the difference between a canary with two wings and a canary with one.

A difference of a pinion.

* * *

IF a bird craps on your car, never take her out again.

* * *

DONALD Duck split with Daisy and soon found his way to the brothel.

"I'm down for a good time," he said, "and you can stick it on my bill."

* * *

A BLOKE at the singles bar was making headway with a bird and thought he would put the hard word on her.

"How do you like your eggs in the morning?" he said.

"Unfertilized, thanks," she replied.

* * *

A BLONDE and a brunette were walking along a country path when the brunette stopped and said: "Oh dear, look, a dead bird."

The blonde looked up in the sky and said: "Where? Where?"

24

A BLOKE tried to take his pet duck to the movies but was told in no uncertain manner that ducks were not allowed in the stalls. Like a true duck owner he went to the Gents, stuffed the duck down the front of his trousers and in a defiant mood bought his ticket and entered the theatre.

Unfortunately, half way through the movie the duck became fidgety through lack of air so our man opened his fly and let the duck stick its head out.

The woman seated next to him nudged her husband and whispered: "The bloke next to me has his thing sticking out."

Her husband, absorbed in the film, said not to worry about it.

"Don't worry about it?" she said. "The bloody thing is eating my popcorn."

*　　*　　*

TWO naked statues, male and female, had graced a park for centuries. One day a bolt of lightning struck them and the booming voice of the Almighty said: "Statues. In recognition of your long service you can come alive for an hour."

They jumped down from their pedestals, held hands and rushed into the bushes where, for the next hour there came sounds and strains of grunting and moaning.

"Look at the time," said the man, "we've only two minutes to go. Shall we do it one more time?"

"Yes," she said with enthusiasm, "this time I will hold the pigeon and you shit on it."

BIRTHS

THE baby was born on their first wedding anniversary and the proud mother told the husband to lodge a birth notice in the newspaper.

"Gawd they know how to charge," said the husband on his return. "The girl at the newspaper office asked me how many insertions. I said twice a day for 12 months and I didn't get much change from $200."

* * *

JACK and Jill were ecstatic. After five girls the new baby turned out to be boy.

Jill rang her mother to tell her the good news.

"That's wonderful," said her mother. "Who does he look like, you or Jack?"

"Don't know yet, Mum. We haven't looked at his face."

* * *

AN oil rigger setting off for another month on the platform told his pregnant wife: "When the baby arrives send me a telegram. But say 'bicycle arrived' and that will save me buying a round of drinks for everyone."

She said she would, "And I'm sure we are going to have a boy," she said.

A week later he received a telegram: "Bicycle arrived. Punctured back and front."

BONKS

MAN cannot live on bread alone.

He needs a bit of crumpet.

* * *

THEY we adjusting their clothes after a quickie in the back seat. "Gee," he said. "If I knew you were a virgin I would have taken more time."

"If I knew you had more time," she said, "I would have taken off my panty hose."

* * *

THE frustration the first time you can't make it the second time is nothing compared to the second time you can't make it the first time.

* * *

PUT some excitement into your sex life and try riding your wife Rodeo Style.

That's when you mount her from behind then whisper in her ear: "This is how I do it with your sister."

Then try to stay on for ten seconds.

* * *

WHAT I like to hear most of all,
    And I am sure that you'll say that I'm right,
    Is a girl who says, "I shouldn't,
    But for you I will tonight."

* * *

FRED was saying that sex with his wife was like New Year's Eve.

"You mean bells, whistles and fireworks?"

"No. Once a year."

* * *

"WHY are you taking so long?" demanded his wife.

"I'm trying," he said, "but I just can't think of anyone."

* * *

KEENLY in need of feminine company the salesman struck up a conversation with the barman who suggested the blonde in the corner was a good chance.

The salesman quickly made contact and she accepted his offer of dinner at the hotel's expensive restaurant where she ordered practically everything on the menu.

"Do you always eat this much?" asked the salesman, thinking of the bill.

"Only when I've got my period," she said.

* * *

AFTER their first night bonk she said, "Well I figured you were a doctor, but I didn't know you were an anaesthetist."

"How did you know?"

"You washed you hands before and after the event," she said, "and through the entire performance I didn't feel a thing."

* * *

AFTER a week on board the new bosun asked, "What do you do for sex on this ship?"

He was told "On Friday nights we fuck the Chinese cook for $23."

"Why does it cost so much?"

"Well the captain doesn't like it, so we slip him $10, the padre doesn't approve so we slip him $5 and the cook doesn't like it so we slip $2 each for four blokes to hold him down."

*   *   *

A COP walking along the foreshore at night stepped on a bloke's bare bum. A woman's voice said, "Sock it to me again, Sam."

*   *   *

A COP discovered a couple bonking away on the foreshore.

"Hullo, hullo, hullo," he said, but the steamy scene before him nudged his primeval urge and he recognised the woman as one of the more attractive pros.

He checked to see nobody else was about and said to the bloke. "Hey, do you reckon I could be next?"

"Dunno," he replied, "I've never screwed a copper before."

*   *   *

ON the river bank in Alabama he found some soft grass then took off his trousers and hung them on a tree.

"You must be from the north," she said.

"Right on, babe, but how could you tell?"

"A southern boy wouldn't hang up his clothes," said Lulu Belle, "because when we've finished we're gonna be miles from here."

*   *   *

THE Irishman was bonking a Scottish lass in the park and she wasn't impressed with his performance.

"I thought Irishmen were supposed to be big and thick," she grumbled.

"And I thought the Scots were tight," he replied.

*   *   *

"LET'S make love a different way tonight, dear," he said.

"Lovely. What way do you propose, darling," she replied.

"Back to back," he said.

"How do we do that?"

"I've invited another couple," he said.

* * *

A WOMAN was gazing into the window of a shoe store admiring a pair of red shoes when a suave middle-aged man sidled up beside her.

Coming to the point he said: "I'll buy those shoes if you will come to bed with me."

She really wanted the shoes and after a moment's thought said: "Okay. But I have to tell you that I am not very keen on sex."

He bought the shoes and soon had her back in his apartment where they went to bed. Just as she had told him she was very passive and he was getting a little bored himself humping away in the missionary position while she lay so still.

Then suddenly she threw her legs up in the air and sighed: "Wow, lovely, bee-yooti-ful."

"I thought you said you didn't like sex," he said.

"I don't," she replied, "I'm just admiring these beaut new shoes."

* * *

IT was after their first night bonk and the egotistical stud, lying back on the pillow, said: "On a scale of one to ten, how would rate that performance?"

"Three," was the quick answer that shocked him. "But you still have seven more chances to notch the perfect score," she said.

BOOBS

THE Pop Concert was about to start when a female streaker raced down the aisle.

She was caught by the bouncers and chucked out.

* * *

DOLLY Parton has just had a single come out.

* * *

A YOUNG husband watched his flat-chested wife try on her new brassiere.

"Why did you buy that for?" he said. "You've nothing to put in it."

"Listen," she said, "I don't complain about you buying underpants."

* * *

SIGN on Fred's door:

"Knock firmly. I like firm knockers."

* * *

SHE was always trying to enlarge her breasts. "I might try silicon implants," she said.

"Costs too much," said her laconic husband.

"Just get some tissue and rub it along your cleavage."

"Will that make them larger?"

"It did a good job on your arse," he said.

* * *

HER cynical husband asked why she was so bright and cheerful.

"I saw my doctor today and he said I had firm breasts like an 18-year-old."

"Yes," said the husband, "but what did he say about your 45-year-old arse?"

"Your name wasn't mentioned," she said.

* * *

A TABLE top dancer called Valerie
Started to count every calorie
Said her boss in disgust
If you lose half your bust
Then you'll be getting just half of your salary.

* * *

THE foundation garmet store unveiled its latest model

brassier called the Sheepdog. It rounds them up and points them in the right direction.

* * *

"DID she blush when her shoulder straps broke?"

"I didn't notice."

* * *

IT was such a hot day Miss Prim took a cold shower and was relaxing on the sofa in the nude when there was a knock on the door.

"Who is it?" she said in alarm, frantically looking for a gown.

"Just the blind man," said the voice outside.

Relieved at the news she opened the door slightly with one hand while reaching for her purse with the other. It was enough for Fred to barge in.

"Great set of norks, lady," he said, "but where do you want these venetians hung?"

* * *

THERE was once a maid from Assizes
Whose boobs were two different sizes
One was so small
It was nothing at all
While the other was large and won prizes.

* * *

MUM arrived at the function looking the best she had for years. "You look great," said her husband. "You should always leave your bras at home."

"How did you know?" she asked.

"Because you've lost all the wrinkles from your face," he said.

* * *

WHILE they were cuddling under the trees
She said to her boyfriend: "Oh please,
It would give me such bliss
If you play more with this
And give less attention to these.

31

SHE was a buxom young woman with a baby in her arms and when she walked into the clinic the doctor asked what the problem was.

"It's the baby," she said, "he seems under-nourished."

The doc carried out an extensive examination of the baby but could find nothing wrong.

"Is he bottle or breast fed?" asked the doc.

"Breast fed," she replied.

"Then I'd better check you too. Strip off to the waist please."

She looked rather embarrassed but did as she was told to reveal a perfect pair of norks. The doctor weighed each one lightly in his hand, then gave the nipples a gentle squeeze and a tug.

"That's the problem." he said. "You are not giving any milk."

"I'm not expected to," she said, "I'm the baby's aunt, but it's been very nice to meet you."

*   *   *

AFTER years in a seminary three priests were assigned to parishes in Tottenham. At the railway station the girl in the ticket box proved to be a buxom wench boasting a pair of very disturbing norks. It brought the priests out in a sweat.

"Three tickets to Titterton," stammered the first before retreating in embarrassment.

"Here, give me the money, I'll have a go," said the second priest approaching the window: "Three titties to Tockerton," he muttered.

"Here, you are making a mess of it," said the third, snatching the money and getting a grip on himself.

"Three tickets to Tottenham, Miss," he said sternly, "and unless you dress more demurely St Finger will point his Peter at you."

*   *   *

EXPERTS were called in from all over the world to diagnose the Pope's illness. Finally, it was agreed that his long life of celibacy had built up such a store of seminal fluid it was choking his arteries.

The only cure was to have intercourse with a woman.

The Pope was aghast. He wouldn't hear of it. Vows and all that.

His physician was convincing: "Your Holiness," he said, "if you persist in celibacy you will be condemning yourself to death. That's suicide, which is also a mortal sin."

The Pope was in great anquish. "I will retire to my room for three days of prayer to help me make a decision," he said.

On the third day the physician was waiting when the Pope emerged. "My decision has been made," he announced. "I will be guided by your advice, but please be sure that she has big tits."

* * *

SHEILA the feminist insisted on attending the church hatless and in a see-through blouse.

"You can't enter the church like that," said the priest.

"I have a divine right," persisted Sheila.

"By what I can see your left is divine too, but you still can't come in."

* * *

PERCY the 'Perv was a short bloke and used to enjoy riding home on the subway in peak hour when, more often than not, his head would be jammed between the breasts of so many buxom office girls.

Once he was nose to nipples with a tall tough blonde.

"Listen, Joe," she sneered, "how would you like a bust in the gob?"

"Oh, you mind-reader you," said our Perce.

* * *

THERE was a young woman called Clair
　Who possessed a magnificent pair
　Or that's what we thought
　Til we saw one get caught

On a thorn and begin losing air.

* * *

AT a city hotel a waiter was dismissed for having his thumb in the soup and a topless waitress was dismissed for two similar offences.

* * *

THERE was an argument at the topless bar when the president of the Beer Appreciators' Society complained that the beer was okay but his waitress was flat.

* * *

A TAXI driver who undid his lady passenger's bra was charged with exceeding the limits in a built up area.

* * *

TO his bride said the sharp-eyed detective
   "Can it be that my eyesight's defective?
   Has your east tit the least bit
   The best of the .west tit?
   Or is it a trick of perspective?"

* * *

MISS Lottsabazooma was so proud of her boobs she always chose a dress to show them off to best advantage.

Trying on a low cut dress she checked it in the mirror and then asked the supervisor if she thought it was cut too low.

"Do you have hair on your chest?" asked the supervisor.

"Of course not."

"Then this dress is too low," she said.

* * *

HE placed his stethoscope on the young women's chest and said, "Big breaths my dear."

"Yeth," she said, "and I'm only thixteen."

* * *

A MOUSE dashed up a girl's leg, passed her navel and came to rest snugly in her cleavage.

She looked down and said: "You must be a titmouse."

"No," he replied, "I'm a Mickey Mouse. I just overshot the mark."

* * *

TWO blokes entered a noisy pub and were surprised to see a buxom waitress bouncing from table to table and getting her boobs felt at each stop.

"Looks like a friendly pub," said one, so they sat down and waited until she reached their table.

"Can I have a feel?" said one.

"Certainly not," she replied.,

"But those other blokes did."

"They didn't ask," she replied.

* * *

AN old man was the only other occupant of the train compartment and he had fallen asleep, so the young mother had no qualms about breastfeeding her baby.

However, he woke halfway through the process.

"What a lovely child," he said, "what do you feed him on?"

"Just milk and orange juice," she replied.

The old man thought about this for a moment. "Which one is the orange juice?" he asked.

* * *

THE two gossips noticed Miss Lottzabazooma in the park.

"Is that hussy breastfeeding again, right out in public?"

"It's her right enough," said the other sticky-nose, "and look, the boy is at least 25 and not even her son."

* * *

A BUXOM young miss from Valetta
  Loved to parade in a sweater
  Three reasons she had
  To keep warm was not bad
  But the other two reasons were better.

* * *

AND lastly, as all parents well know, a baby is someone who must have a bottle or bust.

BRITISH

WHY is British beer like making love in a canoe?

Theyre both fucking close to water.

* * *

WHEN Britain was an empire it was ruled by an emperor.

When it was a kingdom it was ruled by a king.

When it became a country it was ruled by Maggie Thatcher.

* * *

WHY do British bulldogs have flat faces?

From chasing parked cars.

BROTHELS

AFTER months at sea the sailor asked the cab driver to take him to the nearest knocking shop. When he got out and rapped on the door a small panel opened and a female asked what he wanted.

"I want to come in," said the sailor.

"Well, this is a private club and you will have to slip a $50 membership fee through the mail slot."

He did. Minutes passed and nothing happened.

"Hey," he roared, "I want to be screwed."

"What," said the woman's voice through the door. "Again?"

* * *

THE businessman arrived at the brothel at midday only to find a sign on the door: "Out to Lunch. Go Fuck yourself."

So he decided to go to the whorehouse next door only to be greeted by another sign: "Out to lunch. Beat it!"

* * *

WHEN there are clients more than a few

A cunning old madam called Lou

Will establish a line

By displaying a sign

That informs new arrivals: "Fuck Queue."

IT was peak hour on Saturday night and the sign on the brothel door said: "Last butt not leased."

* * *

THE young man was very fit. Indeed he gave his hired lady the best workout she ever had. "Listen," she said, "If you can repeat that I will give it to you for nothing."

"No worries," he said. "But I will need a rest for ten minutes to recharge my batteries and you will have to hang on to my cock."

"I understand why you need a rest," she said, "and you want me to hold your cock to keep it interested?"

"No, it's not that," he replied. "The last prostitute I was with stole my wallet."

* * *

"I'VE never bothered with drawers"
Said one of the prominent whores.
"There isn't much doubt
I do better without
In handling my everyday chores."

* * *

HE was eight-feet tall and he asked the Madam if she had a girl his height.

"No," she replied, "the only two girls unengaged are only around four feet tall."

"Good," he said, "I'll screw them together."

* * *

THE madam brought her girls in for inspection. "This is Susan," she said, "for $200 you may join her in the bath with champagne on the side. This is Lulu. For $250 she will entertain you on a trapeze. And this is Carmen who offers unlimited delights on a chandelier over a water bed for $300 ..."

"Excuse me," said the punter, "got anybody that still does it in the missionary position?"

* * *

A CULTURED young lad from the bush was taken by taxi

cab to a house of ill-repute. He was impressed by the manners of the young woman who called her mother "Madam".

In the morning he dressed and was about to leave when the young woman who had been so nice to him said: "What about some money?"

"Oh I couldn't," he said. "You've been so nice to me already."

* * *

I have no aversions
   To mergins with virgins
   Though it's more fun to pet
   With a well-seasoned vet.

* * *

HE was knocking on the door of the brothel at three in the morning. Madam opened the door to find him with both arms and legs in plaster casts.

"I want a woman," he said.

"Go away," she said. "We're closed."

"I want a woman," he insisted.

"Go away," she repeated. "Anyway, what could you do with a woman in that condition?"

"I knocked on the door didn't I?"

* * *

PAT and Mick were digging up the road outside the local knocking shop when they noticed the vicar approaching furtively before he ducked into the entrance.

"Did yer see that?" said Pat. "The dirty Protestant minister sneaking in for his share o' sin. What a hypocrite."

After further denouncement of the vicar they began digging again until Mick spotted a rabbi make a tentative but swift entry into the brothel.

"Didja see that?" said Mick. "The Jews are no better."

About an hour went by before they spotted Father McGuire hurry in to the whorehouse.

"Mick," said Pat, "take off your hat. One of those poor girls must be dying in there."

* * *

WHEN he entered the high-class brothel he couldn't help but notice an extremely homely woman, hair in curlers and sitting in a shabby chenille dressing gown.

"Oh, that's Madeline," said the Madam, "She's our answer for our clients who suffer from premature ejaculation."

* * *

ISAAC was the first to admit he was a little kinky. "I'm a monster," he told the madam, "I like to beat women and I've got my own whip. Have you got anybody for a wild pervert like me?"

"Olga's just the ticket," said the madam, "but whipping comes pretty high. It will cost you $500."

Olga insisted on the money up front. Once the cash was handed over Isaac went to work with his whip.

After ten minutes an exhausted Olga gasped: "I can't take much more. When are you going to stop?"

"When?" roared Isaac between frenzied strokes. "When you give me my money back."

BUSES

A MAN with eight kids boarded a bus. When they were all seated there was no place for him, so he clung, swaying to a strap.

An alert drunk had sized up the situation and finally leaned across the aisle to tap him on the shoulder. "Fucked yourself out of a seat, didn't you!" he said.

* * *

ALL the team was aboard the bus but it wouldn't leave the hotel. They were waiting for their groupie.

They were waiting for her to get on so that they could all get off.

HEADS turned as the buxom young blonde innocently enquired of the bus driver that she would like to get off on the end of his route.

* * *

PADDY, his wife and their seven kids were waiting at the bus-stop when they were joined by a blind man. When the bus arrived it was almost full and the conductor said only eight could board.

"Okay Teresa," said Paddy to his wife, "You take the kids on board and me and the blind man will walk."

Without giving the blind man an option in the matter Paddy helped his family scramble aboard and the bus took off.

He and the blind man then set off walking down the road and all went well until the constant tap-tap-tap of the blindman's cane began to irritate Paddy.

"Tap-tap-tap, that bloody tapping is driving me crazy. "Can't you put a bit of rubber on the end of it," he complained irritably.

The blindman was quick to respond. "If you had've stuck a bit of rubber on your own stick we would be on that bloody bus."

* * *

THE pretty stenographer left the office and was on her way home in a very tight mini-skirt. She tried to board the high step on a bus but her skirt was too tight. She reached round and loosened the zip, but still couldn't get her leg up on the step.

She reached behind and unzipped it a bit further, but again the skirt was too restrictive.

Then she was suddenly lifted on board by two strong hands on her bottom.

She turned round to the young man responsible and said, "How dare you."

"Well I thought you wouldn't mind after you opened my fly twice," he said.

40

BUSINESS

AS the hooker said to her client: "It's a business doing pleasure with you."

* * *

THE business partners were at the bar for their usual Friday night drink. Suddenly one of them said: "Heck. I will have to go back to the office. I forgot to lock the safe."

His partner, well into his third drink replied, "Take it easy, John. Nothing to worry about. We're both here."

* * *

YOUNG Isaac was learning economics and asked his father for advice on business ethics.

"Ethics?" repeated his father. "Well it's like this my lovely boy. Let me put it this way. Suppose a woman comes in and buys a garment for $95 and pays with a $100 note. She is very excited while I wrap the garment, and as she leaves with the parcel under her arm I notice she has left her $5 change on the counter. This is where the big question of ethics comes in my son. Do I tell my partner or not?"

* * *

IT was Saturday morning and the suave Romeo walked into the jewellery store with a gorgeous blonde on his arm. "Choose any ring you want, darling," he said.

She chose a whopper and the Romeo asked if he could pay the $50,000 by cheque.

"Of course sir," said the manager, "but you will understand that I will have to keep the ring in the safe for you until the cheque is cleared on Monday morning."

It was Tuesday when the Romeo returned.

"Oh, it's you sir," said the manager with a frown. "I'm afraid your cheque bounced."

"That's okay," said the Romeo, "I just wanted to thank you for best weekend I've ever had."

* * *

BUSINESS is business, so when a high-class call girl

41

refused an all night stand with Isaac Goldstein he wanted to know why.

"For everyone else it is one hundred dollars," she said, "But for you it would be two hundred because, frankly, I don't like Jews."

When Isaac put his money down she reluctantly agreed, "on condition the lights are off all night so that I don't have to look at your nose," she said.

However, half way through the night she had to admit that the Jew could certainly ride. He had screwed her 15 times before midnight with only a quick dash to the toilet between each session to make a quick recovery.

Finally, half way through another vigorous session, she had to comment. "My gawd, Isaac, I must admit you are much raunchier than I expected."

"Ah ain't no Isaac, maam," said a black man's voice, "Isaac is in der toilet selling tickets."

BUTCHERS

IT was Friday evening and Bill the butcher went out on his rounds to collect some bad debts.

Miss Lottsabazooma had owed $7-50 for some time and he meant to collect it. She opened the door wearing a short flimsy nightie and invited him in.

She apologised for not having the money, claiming she hadn't been able to get to the bank. "Maybe there is some other way I can square the account?" she said suggestively.

"Okay, but can I borrow your lipstick for a moment?" said Bill. He then drew a circular line around his donger half-way between his knackers and the nob. "You're not getting all of this for $7-50," he said.

IT was many years ago since the embarrassing day when a young woman, with a baby in her arms, entered his butcher shop and confronted him with the news that the baby was his, and what was he going to do about it?

Finally, he capitulated. He promised to provide her with free meat until the boy was 16. She agreed.

He had been ticking the years off on his calander and one day, the teenager who had been collecting the meat each week, came in to the shop and said: "I'll be sixteen tomorrow."

"I know," said the butcher with a smile, "I've been counting too, and tell your mother when you take this parcel of meat home that it is the last free meat she will get, and watch the expression on her face."

When the boy arrived home he told his mother. The woman nodded and said, "Son, go back to the butcher and tell him I have also had free bread, free milk and free groceries for the past 16 years and watch the expression on his face!"

C

CAMELS

A BABY camel said to its mother one day: "Why do I have such long eyelashes?"

"Because they shield your eyes in desert dust storms."

"And why," said the little camel, "do I have such big feet?"

"That's so you won't sink down in the sand."

"And why do I have a hump on my back?"

"That's so you can carry a large quantity of water so you can survive for a month in the desert."

"Well Mummy, what the bloody hell am I doing in the zoo?"

*   *   *

ACHMED the camel driver had piles of gold, which are just as uncomfortable as any other kind. Piles are an occupational hazard for camel drivers and it was folk-lore tradition to treat the complaint by shoving a handful of cold tea leaves up where the sun don't shine.

Achmed did this ritual night and morning, but to no avail. So when the camel train eventually reached Cairo he took the opportunity to see an English doctor.

Dropping his dacks he bent over while the doctor spread his cheeks apart and began to mutter to himself: "Hmm, yes, hmmm."

"Something wrong?" asked Achmed.

"No, quite the contrary," said the doc. "You are going to take a long trip...you will meet a tall, dark romantic stranger..."

* * *

IN the serene atmosphere of the club's reading room one gent leaned over to the other and whispered: "I say, old boy, did you hear Ponsonby has been drummed out of the Royal Hussars in India?"

"Indeed I did not," replied his companion. "What for, ol' man?"

"Rooting camels I believe," said the first.

The second pondered over this for a while, then leaned over, tapped his friend on the shoulder and asked: "Male or female camels?"

"Females of course. There's nothing queer about Ponsonby."

* * *

AN old Arabian classic:
    The sexual urge of a camel
    Is stronger than anyone thinks
    He's lived for years on the desert
    And tried to seduce the Sphinx
    But the Sphinx's centre of pleasure
    Lies buried deep in the Nile
    Which accounts for the hump on the camel
    And the Sphinx's inscrutable smile.

CARS

See MOTORING

WHAT'S the difference between a sheep and a Honda?

You don't mind being seen getting out of the back of a Honda.

* * *

OUTSIDE the pub two Volkswagen beetles had their

45

bumpers locked together and the owners were having difficulty disengaging them.

A drunk took stock of the situation and said: "Throw a bucket of water over them."

* * *

HE stumbled into the bar and after several drinks confided to his mate. "The next time I give her the ultimatum 'Screw or Walk' I must remember to be in my own car and not hers."

* * *

WHEN Henry Ford went to heaven he started to reorganise the place with a production line on harps and angel wings.

God got his nose out of joint over the pushy entrepreneur. "Listen," said God, "you are talking to the inventor of the human female, the most efficient machine ever made."

"Her bodywork might be great," said Ford, "but her input valve is too close to her exhaust and men often get them mixed up."

"Even so," said God, "there are more men riding my machine than anything you ever made."

CATS

LARGE cats can be dangerous,
  but a little pussy never hurt anyone.

* * *

SIMPLE Simon was accosted by a cheeky street-walker.

"Can you help me, love?" she said, "I've got an itchy pussy."

"Sorry," said Simon, "I don't know a thing about Japanese motorbikes."

CHINESE

BLOKE in a Chinese restaurant shouts to the manager:

"This chicken is bloody rubbery," to which the manager smilingly replies, "Thank you very much."

* * *

WHEN visiting the local hospital Fred felt sorry for a Chinese patient who appeared to have no visitors. When he approached the bed in a friendly manner the Chinese mumbled something, went red in the face and then grasped his throat.

Fred asked if he could help, maybe get a doctor.

The Chinese reached for pen and paper and scribbled some Chinese characters, then gave a last gasp and died.

A week later after ordering his usual Chinese takaway he produced the note for Charlie the Chow to interpret.

Charlie squinted at it and said: "Get off. You are standing on my fukin oxygen supply."

* * *

WHAT do you call a Shanghai woman who wins ten million dollars?

A Chinese fortunate cookie.

* * *

ACUPUNCTURE fees in China are so cheap it is called pin money.

* * *

MISTER Wong rushed his wife to the hospital where Mrs Wong gave birth to a bouncing baby boy. All white.

"It must have been the milkman," said Mr Wong sadly. "Two wongs don't make a white."

The doctor consoled him: "Occidents do happen," he said.

* * *

SAID the Chinese maid when she received her marriage licence: "It won't be wrong now."

* * *

CRITICAL about the lack of democracy the western reporter asked the Chinese General: "Well, when did you have your last election?"

47

"Just before blekfast this morning," he replied.

*　　*　　*

THE Chinese cook had been teased unmercifully by the shearers who had put snakes in his bed and mice in his boots. Finally they relented and said enough was enough and assured him they would torment him no more.

"No more spiders under pillow?"

"No," they assured him.

"No more flighten me?"

"No, no more tricks," they said.

"Glood, then I stop pissee in soup."

*　　*　　*

CHINESE Proverb: Man who goes to bed with sex problem on mind wake up with solution in hand.

*　　*　　*

CHARLIE ran a take-away in the red light district. Indeed the girls would often eat there and relate stories about their trade and some of the tricks they got up to.

It got him so horny one night he closed the shop and went home early.

He tapped his wife on the bum and said: "What about a little 69?"

"Why the hell would I want chicken and almonds at this time of night?" she said.

*　　*　　*

THE phone rang at the Chinese Laundry.

"Can I speak to Half-in?"

"No. Half-in's out."

"Is that Half-out?"

"No. Half-out's not in."

"Who's that?"

"I'm Half-up, the secretary."

"Sorry, I'll call back when you're not busy."

*　　*　　*

THE boss said the expedition was to set forth at dawn next morning. The Italian was to drive the truck, the German

48

was to bring the tent and the Chinaman was put in charge of supplies.

Next morning the Italian and the German were punctual at dawn, but there was no sign of the Chinaman. After waiting an hour the boss ordered the expedition to start. The truck had gone only a few hundred metres when the Chinaman jumped out from behind a tree yelling: "Surplise! Surplise!"

* * *

LEE Pung used to eat regularly at a Greek restaurant and always ordered fried rice as a side dish. Each night Con the Greek used to fall about laughing when Lee would order his "flied lice."

Sometimes Con would have two or three friends gather around to hear Lee say "flied lice."

Lee got sick and tired of the taunting and took a month off for an intensified course in Oxford English.

When he returned he ordered, loud and clear, "and a large serve of fried rice."

"What did you say?" said a very surprised Con.

"I said fried rice, you fluckin' Gleek."

CHRISTMAS

WHEN the garbage cart entered the street of a posh suburb on Christmas Eve the eager housewife was waiting at the front gate. One by one she took the garbos by the hand upstairs to her bedroom. When the driver thought it was his turn he was very disappointed to be handed a five dollar note.

"Whats this?" he asked.

"For Christmas," she replied. "My husband said give the driver a fiver and fuck the rest."

* * *

WHEN the three wise men reached the stable and stooped

to bob through the small stable door one of them banged his head on the low lintel. "Jesus Christ!" he said.

"Now that's a better name," said Mary. "We were going to call him Fred."

* * *

RUDOLPH the Red Nosed Reindeer always led the sled team, while Rudolph the Brown Nosed Reindeer always brought up the rear.

* * *

ACTUALLY Rudolph the Brown Nosed Reindeer rides in the sleigh with Santa.

* * *

SANTA doesn't have any children of his own.

He only comes once a year, and then it is down a chimney.

CLAIRVOYANTS

ROGER the pharmacy clerk fancied himself as a mind-reader. He would study facial expressions as customers came in.

"Wait," he said to the blonde before she could order. "I know what you want."

He handed her a packet of Kotex.

"No," she replied. "I want a roll of toilet paper."

"Darn," said Roger. "Missed it by a whisker."

* * *

WHEN a midget fortune teller escaped from jail the newspaper headline read: "Small Medium at Large."

* * *

GYPSIES are good at predicting the future because their fathers had crystal balls.

* * *

IN court last week a clairvoyant sued for divorce on the grounds of her husband's adultery next week.

THE local Society for the Investigation of Psychic Phenomena was meeting in the village hall and being addressed by a leading spiritualist.

At the conclusion of a quite spooky address the spiritualist asked: "Now I am quite sure some of you have had quite intimate relationships with a ghost. Don't be shy, come tell us about it."

From the back of the hall came a voice, "Well, actually I have, but I'd rather not talk about it."

While the speaker cajoled him to come forward there was applause and encouragement from the audience.

The timid man eventually approached the stage. "And now," said the chairman, "Mr Smithers will tell us of his intimate relationship with a ghost."

"Ghost?" said Smithers turning on his heel and heading back to the stalls, "I thought you said goat."

* * *

HE asked Madame Celeste to look into her crystal ball.

"I fear I am going to die," he said.

"Rubbish," she said confidently, "That's the last thing you'll do."

She took his palm, gazed into it for some time and said: "You will live to be ninety."

"But I am ninety."

"Well there you are then, what did I bloody well tell you."

CLUBS

WUTHERING-Smith was reminiscing. "Remember that lovely barmaid, Belle, who served here for so long?"

Frobisher remembered. "She used to wear a black garter."

"Indeed she did, Frobisher, why was that?"

"It was in memory of all the chaps who passed beyond!"

IT was at a gentleman's club. "Sorry, old boy, to hear you had to bury your wife yesterday."

"Had to," replied the other gent. "Dead you know."

CONDOMS

THE condom vending machine in the pub carried the notice: "If machine is out of order, see publican."

And scribbled below: "If the machine is in order, see the barmaid."

* * *

BUY condoms and avoid the issue.

* * *

BUY one for fun.

Buy 144 and be gross.

* * *

IF the cap fits, wear it.

* * *

IN case of malfunction, marry.

* * *

McTAVISH bought a packet of condoms.

"That will be $5.50, with tax," said the clerk.

"Forget the tacks. I'll tie 'em on with string."

* * *

THEY were having their post coital cigarette when she asked: "If I am pregnant and we have a baby what will we call him?"

He ripped off his condom, tied it in a knot and flung it out the window. "If he gets out of that we'll call him Houdini."

* * *

"HAVE you seen the printed warning on condoms?"

"No."

"Don't you roll them right down?"

* * *

WHAT do Scotsmen do with their old condoms?

They keep rooting with them.

*   *   *

THE priest gathered everybody into the village hall for the Pope's latest decree. "The men must not use condoms and the women must not use the pill."

A shapely young woman stood up at the rear of the hall and replied: "If you don't play the game you don't make the rules."

*   *   *

WE know a bloke who put a condom on inside out, and went.

*   *   *

ON a sure thing he hurried to the gent's room at the pub only to find a drunk at the condom vending machine. The drunk was feeding coins into the machine and thrusting the packets of condoms into his coat pocket.

Afraid the drunk would empty the machine the young man tapped him on the shoulder and asked if he could use it just once.

"No way," replied the drunk, "not when I'm on a winning streak."

*   *   *

LOUIS Lane noticed that Superman fitted a condom before he got down to the business.

"How nice," she said, "Is that for safe sex?"

"No," replied Superman, "it's to protect my dick of steel from rust."

*   *   *

LUIGI's wife was having too many children so the doctor advised him to use a condom. "Wear this sheath and as long as you wear it your wife cannot conceive," instructed the medic.

Three months later when his wife became pregnant again the doctor called Luigi to explain.

"I swear I no take it off," he told the doctor. "It's still on now. But every morning I needa piss so I cut the end off it."

* * *

WHEN Fred said he was getting married the boys at the factory took up a collection and bought him a 13-piece bedroom set; a dozen condoms and a sleeping bag.

* * *

AN entrepreneur is distributing his own brand of condom and has called his product Planned Parent Hood.

* * *

WHEN Gino brought Gina into the clinic to tell the doctor that she was once more in the family way the doctor exploded. "Didn't you use the condom as I instructed?"

"Si, Doc," said Gino, "but we haven't got an organ so I stuck it over the tamborine. It's the only musical instrument I've got."

* * *

A DUCK had been such a regular customer at the local pharmacy that he had his own private account.

One day he waddled in to buy a condom.

"Will I stick it on your bill?" said the chemist.

"What d'yer think I am, a dick-head?" said the duck.

* * *

THE little girl said to her mum, "Daddy must be going to buy a very small car."

"Why is that, dear."

"Because," said the girl, "I just found this very small inner tube in his pocket."

* * *

THE young teenagers met in the back stalls of the theatre and after a hot petting session he wanted to go on with it.

"Not here," she said. "Come around tomorrow. It's Sunday and my parents go to Evensong. We can have the house to ourselves. Oh, and don't forget the condom."

Next evening the lad arrived at the front door just as her father announced that they were off to church.

"I'll come with you," said the lad smartly.

At the first opportunity the young girl whispered, "Why the change of plan and how long have you been religious?"

To which the lad whispered in reply: "How long has your father been a chemist?"

CONFESSION

IT is hard to envisage the torture of a man giving up his sex life only to have people come in and tell him the highlights of theirs. But here we go:

* * *

THERE is so much sin around these days that the local church has put in two more confessionals.

And a sign over one reads: "Eight items or less."

* * *

WHILE on an athletics camp Gina the gymnast had her first sexual encounter with Pete the pole vaulter. Next morning she felt shame and couldn't get to her local church and confession quickly enough.

The priest was sympathetic and gave her absolution. Gina was so elated she did spontaneous cartwheels down the aisle.

Mrs O'Flaherty witnessed it. "Oh Gawd, is that today's penance? The very day I've forgotten to wear my drawers?"

* * *

MURPHY nicked round to the priest's house and stole one of his chickens. He then went straight to confession.

"Forgive me father, for I have sinned. I have stolen a chook and I'm very sorry. Can I give it to you for repentance?"

"Certainly not," said the priest. "You must give it back to the person you stole it from."

"I have offered it to him, father, but he doesn't want it."

"Oh well, then you'd best keep it. Say 10 Hail Mary's."

* * *

PRIEST: "Are you troubled by improper thoughts?"

Fred: "No. I rather enjoy them."

* * *

WHEN the sliding door opened in the confessional box he started: "Father, I had sex with a pair of lovely 18 year-old nymphomaniac twins five times last week."

"What kind of Catholic are you?" demanded the priest.

"I am not a Catholic," he replied.

"Then why are you telling me this?"

"I am telling everyone!"

* * *

GOING to confession the young man confessed that he had committed sins of the flesh with a new woman in town. "Her name is Pussy Pink and she is a seductive, voluptuous redhead, and if you saw her father you would understand."

The priest granted absolution but was intrigued about the description of the town's new vamp.

The following Sunday he saw a well-built redhead sway down the aisle all the way to the front pew.

Nudging the organist he said: "Hey, Reynolds, is that Pussy Pink?"

Reynolds turned and squinted at the woman as she crossed her legs. "No, Father," he said. "It's just the sunlight coming through the stained-glass windows."

* * *

O'FLAHERTY was in confession and the priest asked: "Now tell me son, did you ever sleep with a woman?"

"No, not me, Father."

"Now son, I'll ask you again," said the priest, "did you ever sleep with a woman?"

"No, er, well, no, Father."

"Now son, there's just me and God listening. I will ask you for the last time, did you ever sleep with a woman?"

"Well, come to think if it, Father," said O'Flaherty, "I believe I did doze off once or twice."

"FATHER," said Murphy, "I feel I don't need forgiveness for the various adulteries I have scored this month."

"And why not?" asked the astonished priest.

"'Cos all the married women I slept with were Jews," he said.

"Ar, you're right me son," said the priest. "That's the only way to screw the Jews."

* * *

BRIGID was still a new bride and sought some advice from Father McGinty in the confessional box.

"Father," she whispered, with a little embarrassment, "is it alright to have intercourse before receiving communion?"

"Certainly, my lass," he replied, "just as long as you don't block the aisle."

* * *

A DRUNK staggered into the church, bumped his way down the aisle, entered the confessional took a seat and promptly went to sleep.

A short time later he was rudely woken by the priest rapping on the partition.

"It's no use banging," said the drunk, "There's no paper in here either."

* * *

EVERY Saturday night the three lads went out on the town together, but Shamus always made a point of going past the church first so he could duck into confession while the other two waited outside.

"It's been a week since my last confession, Father," said Shamus, "and I'm sorry to say that I have sinned of the flesh once again."

"Was it that O'Flannagan hussy from the dairy?"

"No Father."

"Was it the cheeky Costanzo girls in the fruit shop?"

"No Father."

"Don't tell me it was the widow Murphy flauntin' her wares again?"

"No Father."

"Well do your usual penance and be off with you then," said the priest.

Shamus rushed out of the church to his waiting mates. "Got three certainties for tonight," he said.

* * *

"FATHER, yesterday I made love to my wife,"

The priest explained that there was nothing wrong with that.

"But Father, I did it with...lust."

Again the priest re-assured the man that it was no sin.

"But Father, it was the middle of the day."

The priest was growing uncomfortable with the description but assured his parishioner that it was a natural act for man and wife.

"But Father, it was sheer passion. As she leant over the deep freeze I just jumped on her and we did it on the floor. Am I banned from the church?"

"Of course not," said the exasperated priest.

"Oh good. We're both banned from Safeways."

* * *

WHEN the priest finally noticed the little boy sitting close to the confessional box he grabbed him by the ear. "You young rascal," he said, "have you been listening to confessions all evening?"

"No Father," said the kid, "I've only been here since Mrs Murphy told you about doing it with the baker."

* * *

MISS Lottsabazooma went to confession and told the priest that she had been having an affair with a married man.

"But this is the fifth time you have told me this week," said the priest.

"I know," she said, "I like to talk about it."

THERE was a young lady called Tessa
A quite unrepentant transgressor
When sent to the priest
The rude little piece
Would try to undress her confessor

CONMEN

LARRY was the slickest talker in the world. He even made his wife feel sorry for the hitch-hiker who lost her bra and panties in his car.

* * *

THE debutante was learning to swim and was being held by the handsome swimming instructor, Ron the Con. While he displayed a benign smile there was a look of puzzlement on her face.

"Will I really sink if you take your finger out?" she asked.

* * *

AT the City Magistrate's Court today Slippery Samuel, the world's greatest confidence trickster, sentenced the chief magistrate to two year's hard labour.

* * *

IT was one of those swinging house-parties. He sidled up to the newly arrived blonde and said: "Why don't we pop into the bedroom while its empty. We've got the rest of the evening to get acquainted."

* * *

RON the con had it all sussed out. His millionaire father was terminally ill, only had a month to live. He could hardly wait to get his hands on the money and start living it up with wine, women and fast cars.

In the bar that night he saw a ravishingly beautiful woman and with the confidence of his impending wealth decided on the bold approach.

"I might be an ordinary clerk at the moment," he said,

"but within one month I will inherit five million dollars. Interested?"

Indeed she was. She even went home with Ron that night. Next day she became his stepmother.

*   *   *

McTAVISH was the meanest of Scottish conmen. When he had need to write a letter to his brother Hamish he would use the post office pen, then seal the letter in an envelope addressed to himself and post it without a stamp.

When it was duly delivered to his address McTavish refused to pay the duty and refused to accept the letter. It was therefore returned to sender whose name was on the back.

*   *   *

A YOUNG woman was walking along the street when she saw a ladder with a notice attached to the bottom rungs. It said CLIMB THE LADDER TO SUCCESS.

It so intrigued her she climbed to the top of a flat roof where she found a naked man.

"Who are you?" she asked.

"I'm Cess," he replied.

*   *   *

RON the Con has some advice for husbands too.

Always have a packet of aspirin on hand, he says. Then when you get randy you simply hand two tablets to the Missus.

When she says: "What's that for?" you say, "for your headache."

"But I haven't got a headache."

"Good, then lets screw."

*   *   *

FOR months now he had noticed a very attractive nurse travelling on the same tram he caught every night and he would seek a seat where he could quietly admire her.

He was enjoying some lecherous fantasies when he was

startled by the tram conductor's first words: "She does it yer know!"

The tram conductor continued. "I can read your thoughts. You would like to get off with that nurse. She's a nympho and kinky you know."

It was a shock to hear the tram conductor's next statement. "She turns it on for the tram conductors every Friday night behind the depot."

When he got off the tram his mind was full of visions of the nurse and his ears were ringing with the tram conductor's words.

Next morning was Friday, so as soon as dusk had settled into night he made his way to the park behind the tram depot.

Sure enough, there she was in the park. Worse, as he came up behind her he knew she heard him approaching, yet she hiked up her skirt so that he could make out the two white orbs of her bum. The temptation was too much. He virtually jumped on her and went at it like a jack hammer.

He was lying back having a quiet smoke when he began to chuckle.

"What are you laughing at," she said.

"I am not really a tram conductor," he confessed.

"That's okay," came the reply, "I'm not really a nurse. Actually I'm a tram conductor."

COURT

See LAWYERS

"HAVE you got anything to say for yourself?" said the judge sternly after hearing the case.

"Fuck all," muttered the defendant.

"What did he say?" asked the judge learning forward to the clerk.

The clerk stood up, turned, and whispered quietly to the judge: "He said 'fuck all' your worship."

"That's funny," said the judge, "I'm sure I saw his lips move."

* * *

THE young woman, accusing her boss of sexual harassment, told the court that she was too embarrassed to repeat the words he said to her. The judge suggested she write them down and that the words be passed to himself and the jury.

Fred was a member of the jury. When the note was passed to him he read: "Get your pants off and have a drink with me tonight." Fred passed it on to fellow jury person, elderly Miss Smithers, who unfortunately had nodded off. He had to nudge her. She woke, read the note, smiled at Fred and put it in her handbag.

* * *

RASTUS was giving evidence in a rape case but was reprimanded by the judge for openly using the magic word.

He began the second time. "Yes, yer Honour, on the night of the thirteenth I seen them on the beach and they was fucken..."

The judge was aghast at the frank language and rapped the bench with his gavel again.

"I will adjourn the case for five minutes to allow time for this witness to come up with a more palatable description," he announced.

After the break, Rastus resumed his evidence:
"Her pants were down
His arse was bare
His balls were flying in the air
His you-know-what
Was you-know-where
And if that ain't fucking
Then I wasn't there!"

* * *

IN a small country town the farmer was asked to testify about the character of a woman defendant.

62

"What about her veracity?" he was asked.

The farmer thought for a moment and said:

"Some says she does, some says she doesn't."

* * *

A MOTHER of three filed paternity charges on a prominent test cricketer.

"On what grounds?" she was asked.

"Lords, Old Trafford and the MCG," she replied.

* * *

THE company director who had just been found responsible in a paternity case was told by the judge: "There is no such thing as a free lunge."

* * *

IN the dock was a 13 year-old boy on a paternity charge.

To emphasise the ridiculousness of the case the defence counsel asked the boy to stand up then unzipped his fly and took out the alleged weapon.

Taking the limp tool in his hand he began: "Ladies and gentlemen of the jury, I ask you to study this undeveloped penis."

Emphasising his point by rattling the flacid dick around he continued: "Ask yourself, is it possible he could have fathered a baby with this?"

The defendant tapped him on the shoulder and whispered,"If you don't let go we are going to lose this case."

* * *

THE judge called the court to order to make a serious announcement. He said he had been bribed $2000 by the defendant and $3000 by the plaintiff.

"This is a serious matter and I have given it earnest consideration" he said. "I've decided to return $1000 to the plaintiff, and judge the case on its merits!"

* * *

DAN Murphy was charged with stealing cattle. After the bush jury heard the evidence the foreman stood up and said: "Not guilty. So long as he returns the cattle."

The circuit magistrate was infuriated with that finding and demanded that they go back and reconsider their verdict.

After a short wrangle among themselves the foreman stood once more. "Okay, not guilty, and he can keep the bloody cattle."

* * *

"YOU seem to have more than an average share of intelligence for a man of your background," sneered the lawyer at the witness stand.

"Thank you," said the witness. "If I wasn't under oath I'd return the compliment."

* * *

THE clerk turned to the little bloke in the dock. "Prisoner at the bar," he said, "do you wish to challenge the jury?"

Fred eyed the jury. "Not all of them at once," he said, "but I think I could go a few rounds with the little fat geezer in the middle."

* * *

A BLOKE due to appear in court was talking about the case in the bar and was advised by his drinking mate: "If you want to get off, just send the judge a case of whisky."

The defendant discussed this with his solicitor next morning. "On no account do anything like that," said the legal man. "We've got a thin argument already without complicating it with a bribe."

To the solicitor's astonishment our bloke won his case. "We would have lost if you sent that case of whisky."

"Oh, but I did," said our bloke, "but I put the other party's name on the card."

* * *

JUDGE: "Can't you settle this out of court?"

"That's what we were doing when the police interfered."

* * *

THE defendant had just been convicted and fined and was

asked by the judge if he could pay anything at all towards the penalty and costs.

"Not a brass razoo," he replied. "All the money I had has gone to my lawyer and five of the jurors."

*　*　*

CHARGED with stealing a barrel of beer from the back of the pub the old defendant was not familiar with legal jargon. So when the judge said he would have to dismiss the case due to insufficient evidence the old lag scratched his head and said "What d'yer mean?"

The clerk explained: "It means you are let off."

"And does it mean I can keep the grog?"

*　*　*

"HAVE you ever been cross-examined before?"

"Yes, your honour, I'm a married man."

*　*　*

"DO you plead guilty or not guilty?"

"WHAT else have you got?"

*　*　*

"DO you plead guilty or not guilty?"

"How do I know. I haven't heard the evidence yet."

*　*　*

"HAVE you anything to offer before judgement is passed?"

"No, judge, my lawyer has left me skint."

*　*　*

"GUILTY. Ten days or two hundred dollars."

"I'll take the two hundred thanks, judge."

*　*　*

"ORDER, order in the court."

"Whisky on the rocks for me thanks."

*　*　*

JUDGE: you are charged with habitual drunkeness, what is your excuse?"

"Habitual thirst, yer worship!"

65

JUDGE, to jury: "What possible reason could you have for acquitting this man?"

"Insanity," said the foreman.

"What, all of you?"

* * *

TWO tramps were hauled before the court and charged with vagrancy.

"And where do you live?" asked the judge.

"Nowhere," said the first tramp.

"And where do you live," he asked the second tramp.

"Next door to him!"

* * *

TWO magistrates were rolling home from a reunion, arms around each other, singing *Sweet Adeline*.

"Hey," said one. "I think we're drunk."

"You're right. And according to law I will have to charge you with being drunk and disorderly," said his mate.

"And you will have to appear before me at 10 tomorrow," said the first.

Next morning in court the first pleaded guilty to the charge and was fined $10. They then changed places.

"Drunk and disorderly, eh, fined $20."

"Hey," protested the first. "When I was in the chair I only fined you $10."

"Yes," said the second magistrate. "But the offence is getting too prevalent. You are the second drunk to appear before this court this morning!"

* * *

JUDGE to habitual defendant: "Is this the first time you have been up before me?"

"I dunno yer Honour. What time do you get up?"

* * *

ON his second murder charge the accused decided that the only way to avoid a life sentence was to bribe a juror to reduce the conviction to manslaughter.

His hopes were raised when the jury was out for three

days. Then they finally announced the verdict was guilty of manslaughter.

"Thanks," said the accused later. "How did you manage it?"

"It was bloody difficult, I can tell you," he replied. "The others were hell-bent on acquitting you."

* * *

THE judge, he populates
   The city jails
   By grave decisions
   Heads or tails

COURTING

See ENGAGEMENTS, NEWLY-WEDS

WHEN asked to explain why the relationship was over she told him straight:
   "Because you are no good in bed."
   He was miffed. "But how can you tell after 15 seconds?"

* * *

HE: "Don't the stars look lovely tonight?"
   She: "Can't tell. I'm in no position to say."

* * *

THEY were both nervous on their first night together. When he parked the car in a shady lane he summoned up the courage to say: "Would you like to get in the back seat?"

"No," she said. "I'd rather stay in the front with you."

* * *

THEY were cuddled up in the back seat of the car when he proffered it to her.

"But if I do perform oral sex on you," she said squinting at the monster in front of her, "won't you lose respect for me in the morning?"

"Of course not," he said, "provided you are good at it."

* * *

SOME joy rides can extend from here to maternity.

THINGS were not going too well in the motel bed.

"Maybe I am not the greatest lover," he said, "but things would improve if you would grind your arse instead of your teeth."

*   *   *

"DARLING," he said, "am I the first man to make love to you?"

"Of course you are. Why do you men ask the same stupid question?"

*   *   *

THE couple were having a heavy petting session in the park.

"Gee, I wish I had a torch," he said.

"So do I," she said, "You've been eating grass for the last ten minutes."

*   *   *

OUT on her first date her mother's words were ringing in her ears: "Say no to everything he suggests."

So as she got into his car he said: "I suppose a root is out of the question?"

*   *   *

HE was a man of few words.

"What about a root?" he said.

"Your place or mine?" she replied.

"If you are going to argue about it, forget it," he said.

*   *   *

FRED was making a timid advance. "What would you say, sweetheart, if I stole a kiss?"

"The same thing I'd say to any dickhead who had the chance to steal a car and only took the hub caps," she said.

*   *   *

THEY were sitting in his car when she took the initiative and slid her hand down inside his trousers and grabbed his dong.

"What are you doing?" he enquired tentatively.

"Oh, nothing," she said. "For a moment I thought this might be the start of something big."

* * *

IT was their first date and her stern father was intent on having the last word:

"Young man. I want Beryl to be home early tonight."

"Don't worry," said the young suitor, "I'll have her in bed by ten."

* * *

THEY were fondling in the back seat of the car.

"Oh," she said. "Don't do that or I'll go to pieces."

"Go ahead," he panted, "I've got hold of the bit I want."

* * *

AFTER two hours of struggling in a parked car she managed to protest to her date:

"Do you know what good clean fun is?"

"No," he said, "what good is it?"

* * *

THERE was a young woman named Gloria
Whose new man said: "May I explore ya?"
She replied to the chap:
"I'll draw you a map
Of where others have been to before ya."

* * *

SHE finally got fed up with her boyfriend's fumbling advances and decided to put him in her place.

* * *

HE: "It's so dark I can't see my hand in front of my face."

She: "Don't worry, I know where it is."

* * *

JAKE said "How about a good night kiss?"

She refused. "I don't do that sort of thing on my first date."

"Well," replied Jake, "how about your last?"

IT was their first date and as he delivered her to her front door she gave him a lingering kiss.

"Is there anything else I can do for you?" he asked hopefully.

She leaned close to his ear and whispered: "I want you to weigh me."

Anxious to impress, he drove her back to town and found a pharmacy which had a pair of scales.

When she finally got home her mother asked if she had a nice time.

"Absowoutwy wousy," she said.

*   *   *

HE told his doctor that he had just met the love of his life but was very worried. He didn't know if she had VD or TB.

The doctor listened to the symptoms the young man had observed and then gave his diagnosis.

"If she coughs you can screw her," he said.

*   *   *

AFTER their first date and a wild night together he lay back enjoying an after-coitus cigarette.

"Do you tell your mother everything you do?" he asked.

"Of course," she said. "My mother couldn't care less. It's my husband who is so damned inquisitive."

*   *   *

HE sidled up to the bar beside the brunette and struck up a conversation.

"Before we go too far," she said, "I think you should know I am a lesbian."

"That's okay. I've got a cousin in Beirut," he said.

*   *   *

ON their first date they were getting to know each other.

"Are you a virgin?" he asked.

"Yes," she replied, "but I'm not a fanatic about it."

"BUT John," she said, "why did you park here where there are so many nicer spots down the road?"

"I believe in love at first site."

* * *

SHE cuddled up to him and said: "Do you think of me when you're away?"

He replied: "I always bare you in mind."

* * *

HE begged and pleaded for more
But she said: "You've already had four
And I'm sure that you've heard
Although it's absurd,
That Eros spelt backwards is Sore."

* * *

"I don't believe we've met. I'm Mr Right."

* * *

HE had been watching the blonde at the other end of the bar for some time before he got sufficient courage to approach her.

"Would you like a Harvey Wallbanger?" he asked.

"Love one," she said. "But let's have a drink first."

* * *

HE snuggled up to her and said: "I'm yours for the asking."

She snuggled back and said: "I'm asking fifty bucks!"

* * *

IT was love at first sight and they had taken the big step and slept together for the first time. They were still in bed when the phone rang next morning.

He reached out and picked up the receiver, listened for a moment, then gave her a shake.

"It's for a Miss Sheila Kelly," he said. "Is that you?"

* * *

WHEN Myrtle finally brought a bloke home her parents were relieved that this might be the Mr Right who would take her off their hands. But when they took a closer look they took Myrtle aside.

"He's not exactly a young man," whispered Mum to her daughter. "He's fat, he's bald and he's pretty old isn't he?"

"There's no need to whisper, Mum," said Myrtle, "he's bloody deaf too."

*   *   *

IT was only three weeks after Fred got engaged to the circus contortionist that she broke it off.

*   *   *

CUDDLING on the couch he was using his best lines and favourite moves. But he was getting nowhere. When she yawned and a light shone out of her mouth he knew it was time to go.

CRICKET

SHE was only a cricketer's daughter,
  but she could take a full toss in the crease.

*   *   *

THE district cricket secretary was preparing the match reports to send on to the local newspaper when he noticed the scribe from Wonga Creek had written "boeling."

"That's the worst spell of bowling I've seen for a long time," he mused.

*   *   *

THE club's best batsman was on the phone to his captain trying to explain why he couldn't play next day.

"No, I can't let you off the game," said the captain who was made of stern stuff. "If I did, then I would have to do the same for any other player whose wife dies."

*   *   *

THEIR marriage had been shaky and it was one of those embarrassing truces while they washed the dishes in silence. But when she passed him a plate and he dropped it, crash, on the floor, her nerve broke.

"And where do you go Tuesday and Thursday nights?" she blurted out.

"Down to the brothel, like I told you," he said. "I just go down for a bit of extra sex."

"I don't believe you," she said spitefully. "And what about Saturday afternoons. Where do you go then?"

"Just looking for the odd root, to pick up a tart or two. I promise."

"Are you sure you haven't been playing cricket?"

"Of course not," he said, putting his arm around her.

This seemed to settle her down. She continued with the dishes and handed him a plate.

He reached for it, fumbled, took a second grab, missed, and it crashed to the floor.

"You bastard," she roared. "You've been playing with the English Eleven* all this time."

(* or any other team, cricket or football, currently on the bottom of the ladder).

CROCODILES

TARZAN lumbered home after a hard day's work just in time to see a crocodile snap one of his 15 kids off the river bank.

"Hey Jane," he complained, "did you see that?"

"Oh come to bed and let's make another one," said Jane.

The very next day as he was coming home it happened again. A croc took another kid in the shallows.

He complained to Jane but she merely replied: "Oh let's go to bed and make another one."

Tarzan put his foot down. "I'm not working all day and rooting all night just to feed the bloody crocodiles," he said.

*   *   *

TARZAN rushed into the Jungle Fast Food outlet: "I'll have a crocodile sandwich. And make it snappy," he said.

*   *   *

THE crocodile sauntered into the men's wear shop.

"Do you have any shirts with little men on the pockets?" he asked.

CUSTOMS

BLOKE carrying two heavy suitcases is stopped by customs.

"What's in the bags, sir?"

"Chook food," he says.

When the bloke was asked to open the cases the customs agents found radios, calculators, gold wrist watches, miniature computers, and a range of electrical gadgets.

"Okay," he says. "I feed it to the chooks, but if they don't like it I try to sell it."

* * *

CUSTOMS officer was inspecting a sweet young thing's suitcase and discovered six pair of French knickers. "What are these for?" he asked.

"Sunday, Monday, Tuesday, Wednesday, Thursday and Friday," she replied.

"And what about Saturday?" he asked.

"I dont wear any on Saturday," she replied with a smile and a wink and minced by.

Next was a big German frau who flung her suitcase onto the counter.

"And what are these for?" asked the customs officer discovering 12 pairs of thick flannel bloomers.

She replied: "January, February, March, April........."

* * *

AN importer lost a trunkful of pornographic books due to luggage mishandling but the authorities eventually found them.

His trunk came up on Thursday and his case comes up on Friday.

74

LONG John decided to smuggle five gold watches into the country, but the trick was how to sneak them past Customs.

Wearing his most nonchalent expression he approached the officer he thought looked most amiable and friendly.

"G'day," said the officer, "got the time on yer dick?"

"Damn. You bastards know everything."

* * *

A MARRIED couple, Freda and Fred, had been successfully smuggling native birds out of Australia to the United States for years.

Fred suggested they could double their earnings by smuggling some American wildlife on the return trips.

"For example," he said. "I've got a squirrel here and I am going to hide it by stuffing it down the front of my pants."

"And this is for you," he said, handing Freda a skunk. "That will bring big money in Australia. Stuff it down the front of your panties."

Freda protested: "What about the smell?"

Fred shrugged his shoulders. "If it dies ... it dies."

CYCLISTS

TWO gays were arrested for riding a bisexual built for two.

* * *

TWO young women were riding their bicycles off the beaten track.

Admiring the scenery one said: "I"ve never come this way before."

"Neither have I," said her friend, "it must be the cobble-stones."

* * *

THE Vaseline and Malvern Star classic:

MR and Mrs Coddle lived with their daughter Molly in a neat little suburban street next to a lad called Albert.

For years Molly had romantic designs on Albert, after all he was The Boy Next Door.

But Albert was oblivious to these overtures and more obsessed with his Malvern Star bicycle which he cared for with a passion.

One day he was polishing his bike as usual when Molly looked over the fence and asked if he would like to come to tea next Saturday night.

"Can I bring my bike?" was Albert's immediate reply.

"I guess so," said Molly.

Saturday night came around and sure enough Albert arrived at the front step with his Malvern Star. "Can I bring my bike inside?" he asked.

"No. Leave it on the porch," said Mr Coddle from inside the house.

"Okay," said Albert. "But if it is staying out in the moist air I need to give it another rub with Vaseline to keep the rust away. I do this every day," he said as he began busily polishing.

It was a lovely meal, but as they pushed away the empty plates from the third course, Mrs Coddle said: "Well, that was nice, but I'm not doing the dishes."

"Well I'm not," said Molly.

"And I'm not," said the father.

"And I am certainly not," said Albert. "It looks like rain outside and I want to polish my bike."

"Well I cooked the meal and I'm not doing the dishes," insisted Mrs Coddle.

"Enough!" roared Mr Coddle. "No more argument. Not another word. In fact, whoever utters the next word will do the dishes."

They all sat there, tight-lipped. Silence.

Outside there were some storm clouds gathering and Albert became agitated about the possible dampness on his bike. He desperately wanted to get the Vaseline jar and rub the frame over.

But grim silence persisted.

Another look at the threatening clouds and Albert decided he would be forced to make somebody speak.

He leapt on Molly, wrestled her to the floor and deflowered her.

Mr and Mrs Coddle were aghast; but not a word was uttered.

Another period of grim silence ensued.

Albert took his second desperate action. He jumped on Mrs Coddle wrestled her to the floor and gave her one too.

Father's jaw dropped open but he gritted his teeth again and nary a word escaped.

What else could Albert do? He was defeated for it began to sprinkle rain and there was a distinct chance his bike was not fully under cover on the porch.

"Okay, I've got to get the Vaseline," he said.

"I'll do the dishes. I'll do the dishes," said Mr Coddle jumping up and running into the kitchen.

D

DANCING

A BUCK rabbit went to the square dance but was soon asked to leave. He kept doing the dozy doe in the corner.

* * *

FRED has been barred from the hokey cokey dancing class.

He was putting it in when he should have been shaking it all about.

* * *

THE chorus girl said her left leg wasn't bad, her right was a little better, and between the two she could make a fortune.

* * *

DISCO dancing is for jerks.

* * *

SHE said she didn't like dancing.

"It's just screwing set to music," she said.

"Well what's wrong with that?" he said.

"It's the music," she said.

* * *

STAR acts at the Dancing Society's Annual Review were Miss Lottzabazooma who performed the Dance of the Virgin entirely from memory, partnered by Alfonso who danced the fandango with his fan in one hand and his dango in the other.

* * *

FRED went to the annual dance at the Deaf and Dumb

Institute and was impressed by the way the members were able to feel the vibration, the rhythm and beat of the music.

He spotted an attractive girl and with gestures and signs asked her to dance. She nodded and they were soon whirling around the floor.

After a bracket of numbers he made signs of drinking. She nodded and he took her arm and they headed for the bar.

On the way a young man tapped the woman on the shoulder. "What's this?" he said, "I thought you were going to have a drink with me?"

"I intend to," she answered, "as soon as I can get rid of this deaf and dumb bastard."

*　*　*

THE director of entertainment walked into the hotel' s dance hall. "What's going on?" he said.

The choreographer replied: "The chorus girls are rehearsing the Dance of the Virgins."

"That's tough," said the MC. "They would all be doing it from memory."

*　*　*

TO overcome an embarrassing shyness Charles was advised to take up dancing. He plucked up courage to ask a buxom young wench to waltz when halfway through the number her necklace became unfastened and slid down the back of her dress.

"Be a darling and reach down and get it," she said.

His first fumbling attempt failed.

"Further down, further down," she said.

Aware that he was being watched he said, "I feel a perfect arse."

"My tits aren't bad either," she said, "but just get the necklace."

*　*　*

TWO old ladies were discussing the good old dancing days.

"Remember the Pride of Erin," said one, "and the barn dance?"

"Yes, great old times," said the other, "And what about the Minuet?"

"What? You expect me to remember the men I eat. I can hardly remember the men I fucked."

DEFINITIONS

ABSENTEE: A missing golfing accessory.

ABUNDANCE: A local hop usually staged in a barn.

ACME: Pimples on the face running towards the top.

ADAMANT: The very first insect.

ADIEU: Hymie Finklestein.

ADORN: What comes after the darkest hour.

ADVERTISEMENT: Something that makes you think you've longed for it for years, but never heard of it before.

ALIMONY: A mistake by two people paid for by one.

ALPHABET: Not quite the complete wager.

ANTI-FREEZE: When you don't talk to your uncle's wife.

APEX: The female of the gorilla species.

AROMATIC: An automatic longbow.

ARTFUL: A painting exhibition.

AUTOBIOGRAPHY: The car's logbook.

AUTOMATIC SHIFT: When the driver moves closer to his girlfriend.

AVAIL: Helpful for ugly women.

AWE-STRUCK: Being hit with a paddle.

BACTERIA: A modern self-service TAB.

BADMINTON: The reason the lamb tasted off.

BALANCE: Something you lose if the bank pushes you.

BARBARIAN: The man who cuts your hair.

BIGAMIST: A fog over Italy.

BIGOTRY: An Italian redwood.

BLUNDERBUSS: A coach which goes from Melbourne to Sydney, via Port Augusta.

BOOKCASE: Litigation about a novel which ensures wide sales.

BOXER: A bloke who stands up for the other fellow's rights.

BRAZIER: Something to warm your hands on.

BRUSSELS-SPROUTS: A world famous statue found in that city.

BURLESQUE SHOW: Where attendance falls off if nothing else does.

CABBAGE: The fare you pay a taxi driver.

CLIMATE: The best thing to do with a ladder.

CONDOM: An item to be worn on every conceivable occasion.

CONDOM: A sock in the puss.

CONDOMS: Homes for Retired Semen.

CONSCIENCE: The thing that aches when everything else feels good.

COPULATE: What an Italian police chief says to an officer who doesn't get to work on time.

COWARD: A man who thinks with his legs.

DETEST: The West Indies playing India.

DIAPHRAGMS: Trampolines for dickheads.

DUCK DICK: A game warden.

ECSTACY: It's the feeling you feel when you feel you are going to feel a feeling you have never felt before.

ELECTRICIAN: A switch doctor.

ENGLISH GENT: One who gets out of the bath to piss in the sink.

EUNUCH: Massive vassel with a passive tassel.

FASTIDIOUS: A girl who is fast and hideous.

FAUCET: What you have to do if the tap won't turn.

FELLATIO: The French Connection.

FETE: A boring picnic worse than death.

FLOOZIE: A sweet girl with the gift of the grab.

GALLERY: A hostel for young women.

GAY MILKMAN: Dairy Queen.

GRANARY: A home for senior female citizens.

HEBREW: a male teabag.

HEN'S Party: A bunch of birds cackling about who is laying whom.

HIGH FIDELITY: A drunk who always goes home to his wife.

HORIZON: Callgirl getting up in the morning.

HUMBUG: A singing cockroach.

HYACINTH: A yank greeting a gal called Cynthia.

IDOLISE: Eyes that refuse to look at anything.

INCOME: What you have to make first, because you can't make it last.

INNUENDO: An Italian suppository.

JEALOUSY: The friendship one woman shares with another.

JEWISH DILEMMA: Free Pork.

LACTIC: A grandfather clock which doesn't work.

LIBERAL: A Conservative who's been arrested.

LESBIAN COCKTAIL LOUNGE: Her-She Bar.

LESBIANS: Insurmountable odds.

LESBIAN: A manic depressive with illusions of gender.

MADAM: One who offers vice to the lovelorn.

MARCONI: The first man to send a message through a length of spaghetti without it touching the sides.

MINE SHAFT: What a German calls his dick.

MONOLOGUE: A discussion between man and wife.

NONDESCRIPT: A television play.

ODIOUS: Not very good poetry.

ORGY: Grope therapy.

PARENTS: Couples who practise the Rythym Method.

PEDESTRIAN: A motorist with teenage sons.

PIMP: Nookie Bookie.

PIMP: Public relations man for a public relations girl.

PORNOGRAPHY: Cliterature.

PREMATURE Ejaculation: The come before the scorn.

RACIAL DISPUTE: When the course judge calls for a photo.

RED RIDING HOOD: A Russian condom.

REFLECTION: What a girl looks at, but is not given to.

SAGE: A bloke who knows his onions.

SITTING Pretty: Sitting Bull's gay brother.

SNOW JOB: How a woman defrosts her man.

SNUFF: Sufficient unto the day.

SONATA: A song sung by Frank.

SPECIMEN: An Italian astronaut.

STALEMATE: A husband who has lost his ardour.

TEAR JERKER: A bloke who cries while wanking.

TRUE LOVE: An injection with affection to the midsection from a projection without objection.

VICE SQUAD: The pussy posse.

VICE VERSA: Dirty poetry from Italy.

VIRGIN: A girl who whispers sweet nothing doings.

VIRGIN: A girl who won't take in what a guy takes out.

VIRGIN: Any Hicksville girl who can outrun her brothers.

VIRGIN SQUAW: Wouldn't Indian.

WELSH RAREBIT: A Cardiff virgin.

WET DREAM: A snorgasm.

ANTI-CLIMAX: Bore-gasm.

CORPORATE VIRGIN: New girl in the office.

DESPERATE Straights: Sex-starved heterosexuals.

GAELIC: An Irish Lesbian.

INCEST: Relatively boring.

LUBRICATED CONDOMS: Bedroom slippers.

MASTURBATION: I-balling.

SELF-DECEPTION: Faking an organism during masturbation.

DENTISTS

JOE wasn't keen on having his tooth pulled out. In fact

every time the dentist tried to get the pliers near the tooth Joe would clamp his mouth shut.

The dentist whispered an instruction to his nurse, then got his pliers ready and gave the nurse the nod.

She took a firm grasp of Joe's balls and gave them a sharp twist. When he let out a yell the dentist swiftly siezed the tooth and yanked it out.

"That wasn't so bad?" said the dentist.

"No," said Joe. "But by Jeeze the roots went down a long way."

*　*　*

OLD Fred had always feared the dentist and had delayed making a visit until the last of his aching teeth forced the issue. The dentist took one look and declared they all needed root canal work.

"No way," protested the old man, "I am too much of a coward. I can't stand pain."

"Who said anything about pain. I am the painless dentist."

But the old man could not be convinced.

"Listen," said the dentist, "I did a multi-tooth replacement on a rabbit trapper up north. He will vouch for me. Here, I'll phone him now."

The dentist dialed, then handed Fred the phone.

"You don't know me," Fred began, "but I am in the office of your dentist. He told me he did a job on your teeth and it didn't hurt. Is that true?"

"Well, put it this way," said the gruff voice on the other end of the phone. "I'm a rabbit trapper by trade. I was trudging through the scrub a few days ago and I had a sudden urge to have a crap. I moved in behind a bush, dropped my trousers and squatted down ..."

"Yes," said Fred, "but about your teeth ..."

"I'm getting to it. I was just about to have this crap when my foot trips the trigger of a rabbit trap I set on that exact spot a week before. The steel jaws snap shut, right on my balls. I let out a scream and try to make a mighty leap only to find the trap is on a very short chain to the steel anchor peg. To get to the point, it was the first time in months that my teeth didn't hurt."

* * *

A DASHING young dentist, Malone
  Attends all the nice women alone
  And tries, from depravity
  To fill the wrong cavity
  It's the reason his practice has grown.

* * *

THERE was a young lady called Billing
  Who went to a dentist for drilling
  Out of depravity
  He filled the wrong cavity
  And now Billing's nursing her filling.

DESERT ISLANDS

A SAILOR stranded on a desert island for years had only a pig and an Alsatian for company. He formed a romantic attachment for the pig, and rightly so, because Porky was female. But every time he tried to root the pig the dog would snap at his heels.

One day a beautiful blonde waded ashore. She was the answer to his prayer. His problem was solved.

She thanked him for the fresh food: "I owe my life to you," she said, and noticing his tanned nude body and his rising endowment added, "is there any way I can repay you?"

The sailor got straight to the point with the vital question: "Would ya mind taking the dog for a walk while I fuck this pig?"

* * *

SEVEN survivors staggered ashore from the shipwreck, six women and a man. They were civilised about it. The women decided they would each have the bloke for one night each and he could rest on Sundays. The bloke agreed with relish, but as the weeks went on he realised what a physical commitment he had undertaken.

Then one day he spotted a raft with a lone figure paddling toward the island. It was a man.

Elated at finding unexpected help the bloke ran into the shallows to help him ashore.

The guy on the raft waved a handkerchief to him and said: "Oh, Hello Big Boy!"

"Oh shit," said the rescuer, "there goes my Sundays."

* * *

A GOLFER fell overboard from a Sitmar cruise and finally drifted ashore on a tropical island. He was eventually revived by a beautiful bare-breasted native girl.

She took him to her hut where she supplied him with food.

Then she produced a bottle of Scotch from a crate which had also drifted onto the beach.

Then she said: "Would you like to play around with me?"

The golfer was frankly astonished. "Don't tell me you've got a set of golf clubs too?"

* * *

BLOKE walking along a deserted beach picks up a bottle and rubs it. Sure enough, out pops a genie and offers him two wishes.

"I wish I was always hard, and I wish I could get all the arse I wanted."

"Whatever turns you on," said the genie and turned him into a toilet seat.

DICKS AND DONGERS

AN erection is like the Theory of Relativity;
    the more you think about it the harder it gets.

A YOUNG mother took her five-year-old son to the doctor because she was concerned at the small size of his penis.

The doctor said size was not important. She was unconvinced so he placated her with a line that plenty of Vegemite would do the trick. "Give it to him on toast," he said.

Next morning little Johnny was surprised to see 16 slices of toast and Vegemite on the table.

"I can't eat all that, Mum," he complained.

"Shut up," she said, giving him a clip over the ear, "Two slices are for you. The rest are for your father!"

* * *

FRED dropped his dacks to show the doctor the damage to his donger.

With embarrassment he explained that he was climbing out the bedroom window when the husband fired an accurate shotgun blast that hit him in the privates.

The doctor looked closely then reached for his pad and scribbled a name.

"Is he a specialist?" asked Fred.

"No," replied the doc. "He's a a top piccolo player. He will show you where to put your fingers next time you want a leak."

* * *

"HEY Mum," he said as he rushed in from school. "I've got the biggest dick in grade five."

"Well so you should, ya dickhead," she said, "you'll be 21 next August."

* * *

HE rushed in to the clinic. "Can you take a look at my dick, doctor."

"Of course," said the doctor, and after examining it for five minutes said: "There's nothing wrong with that."

"I know," said the man, "but it's a fucken beauty isn't it!"

HE then went into a chiropodist and plonked his donger on the counter.

"Why, that's not a foot," said the doctor.

"I know, but it's a good ten inches."

* * *

JAKE and Fred went behind a fence for a leak. While they stood side by side Jake said: "I wish I had a big one like my brother. It's so big he has to hold it with all five fingers."

Fred looked down. "But you are holding yours with all five fingers."

"Yes, but I'm pissing on three of them."

* * *

HOWEVER hard you shake your peg

At least one drop goes down your leg.

* * *

ON their wedding night he dropped his trousers and climbed in beside her.

"Oh, what a nice pee-wee," she said.

"My dear," he said, mustering all the authority of a new husband. "The first thing you must learn is that it isn't called a pee-wee. It's a cock."

"Oh, no," she said. "A cock is long, black and fat. That's a pee-wee."

* * *

THE girls were comparing notes, "I hear your new boy friend is very well hung?"

"You bet. You should see his fiveskin."

* * *

WE know a bloke who has five dicks.

His underpants fit him like a glove.

* * *

HE complained to his psychiatrist that he had an inferiority complex because of the diminutive size of his penis.

The shrink looked at it for a moment and said: "Oh, I wouldn't let a little thing like that worry you."

DID you know that former US Vice President Spiro Agnew was an anagram for "Grow a Penis?"

* * *

A POLICEMAN from North Bondi Junction
  Whose organ had long ceased to function
  Deceived his poor wife
  For the rest of her life
  With intelligent use of his truncheon.

* * *

HE picked her up in the singles bar and they had walked to his apartment in silence. "You are not the communicative type," she said as they were undressing.

"No," he replied, and lapsed back into silence until he dropped his underpants.

"I do all my talking with this," he said.

The girl leant forward, squinted, and said, "Gawd. Don't tell me that's all you've got to say?"

* * *

ALTHOUGH it was their first date she was anything but shy and soon had his donger in her hand.

"What's your pet name for it?" she asked. "I know some fellows call it Dick, their Willie or their Peter. What do you call yours?"

"I don't call mine anything," he said. "It always comes without being called."

* * *

OF course men give their dicks names because they don't want a stranger making 99 per cent of their decisions for them.

* * *

SHE said her current boyfriend said he had no need to call his organ Willie, Peter or Dick. "He calls it Confidence," she confided to her girlfriend.

"Is that because he has no trouble getting it up?"

"No," she replied, "it's because he likes instilling it in me."

A BLOKE went to a country dunny and got bitten on the donger by a spider under the toilet seat. He spent a week in hospital and the circumstances of his injury soon became the talk of the town.

On his first return visit to the pub one of the regulars, Spinster Sal, said she heard about his injury but insisted to know where he was bitten.

"Well Sal," he replied. "If you got bit where I got bit you wouldn't have been bitten at all."

*   *   *

A HORNY young man named Fats Wallow
Told a maid as they kissed in a hollow
"Did you know that my dick
"Is three inches thick?"
She said. "Gee, that's a hard one to swallow."

*   *   *

ADOPTING the metric system was the best thing that ever happened to Fred. He claims he has 18 centimetres instead of seven inches.

*   *   *

AN elephant and a rat had become good mates and while wandering through the jungle together the elephant fell into a deep hole. The rat rushed out to a nearby highway, flagged down a Mercedes Benz and with the elephant hanging on to a rope the car pulled him out.

A year later the rat fell down and it was the elephant's turn to rescue him. The elephant simply dropped his dick down for the rat to climb up.

The moral of this story is: If you've got a big dick you don't need a Mercedes Benz.

*   *   *

THE upwardly mobile manager finally arranged a dirty weekend with his secretary. Despite champagne, silk sheets, her alluring lingerie and suggestive poses he was unable to raise an erection for the entire weekend.

When he arrived home he took a shower and entered his

bedroom to find his wife, hair in curlers, in a crumpled flannel housecoat lying on the bed reading.

He looked down to find he was sporting a spectacular erection. "You bloody confused thing," he said. "No wonder they call you a prick."

* * *

IN the deep south Rastus was rambling along the road and almost stumbled over a $20 note. His sore feet prompted him to say: "Feet. At last I can buy you a comfy pair of shoes."

A little further, with the hot sun on his forehead he said. "And Head, we'll get a nice shady hat."

A bit further and the pangs of hunger prompted another promise. "Okay Belly, "we'll get ourselves some soul food."

Then he looked down and noticed he had an erection.

"Okay Big Dick. Who told you we come into money?"

* * *

UNBEKNOWN to Fred the zip on his fly was broken. The woman sitting opposite on the train could stand it no longer.

"Young man," she protested, "your member is sticking out."

Fred looked down: "Don't flatter yourself. It's only hanging out."

* * *

THEY were camping in the outback and enjoying a few beers when Kev got up to go for a leak. When he returned he had forgotten to do up the fly in his shorts and as he sat down Dave told him that a big snake had just wriggled through the camp.

"It was one of the biggest I've seen," enthused Dave. "It was right near your chair. Heck! There it is, I can see the head there now," and reaching for a beer bottle said, "hold still, I'll kill it."

Dave brought the bottle crashing down and Kev let out a wail.

"Hit it again," screamed Kev. "It just bit me."

* * *

THE salesman was put up for the night by an old farmer who only had one bed. Just before dawn the old man woke and began shouting: "Bring me a woman! Look at that erection, I haven't had an erection like that for years. I need a woman."

The traveller told him to calm down. "It's an erection alright," he said, "but it's not yours, it's mine."

* * *

THE politician went to Harley St, London, for a dick transplant. It rejected him.

* * *

NORMAN had to summon up considerable courage to go to the clinic. "You promise not to laugh?" he tentatively asked the doctor.

"Of course not. I'm a professional. Now come along, what's the problem?"

"It's like this. I'm worried about the size of my penis," said Norman.

"Understandable," said the doctor. "It is a common problem. Now drop your trousers and we'll check it out."

Norman did so and the astonished doctor had to struggle to contain a burst of laughter as he found himself looking at a tiny button, the smallest dick he had ever seen.

Choking back a tear the doctor said: "How long has it been like that?"

Norman replied: "It's been swelling up like that for weeks."

* * *

WITH his ten-gallon hat and his high heeled boots the big man leaning on the bar was obviously a Texan. And he soon had a woman by his side.

"Tell me," she said. "Is it true that everything is big in Texas?"

"Yes, Ma'am."

One thing led to another and they were soon back at her her flat where he took off his big Texas hat, and his big Texas boots. He took of his Big Texas pants to reveal that indeed, everything was big in Texas.

They were having their post-bonk cigarette when he said: "By the way, Ma'am. What part of Texas do you come from?"

* * *

ON business in Hong Kong he had been playing around too much and one day noticed his dick had turned yellow.

He went to an expatriate doctor who quickly diagnosed the trouble as Hong Kong Dong and told him that his dick would have to be amputated.

Shocked he sought a second opinion, only to receive the same advice on amputation.

As a last resort he went to a Chinese doctor who confirmed that the complaint was Hong Kong Dong, but there was no need for amputation.

"Oh, I'm so relieved," said the businessman.

"Yes, no need to cut off dick," said the Chinese medic, "in few days it fall off by itself."

* * *

OCKER had just taken up the job as a guide at an Outback wildlife sanctuary and was explaining the difference between an echidna and a porcupine to a group of American tourists. "The echidna is a different colour, different size and anyway," said Ocker with authority, "their pricks are longer."

This caused some embarrassment among the mixed group which quickly dispersed to look at the kangaroos, giving a chance for the supervisor to reprimand Ocker on his choice of words.

"Quills," he said. "Use a bit of decorum. They are quills," and he stood by to listen as Ocker guided the next group through.

"Is that a dog'gone porcupine?" drawled a yank when he saw the echidna.

"Different animal altogether," said Ocker authoritively. "The echidna is smaller, lighter in colour and its quills are longer, but their pricks are about the same size!"

* * *

THERE was a young stud called Sir Lancelot
Women would glance him askance a lot.
For whenever he'd pass
A presentable arse
The front of his pants would advance a lot.

* * *

AN old archeologist named Tossel
Discovered a marvelous fossil
He knew from its bend
And the knob on the end
'Twas the peter of Paul the apostle.

* * *

FOUR blokes had been playing golf together each week for years. At the end of the game three would have a shower and a few drinks at the bar while the fourth would always dash away.

Finally they asked him why he didn't join in the social hour. "To tell you the truth," he admitted. "I don't shower at the club because my penis is so small and I would be embarrassed."

"Does it work?" asked one of his mates.

"Of course it works."

"Well how would you like to swap it for one that looks good in the shower?"

* * *

THE young body builder was proud of his physique and when he took his new girlfriend home she was surprised to see NIKE tattooed on his biceps. "I've won an advertising contract," he explained, "$1000 for each arm."

Then he took off his shirt to display SLAZENGER tattooed across his chest. "I got $5000 for that one," he said.

When he removed his shoes and socks she saw PUMA on his calf muscles. But she was aghast to see AIDS tattooed on his most prized possession.

"No, no. don't go," he said, as she attempted to leave. "If you hang on a bit you will see why I got another $5000 from Adidas."

* * *

THEY had been having a few beers at the bar together recounting old times when the call of nature caused them to line up at the same time, still deep in conversation. But Fred could hardly ignore the fact that Chas was very well endowed.

"I say, that's a remarkable donger you have there old boy," Fred was prompted to remark.

"Wasn't always that way," replied Chas. "Medical science can do wonders with transplants these days," he said. "I got this done over in Harley St, England. Cost a thousand bucks, but as you can see, well worth every cent."

Fred was envious. In fact, he packed his bag that night and flew off to the Old Dart first thing.

It was a good six months later before he ran into his old cobber once again and Fred could hardly wait to tell him that he had taken his advice and was well pleased with the result.

"But Chas, I will tell you something else," said Fred. "You were diddled. I got mine for $500, not a thousand."

Chas couldn't believe it. Same address in Harley St, same doctor. Complaining that he had been ripped off, he asked Fred if he could have a look.

Once more they lined up at the porcelain and when Chas took a peek over the partition the worried frown which had creased his face disappeared.

"No wonder," he laughed. "That's my old one!"

A YOUNG bloke was infatuated with his new girlfriend, but the problem was, he was ashamed of his small penis.

One dark night in the back seat of his car he finally took his courage in hand and put it in her hand.

"No thanks," she said, "I don't smoke."

* * *

FRED had dropped his dacks and the doctor had taken a long hard look before announcing the bad news. "I'm afraid it's got to come off," he said.

Fred was terrified. "Not to worry," said the doc. "We live in the age of transplants. We can get a new one on order."

"How much," asked Fred timidly.

"$500 for the standard model, $1000 for the super model and $1,500 for Every Woman's Delight," said the doctor.

Fred pondered this for a moment. "Do you mind if I talk it over with the wife?"

Fred returned next day. "We've decided to have a new kitchen," he said.

DIPLOMACY

SCHULTZ from the CIA had finally got invited to the diplomatic corp dinner where he intended to make some valuable contacts. However the pre-dinner cocktails had the effect of getting him in a randy mood and he made sure he sat next to the long-legged blonde.

When his hand wandered under the table and came to rest on her knee he was encouraged by the lack of resistence. He moved a little further up her thigh. Again no rejection. He moved further, to her stocking tops.

His heart quickened as he saw her write a note and pass it to him.

It read: "Don't give the show away when you reach my balls. Smithers from MI5."

* * *

LATE one dark night a secret operative disguised as an

Arab slipped into the entrance of a Tel Aviv apartment and crept up to the stairs to the fifth floor.

He counted the doors until he arrived at No.7 where he knocked quietly; two loud knocks, a pause then three soft.

The door opened and an old man said: "I'm Goldstein the pawnbroker, what do you want?"

The shadowy visitor said: "Wet pigeons never fly at night."

"What?" said Goldstein who had been disturbed from his favourite television program.

"Wet pigeons never fly ..."

"Oh no," said the old man, "I'm Goldstein the pawnbroker. You want Goldstein the spy, No.7 down on the fifth floor," said the old man.

*   *   *

A YOUNG bloke had just become engaged and met his fiancee's mother for the first time. "How old do you think I am?" she asked the lad.

"Well," he said after a moment's thought, "I am wondering whether to make you ten years younger to fit with your looks and figure, or ten years older on account of your wise intelligence."

*   *   *

THE white missionary had lived with the Bullabukanki tribe for 18 months when the chief took him aside and said the reverend was in big heaps of trouble.

"Yesterday a white baby was born to my sister, and you are the only white man in this village," said the chief, sharpening his axe.

The missionary broke out in a sweat. "Look, old man, I know it looks bad, but see your flock of sheep down by the river?"

"Yeah, I see them," said the chief.

"Well can you see the black sheep in the flock. There is only one and ..."

"Okay, okay," said the chief, "I'll keep quiet if you'll keep quiet."

DISCRIMINATION

WHEN their car broke down a Jew, an Indian and an Australian knocked on a farmer's door to ask for accommodation for the night.

"One will have to sleep in the barn," said the farmer.

"I will," said the Jew.

But five minutes later there was a knock on the door.

"There's a pig in the barn," said the Jew.

"Okay, I'll go," said the Indian.

Five minutes later there was a knock on the door.

"There is an un-sacred cow in the barn," he said.

"I'll go," said the Australian.

Five minutes later there was yet another knock on the door. It was the pig and the cow.

*   *   *

WHAT is a nigger?

A black man who has just left the room.

*   *   *

WHEN does a Pommie become a Briton?

When he marries your daughter.

*   *   *

THE notice outside the Lion Safari Park read: Coaches $50, private cars $5, Pommies on bikes, free."

*   *   *

THE new migrant was getting familiar with filling in official forms.

Where it said, "Name?" he wrote: Chizkinsky, Boris.

Where it said "Nickname?" he wrote: Hole Arse.

*   *   *

LUIGI was a recent migrant to the country and they asked him how he was settling in.

"I dunno understand," he said. "They call a bald man

Curly, they call a man with red hair Bluey, they call a big man Tiny, and me who has been here for a year with no girl friend they call a Fucking Wog."

* * *

MOISHE Isaacson was walking down a street in Belfast when he suddenly felt a pistol in his back.

"Catholic or Protestant?" demanded the voice behind him.

"Jewish," replied Moishe.

"Well then. I am surely the luckiest Arab in the whole of Ireland."

* * *

AN Englishman, a Scotsman and an Australian went for a job. The boss asked them all the same question: What is the capital of Ireland?"

"New York," said the Scot.

"No. It's Vancouver," said the Englishman.

"Fools," said the Australian, "anybody knows the capital of Ireland is Brussels."

The Australian got the job because he was closest.

* * *

A JEW had settled in a train compartment when an American negro entered and sat opposite. The blackman opened a bag and took out a Yiddish newspaper and began to read it.

The Jew was intrigued. He watched for ten minutes before he leant over and said: "Being black isn't enough?"

* * *

A LION in the London Zoo was lazing in the sun and licking its arse when a visitor turned to the keeper and said, "that's a docile old thing isn't it?"

"No way," said the keeper, "it is the most ferocious beast in the zoo. Why just an hour ago it dragged an Australian tourist into the cage and completely devoured him."

"Hardly seems possible," said the astonished visitor, "but why is he lying there licking his arse?"

"The poor thing is trying to get the taste out of his mouth," said the keeper.

* * *

AN UPPER-class Pom went into a butcher shop in Dublin and with a haughty accent said: "I'd like a sheep's head, my man. And make sure it is an English sheep."

So the butcher shouted to his apprentice; "One sheep's head, O'Reilly, and take the brains out."

* * *

MURPHY was on his death bed. "Teresa, call the vicar," he said.

"Don't you mean the priest?"

"No, the vicar. I want to become a Protestant," said Murphy, "better one of them bastards die instead of one of ours."

* * *

A CIVIL Rights official phoned the State Library and told the chief librarian that there were 15,000 books with the word "nigger" in them and that the books would have to be removed within a month.

"What?" said the librarian, "but there are fifty thousand volumes with the word bastard in them."

"I know," said the Civil Rights man, "but you bastards aren't organised."

DIVORCE

ALTHOUGH she divorced him on the grounds that he couldn't consummate the marriage he had no hard feelings.

* * *

MICKEY Mouse had separated from Minnie and told his lawyer he wanted a divorce.

"But Daisy's not insane," said the mouse's brief.

"I didn't say she was insane," protested Mickey. "I said she was fucking Goofy."

THE judge asked Fred's wife to explain her grounds for wanting a divorce. "You say it's due to poor health and exhaustion. What do you mean?" asked the judge.

"I'm sick and tired of the little bastard," she said.

* * *

SHE told the Family Law judge that she wanted a divorce on the grounds that her husband was wrecking her life with his unbridled lust.

"How often?" asked the judge.

"Twice a week," she replied.

"Good God," said the judge. "Women have stood where you are standing now and called twice a week desertion."

* * *

SHE was suing for divorce. She told the judge that every time she and her husband drove past one of his girlfriends, he made her duck her head.

* * *

BE warned. Fred Nurk failed to keep up his maintenance payments and was repossessed by his wife.

* * *

VINNIE and Louie were whiling away a few hours at the new singles bar and starring into their drinks.

"Ever seen an ice cube with a hole in it?" said Vinnie.

"I was married to one," said Lou.

* * *

"DOCTOR, I have a small, embarrassing wart."

"Divorce him."

* * *

HER lawyer asked her what ground she had for wanting a divorce.

"Well he wants sex every night and he is as big as a horse. It hurts unbearably," she said.

The lawyer said: "In that case I will file your petition."

"File my partition? No, no, let the bastard sandpaper his."

IT was an amicable divorce. They parted good friends. Indeed a few years later when he broke his arm he rang her and asked if he could stay at her apartment for a time. He was having trouble cooking and caring for himself.

She readily agreed and even helped him into the bath one night. While scrubbing his back she noticed he was beginning to get an erection.

"Now isn't that sweet," she said. "Look John, it still recognises me."

* * *

CHAP met his ex-wife at a party and after a few drinks he suggested they go to bed.

"Over my dead body," she sneered.

He downed his drink and replied, "I see you haven't changed."

DOCTORS
See HOSPITALS, HEALTH

BRUNO told the doctor he felt weak and run-down.

When questioned about his sex life Bruno admitted he had sex with five, sometimes six, different girls every night.

"Well," said the medic, "that's obviously the cause of your trouble."

"I'm glad to hear that, doc," said the hot-blooded youth, "I was afraid it might be the masturbation."

* * *

FRED visited his doctor. He was tired and run down.

"How's your sex life?" asked the doc.

"Every Monday, Wednesday and Friday, without fail."

"That might be too much, why not cut out Wednesdays?"

"I can't Doc. That's the only night I'm home."

* * *

FRED's wife went to see her doctor and after an examination he diagnosed her condition as run-down.

"Can you stop having sex with your husband for a month?"

"Sure," she said, "I've got a couple of boyfriends who could stand in for that long."

* * *

THE doctor's phone rang. "Doc, I gotta see you. I think I've got the clap."

"Okay, but first you will have to make date with my nurse."

"I did. That's how I got it."

* * *

AN old Frenchman told his doctor he was worried about his libido and his sexual ability.

"Then show me your sex organs," said le doc.

The aged rogue presented his index finger and stuck out his tongue.

* * *

MRS Lottsabazooma was complaining to the doctor in a very deep voice. "I think you have over-prescribed the hormone pills."

"Don't worry," said the Doc, "a baritone voice is a natural development. It won't last long."

"But I also have hair on my chest," she protested.

"Show me," he said, surprised, "how far down does it reach?"

"All the way to my balls," she said.

* * *

"THERE is something wrong with my aviaries," she said.

"You mean ovaries," said the doc.

She insisted it was "aviaries," so rather than continue the argument he said okay, lift your dress.

"By cripes, you're right," he said. "Looks like there's been a cock-a-too up there!"

* * *

A DOCTOR is a man who gets women to take off their their clothes, then bills their husbands for it.

"OH, Doctor," she said coyly, "Where will I put my clothes?"

"Put them over there, next to mine!"

* * *

THE doctor scratched his head as he studied two reports.

"What's up, Doc," asked the patient.

"It appears the test results are mixed up with those of another patient," the doc said with a frown. "Either you've got Alzheimer's disease, or AIDS."

"That's terrible," said the patient. "What shall I do?"

"All I can suggest at this stage," said the doc, "is if you can find your way home, don't screw your wife."

* * *

TWO doctors were seated on a park bench when one noticed an old man approaching. His knees were pressed together and his fists were tightly clenched and bent inwards.

One doctor nudged the other. "You still reckon you can diagnose on sight?"

"Sure, why?"

"Take a look at this chap."

"Arthritis, no doubt about it," said the first doctor.

"Cerebral palsy. I'll bet on it," said the second.

They were about to ask when the man shuffled right up to them and said through gritted teeth: "Pardon me, do you know where the shithouse is?"

* * *

HE went to the doctor with stomach trouble.

"Are your bowel movements regular?"

"Yes, Doc, every morning at eight o'clock."

"Then what's your problem?"

"I don't get up till nine."

* * *

THE aging playboy was having his annual medical check.

"Sex?" asked the doctor.

"Infrequently," came the reply.

"Hmmm," said the doctor, "is that one word or two?"

*   *   *

DOC: "Have you ever been incontinent?"

Patient: "Nope. Never been interstate for that matter."

*   *   *

EXAMINING Luigi for constipation the doctor gave him three suppositories. "You put them up the back passage, do you understand what I mean?" said the doc.

"No worries," said Luigi.

A week later Luigi was back, to complain he still had the constipation. "The pills were useless," he said. "I did what you told me, but for all the good they were I might as well have stuck them up my arse!"

*   *   *

THE doctor told him he had good news and bad news. Which did he want first.

The patient opted for the bad news first and the doc told him he had three weeks to live. "Hell, what's the bloody good news then?" he asked.

The doctor leaned close and whispered. "See that blonde nurse with the big tits. I'm screwing the arse off her tonight."

*   *   *

AFTER a lengthy examination the doctor came out of the surgery and said to the patient's wife, "I don't like the look of your husband."

"Neither do I, but he's nice to the kids," she said.

*   *   *

SHE told the doctor that every time she sneezed she had an orgasm.

"What have you been taking for it?" he asked.

"Pepper," she replied.

*   *   *

"DOCTOR, is it okay to file my nails?"

"Of course, but why don't you throw them out like everybody else?"

PENSIONER patient was told to bring a specimen to the clinic. He arrives next day with a full jerry pot.

"God, man, did you walk down here with that?"

"No, I took the tram!"

* * *

A DEAF pensioner was told that the doctor wanted a stool specimen, a urine specimen and a sperm specimen.

"What's he talking about?" said the deaf pensioner to his wife.

"He wants you to leave your underpants here," she said.

* * *

WITH great embarrassment the woman had to explain how she had the skin off her knees and elbows. "It's because we have sex doggie fashion in the garage on the concrete floor," she said.

The doctor was a little surprised.

"Goodness, madam, why don't you do it in the conventional fashion?"

"I'd like to, but my dog's quite ugly and I can't stand his breath."

DOGS

A MAN came home early one day and found his wife in bed with his best friend.

He shot the wife, but decided to give the dog another chance.

* * *

TWO drovers stood on the veranda of the bush pub with pots in their hands. Nearby a kelpie sheepdog was sitting in the shade licking its balls.

"You know Jake," said one of the drovers watching the dog, "I'd like to be able to do that."

"Well why don't ya," said his mate. "It's your dog."

* * *

A FOX terrier went in to a post office and took down a blank form and wrote, "woof, woof, woof, woof-woof, woof, woof, woof-woof, woof, woof-woof."

He handed it to the clerk who studied it for a while.

"You have nine words here. You can have another word for the same price."

"Yeah," said the fox terrier, "but it wouldn't make any bloody sense, would it."

* * *

WHEN Mrs Murphy bought a dozen cans of dog food the grocer said he didn't know she had a dog.

"I haven't," she said. "I feed it to my husband. It's cheap and he doesn't know the difference."

The grocer was aghast. "Oh, you shouldn't do that," he cautioned, "It could kill him."

Mrs Murphy took no notice and bought a dozen cans a week until she entered the shop one day dressed in black.

The grocer, fearing the worst, asked about her husband.

"He's dead," she said.

"I told you," said the grocer, "I told you it would kill him."

"Oh no. It wasn't the dog food at all," she said. "He sat down on the road to lick his balls and a truck ran over him."

* * *

FRED's lovelife had waned. "The wife doesn't seem interested anymore," he confided to his neighbour.

"Probably because you've been doing it the same way for years," said his neighbour. "You've got to vary your technique. You've got to try new positions. Just then the neighbour spotted two dogs at it on the front lawn.

"There," he said, "have you tried that?"

Fred said he would think about it.

A few weeks later the neighbour enquired if things had improved.

"Yeah," said Fred, "I love it doggie fashion, but by gee it's costly. It takes a full bottle of whisky before she will get out on the lawn."

THE workmates were chatting at the bar.

"So, have you talked your wife into doing it doggie style?" asked one.

"Actually, she's the one that started the doggie tricks," replied the other. "Every night I have to sit up and beg for it, then she rolls over and plays dead."

*　　*　　*

LITTLE Johnny was waiting at the gate for his dad with a tear in his eye. He couldn't wait to tell that his new pup had died. There it was, on its back, legs in the air, stone dead.

"It's gone to heaven," consoled his dad. "Don't worry. I'll buy you another one.

A week later Little Johnny was at the gate waiting for Dad again.

"Gee Dad," he began, "we nearly lost Mum today. When I came home she was lying on her back, legs in the air calling out 'Gawd, I'm coming' and if it wasn't for Uncle Fred holding her down we could have lost her."

*　　*　　*

THEY sat in the vet's waiting room together, the shapely Miss Trim and prudent Miss Prim.

Miss Prim confided that her miniature poodle had the embarrassing habit of humping her ankles. In fact, it would try to hump everything in sight.

"That's funny," said the shapely Miss Trim, "my Great Dane, Roger, has the same behavioural pattern."

"So you are here to have your dog desexed too?" said Miss Prim.

"No. I'm getting his nails clipped," said Miss Trim.

*　　*　　*

THE sign outside the pet shop said: "Special dog for spinsters," and sure enough, it soon attracted a well-dressed woman in her mid-forties who pretended to browse around the shop before she got to the point.

"And what does this dog do?" she asked.

"He's a big boy. A Great Dane," said Charlie the conman.

"He does little tricks for lonely women, if you get my meaning, nudge, nudge, wink, wink."

"I don't know what you mean, but I'll buy him," she said.

A week later Charlie received a phone call. It was to complain that the so-called special dog was a non-performer. It hadn't done a thing.

"Are you in bed?" asked Charlie.

"Yes," she replied.

"Hmmm, I can't understand it. I'll come right over."

When Charlie arrived the woman was indeed in bed and the dog was sitting on a chair peering out the window.

"Damn it, Roger," said Charlie taking off his clothes, "I'm going to show you this trick just one more time."

* * *

IT was the day the kids brought their pets to school.

Little Mary told the class her poodle was called Mitzi, "because poodles are French and Mitzi is a French name."

Little Jean told the class her Pomeranian was called Puff because it was dainty and had fluffy hair like a lady's powder puff.

Little Fred said his dog was called Porky because it fucks pigs.

* * *

THE barman was quick to act when he saw an old bushman and his dog walk into the bar. "Dogs not allowed in here," he said gruffly.

It was the dog that stopped and said to his master: "Ar, c'mon, let's go somewhere else."

The barman was shocked. "Did that dog talk?" he said incredulously.

"Of course," said the bushie. "He's been talking for years. He's been my only companion."

The barman settled them in the corner and each time he served the old timer with a beer he couldn't resist having a chat to the dog.

It was when the old man went to the loo that the barman

said to the dog. "My brother runs the pub across the road. It would be a great wheeze if you could go over and ask for a beer. He would get the shock of his life."

The barman gave the dog a $20 note and away it went.

When the old timer came back he was alarmed to find the dog missing, and was all the more worried when the barman explained his errand.

"He's a bush dog. He doesn't know city traffic. He could be killed," he said. The old-timer rushed to the door, but his faithful dog hadn't crossed the road. In fact he was humping a cocker spaniel on the footpath.

The old man was shocked.

"I've never seen you do that before," he said.

"I've never had the money before," said the dog.

* * *

A BLIND man had been at the bar drinking all afternoon with his faithful Labrador at his feet. Finally the dog got up, cocked its leg, and pissed on the blind man's trousers.

The man felt the warmth on his leg and began slapping his pockets until he produced a dog biscuit and lowered it to the dog.

A chap who had observed all this said: "Excuse me mate. I wouldn't reward that dog. He just pissed on your leg."

"I know, I know," replied the blind man. "When I find which end his head is, I am going to sink my boot into his knackers!"

* * *

A BLIND man went into the department store and suddenly began swinging his dog around and around above his head.

The superintendent rushed over and ducking each time the dog passed overhead said: "Sir, can I help you?"

"No, I'm just looking around!"

* * *

WHENEVER two drovers get together there is the inevitable argument about who has the best kelpie sheep dog. So the merits of their respective dogs was the subject of the debate at the bar.

"My dog's so smart," said one, "I can give him five instructions at the same time and he will carry them out to perfection."

"That's nothing," said his mate. "I only whistle and point and Bluey anticipates the whole exercise."

Finally they decided to put their dogs to the test. The first drover whistled his dog and told him to dash to the saleyards, select the oldest ram, bring him back into town and load it into the ute which was parked outside the pub.

The dog sped off in a cloud of dust and ten minutes later was seen bringing a large ram down the main street. He jumped into the ute, dropped the tail gate and hunted the ram in.

"Well that's not bad," conceded the second drover. "But watch this."

"Bluey, what about some tucker?"

In a cloud of dust Bluey streaked down the main street to a farm five kilometres out of town. The dog raced into the chook house, nudged a hen off the nest and gently picked up an egg.

The dog then sped back to town and gently placed the egg at his master's feet. But without waiting for a pat on the head the dog gathered a few sticks and lit a fire, grabbed a billy in his teeth and dashed to the creek, set the billy on the fire and dropped the egg into the simmering water.

After exactly three minutes, Bluey rolled the billy off the fire, laid the boiled egg at his master's feet and stood on his head.

"Well, that beats all," conceded the first drover, "but why is he standing on his head?"

"Well he knows I haven't got an egg cup," said the proud owner.

USUALLY, anyone who has a dog calls him Rover or Spot

or some such name. I called mine Sex, and it got me into constant trouble.

One day when he was young I took Sex for a walk and he slipped his collar and ran away. I spent hours looking for him. A policeman came along and aked me what I was doing in an alley at midnight. I told him I was looking for Sex.

That was my first court appearance.

One day I went to the town hall to get my dog registered. I told the clerk I wanted a licence for Sex. He said he would like one too.

When I said he didn't understand, that it was a dog. He said he didn't care what she looked like.

Again I said he didn't understand and that I had had Sex since I was five years old. He said I must have been a strong boy.

When I decided to get married I told the minister that I wanted to have Sex at the wedding. He told me to wait until after the ceremony.

I said that Sex had played a big part in my life and my whole lifestyle revolved around Sex. He said he didn't want to hear about it and he would not allow us to have Sex in the church.

I told him all my friends and relatives coming to the church would enjoy having Sex there. He barred the lot of us and we had to get married in the Registry Office.

Of course, my wife and I took the dog along with us on our honeymoon and when I checked into the motel I told the clerk we wanted an extra room for Sex. The clerk said every room was for sex.

I said you don't understand, Sex keeps me awake at night, and the clerk said "Me too."

When my wife and I divorced we went to court to fight for custody of the dog. I said: "Your honour, I had Sex before I was married," and he replied, "Me too."

Well, now I have been thrown in jail, been married,

divorced, and had more darn troubles with that dog than I ever bargained on. ·

Why, just the other day when I went for my first session with my psychiatrist she asked me what seemed to be the trouble. I replied that Sex had died and left my life. It was like losing my best friend.

She said: "You should buy yourself a dog."

* * *

A WEE little dog
  Passed a wee little tree
  Said the wee little tree
  "Won't you have one on me?"
  "No," said the little dog
  No bigger than a mouse
  "I've just had one.
  And I had it on the house."

DROVERS

IT was the end of the financial year when Jake and Bill, two drovers who spent most of their life on the Outback stock routes, rode into Stumpy Gully for a beer and to lodge their tax return.

They had been given the drum that a tax agent had set up in the town. Indeed, Jake noticed the sign on his shop as they rode by. "Taxidermist" it said.

After several rounds Jake declared he would go and see to the tax business and was soon told by the taxidermist that he was barking up the wrong tree.

"Well, what do you do then?"

"I preserve animals," said the taxidermist. "Like all those you can see around this shop."

"Can you stuff sheep?"

"Yes," was the reply.

"Can you stuff kangaroos and emus?"

"Of course."

When Jake went back to the pub he told Bill that the bloke in the shop wasn't a tax agent at all.

"What is he then?" said Bill.

"Oh he's just another drover," said Jake.

DRINKERS

MY Dad was known as a light drinker.

As soon as it was light he would start to drink.

* * *

A PROSPEROUS man was accosted by a disreputable looking bloke who asked for some money for a meal.

"Here, have a cigarette," said the businessman.

"No, I don't smoke," replied the tramp.

"Then let me buy you a drink."

"No, I don't drink."

"Then let me give you this lottery ticket,"

"No thanks, I never gamble. Couldn't you spare some money for a decent meal?"

The businessman looked at him. "I can do better than that," he said. "You come home with me and I'll cook you the biggest meal you ever saw."

"Wouldn't it be easier if you just gave me the money?"

"Easier, yes," replied the businessman, "but I want to show my wife what happens to a man who doesn't drink, smoke or gamble."

DRUNKS

SITTING in the corner of the pub one drunk said to his alcoholic mate: "I'll never forget the day I turned to the bottle as a substitute for women."

"Why, what happened?"

"I got my dick stuck in one."

STUMBLING onto the bus just as it was leaving the drunk staggered down the aisle, trod on a passengers foot, tripped over a shopping bag and flopped into a seat next to a very disapproving woman.

She said: "You, my man, are going straight to hell."

"Oh Christ," said the drunk trying to stand up, "don't tell me I'm on the wrong bus again."

*   *   *

A DRUNK tottered into the police station to report his car stolen.

"Where did you leave it?" asked the constable.

"It was right on the end of this key," said the drunk, showing the cop his ignition key. "Right on the end of this key," he repeated, holding the key out in front of him.

The cop wasn't impressed. "You should be ashamed of yourself coming into the police station at this time of night in that condition. Look at yourself, why even your fly is open."

The drunk looked down.

"Strewth, they've stolen my girlfriend too!"

*   *   *

THE cops had been instructed to clean up the neighbourhood so it was dead easy when one drunk staggered towards a constable and said: "Excuse me offisher, what time is it?"

The cop replied, "One o'clock," and hit him once over the head with his baton.

"Jeezus," said the drunk, "I'm glad I didn't ask you an hour ago."

*   *   *

TOM, Dick and Harry would often drink together. After a long session one night Harry's elbow slipped off the bar and he fell flat on his face.

"That's one thing about Harry," said Tom. "He always knows when he's had enough."

115

TWO drunks were coming home when they saw a young couple screwing in the park.

"I didn't have sex with my wife before I was married, did you?"

"Don't know," said his mate, "What was her maiden name?"

* * *

THE policeman became suspicious as he watched O'Flaherty cursing and fumbling with the front door lock on a house. When O'Flaherty forced a window and was half way through the cop put the heavy hand on his collar.

"But it's my house, offisher," protested O'Flaherty and invited the cop inside to prove it.

"Look offisher, that's my cat, that's my armchair, this is my bedroom, that's my wife in bed, and that bloke with her, that's me."

* * *

FRED woke his wife. "It's a miracle," he said. "You wouldn't believe it, Muriel. I just went for a leak and the light came on by itself. Didn't touch the switch. Had a leak and as soon as I left the light went out. Untouched by human hands. It's a miracle."

His wife gave an understanding sigh. "For goodness sake go to bed, Fred. "It wasn't a miracle. You've pissed in the fridge again."

DUMB

DUMB Duncan was telling the barman the big city was too expensive. "There's a pub back home where you can get a pot of beer, a ham sandwich and a fuck, all for a tenner."

"Sounds great," said the barman. "How often do you go?"

"Well I haven't been there yet," admitted Duncan, "but my wife goes there regularly."

DUMB Duncan was chuckling to himself at the bar.

"What's the joke?" asked the barman.

Duncan said the joke was on his rival, Fred.

"I have just learned that Fred is paying my Missus $20 for her to sleep with him. She sleeps with me for nothing."

*   *   *

"WHAT can you tell me about current affairs?"

"Not a lot," said the blonde, "I've never had an affair with a currant."

*   *   *

"WHAT can you tell me about Kipling?"

"Not a lot," said the blonde, "I've never kipled."

E

ECONOMY

IT was tough times and the husband was going through the household receipts. "You should clean the house yourself," he said, "and that will save on the cleaning lady."

"You should also learn to cook and that will save on the catering," he said.

"And you should learn to do the ironing so we won't need to pay the ironing woman," he said.

"And you should learn to fuck," she said, "then we could get rid of the gardener."

*   *   *

ECONOMY is a factor in all decisions.

"How much are the bananas?" asked Jean and Jan of the fruiterer.

"Seventy five cents each, or three for a dollar," he replied.

The girls thought it over for a moment. "Oh, lets buy three," said Jan, "we can always eat the other one."

EDUCATION

See Teachers, Schools

THE difference between a university lecturer and a proctologist is that the proctologist only has to deal with one arsehole at a time.

THE professor was giving a lecture on anatomy, but for one prim and proper miss he had dwelt too long on the physiology of the male genitalia.

He continued: "The Mongu tribe in Southern Africa are known to have the longest ..."

It was too much for Miss Prim and she got up to leave the lecture hall.

As she neared the door the professor fired one more shot. "There is no need to hurry, madam, the next plane to Southern Africa doesn't leave until Friday."

ELEPHANTS

WHAT'S grey and comes in buckets?

An elephant.

* * *

AS the elephant said when he saw the naked man:

"How the hell does he eat with that thing?"

* * *

MY first job was a responsible position in the circus. I used to circumcise elephants. The pay wasn't much but the tips were enormous!

* * *

IT is common knowledge that an elephant's genitals are in its feet.

If they step on you, then you're fucked.

* * *

AND male elephants have four feet because six inches would never satisfy a female elephant.

* * *

AFTER a wild night on the town a blonde woke to find an elephant in bed with her.

"Gracious," she said. "What a drinking spree. I must have been tight last night."

"I've had tighter," mumbled the elephant.

THE cub reporter rushed into the office with the news that while the circus was moving to the next town a catastrophe occurred. Seven elephants were lumbering along the road, each hanging on to the other's tail as is their habit.

"When crossing the trainline," said the reporter, "the last one failed to get clear and was struck by the goods train."

"What was the damage?" asked the editor.

"One elephant killed instantly and the arseholes ripped out of the other six."

* * *

AN elephant was drinking from the Zambezi when he noticed a turtle asleep on a log. He ambled over and kicked it clear across the river.

"What did you do that for?" asked a passing giraffe.

"Because I recognised it as the same turtle which took a nip out of my trunk 53 years ago."

"What a memory," exclaimed the giraffe.

"Yes," said the elephant, "turtle recall."

* * *

WHEN young Freddie visited the zoo with his parents he was intrigued by the elephant. He had never seen one before.

"What's that thing hanging down between its legs, Mum?" he asked.

"That's its trunk," said mother with some embarrassment.

"Nar, I mean the other end, at the back."

"That's nothing," said Mum, giving the boy a clip over the ear.

Freddie moved closer to his Dad. "What's that thing hanging down there between his back legs, Dad?"

"That's his donger," said Dad frankly.

"Mum said it's nothing," said young Freddie.

"Yes, your mother's been spoilt," said Dad smugly.

AN elephant escaped from a circus and no trace had been found until a lady who had never seen an elephant before rang the police. She was panic-stricken.

"There is a weird monster is in my back yard," she said. "It is pulling up the cabbages with its tail. But what is worse...I cannot describe what it is doing with them!"

* * *

ALBERT had been engaged to three young women, but when they got to the pre-marital petting stage and the debutantes discovered the diminutive diameter of Albert's willie, they had called the whole thing off.

It was this sad story that Albert confided to his local GP, who could hardly contain his excitement as he referred the matter to Dr Doodlelittle, the eminent transplant surgeon, currently in town on a lecture tour.

"Albert," said the excited GP, "there is also a circus in town and you are certainly the man who could do with a smidgen of elephant's trunk and help us all in the advancement of medical science."

So to make a short story feasible, Albert made medical history by having a smidgen of elephant trunk implanted, and sure enough, his next engagement went through the pre-marital test with flying colours and was running right up to the wedding.

That is, until the night of the bride's kitchen tea. Albert thought he would help out by playing the role of waiter, but as he moved close to the table, something shot out of his trousers and whisked off a small plate of sandwiches.

He stepped back in amazement and hoped nobody saw what he could hardly believe himself. He cautiously approached the table again. It flashed from his fly once more scooping up a Boston bun, three cream cakes and a lamington. It proved to be a show-stopper. Nobody missed it that time.

"Albert!" screamed his would-be mother-in-law. "What are you doing? You are embarrassing us all."

"Embarrassing you?" said Albert. "Where the hell do you think it is stuffing all these goodies?"

ENGAGEMENTS
See COURTING, HONEYMOONS

THE young man was so nervous when he approached his highly formal prospective father-in-law that he blurted out the words: "I am asking for your daughter's hole in handy matrimony!"

* * *

THE suitor had been shown into the lounge room to wait for his date while she got ready. Then her little brother came in.

"Is Jean your oldest sister?" the suitor said to make small talk.

"Yep," said the kid.

"And who comes after her?"

"You and two other blokes."

* * *

THEY got engaged on the eve of his departure for a three month stint with the Antarctic Expedition.

As soon as he returned she broke it off.

* * *

IT was hardly three weeks after Fred got engaged to the circus contortionist that she broke it off.

* * *

THE French maid announced that she was leaving service now that she was engaged.

"Congratulations," said her mistress, "you will have it much easier now that you are getting married."

"Yes, madam, and more frequently as well."

ETIQUETTE
SIR Reginald Snodgrass was the epitome of British eti-

quette, so when he came home unexpectedly and found his young wife entertaining the young duke on the floor it was just too much.

"Sarah," he roared, "arch your back this instant and lift that gentleman's balls off the cold floor."

* * *

WHEN Lady Ponsonby decided to impress the local society by staging a candle-light dinner she hired a maid.

"Don't forget the sugar tongs," ordered her ladyship, but when the girl looked puzzled she had to explain: "When the male guests go to the loo they hold their member with their fingers so we can't have them handling lumps of sugar too can we?"

The explanation didn't entirely satisfy the maid but she went about her business.

Half way through the evening her ladyship summoned the poor girl: "Where are the tongs?" she demanded.

"Hanging in the toilet," she replied.

* * *

THE feuding neighbours had decided to patch up their differences with a few drinks. All was going well until the host broke wind.

"How dare you fart in front of my wife," roared the husband.

"How was I to know it was her bloody turn," he replied.

F

FAIRY TALES

SNOW White gave a sigh, "Gee fellas, I had always dreamed of having seven inches, but not one inch at a time."

* * *

HE had lost all his money. He had lost his job and his wife had left him. In utter despair he climbed onto the bridge railing and was about to end it all in the murky river below.

"John! Don't jump!" cried a womans voice.

He turned to see a scrawny woman behind him.

"How did you know my name?" he said.

The scrawny one waved her arm in a wide arc, there was a flash of light and a flutter of confetti glitter.

"There are five hundred thousand dollars in your bank account this instant," she said with authority.

"Who are you?" said John.

There was another flash and a shower of confetti glitter. "All your problems are solved," she said.

He climbed down from the railing. "Who are you?" he repeated, "and what about my job?"

"You have been reinstated, at a better position and double the salary." There was another flash and John was impressed.

"I am the good fairy," explained the scrawny one, " but I look like this because of a spell cast on me by the wicked fairy, which will remain until I have sex with a man. I have solved your problems, can you help me solve mine?"

"Fair enough," he said.

She took him to a secluded place on the river bank where he humped his heart out until he fell off exhausted. "That's the best I can do," he muttered.

She raised herself on one elbow and dragged on her after-coitus cigarette. "That's alright John," she said, "although it's rare that I get the name right. Anyway, aren't you too old to believe in fairies?"

* * *

BETSY was walking through the woods one day when a large frog jumped into her path.

"Pretty maiden," said the frog, "please save me. I am really a tall prince with blonde hair and broad shoulders but a witch has cast a spell on me. If you take me home and hold me to your bosom all night the spell will be broken by morning."

Betsy gathered up the frog and took it home. She held it to her bosom all night, and sure enough, lying beside her in the morning was her prince, with blonde hair and broad shoulders.

Until this day Betsy's mother has never believed that story.

* * *

THE Big Bad Wolf had hurried through the woods before Little Red Riding Hood could get to her Granny's house.

He burst into the cottage and said: "Okay Granny, out you get. I'm going to lock you in the wardrobe."

But Granny pulled a shotgun from under the blanket with one hand and lifted her nightie with the other.

"Oh no you don't, Mr Wolf. You do like the story says!"

* * *

THE handsome prince had finally come of age and was to meet his promised princess. With great pageantry she was ushered before the throne, but when she was unveiled the prince flinched in terror. She was fat, ugly, nearly bald, cross-eyed and had three teeth missing.

The prince leaned towards the king and noted all her defects. "How could you do this to me father?" he whispered.

"No need to whisper son," said the king, "she's bloody-well deaf too."

*   *   *

TWO young women were walking along a country lane when a large green frog jumped out before them and said: "Please dear maidens. One of you kiss me and I will turn into a handsome prince."

One girl quickly scooped up the frog and put it in her handbag.

"Aren't you going to restore him to a prince?" asked her friend.

"No. Princes are a dime a dozen. But a talking frog, now there is potential for making a dollar."

*   *   *

CINDERELLA was really a nymphomaniac. She was always at it. One day her Fairy Godmother appeared and told her that if she didn't stop screwing she would not be allowed to go to the ball where she would meet the Prince.

Only the next day the Fairy Godmother found her in bed with the chimney sweep.

"That's the last straw," said Fairy Godmother. "I can't stop you going to the ball because it is in the script but at least I can stop you screwing the Prince." And she waved her wand and changed Cinderella's pussy into a pumpkin.

Cinderella returned from the ball with a big smile and a new boyfriend. "Hello Fairy Godmother," she said, "meet Peter Peter."

FAMILIES

"WHATS an orgasm, Mum?"

"I dont know. Ask your Father."

*   *   *

MOTHER was scolding her daughter. "I don't like that boy you are going with. He's too dumb."

"No momma," she said. "He is going to be a doctor and already he has cured me of that little illness I used to get every month."

*   *   *

IT was one of those small towns, and when young Nigel announced he was going to marry Jenny Bloom his dad got all agitated and took him aside.

"You can't my son," he said. "It's difficult to explain. Don't tell your mother, but Jenny is your half-sister." He gave the boy a wink and said, "Er, I used to get around a bit on my bike."

The following year he got really dejected when his dad told him the same story about Rosie O'Grady.

The boy looked so down in the dumps that he spilled the beans to his mother.

"It's no problem," she said."You can marry either of them. Your Dad is not the only one who had a bike, and for that matter, he's no relation of yours at all."

*   *   *

BEFORE Susie was allowed to move out on her own her mother wanted an assurance that she wouldn't bring her boyfriends back to her flat. "It would worry me too much," she said.

Six months later she phoned her daughter. "This new boyfriend of yours, you haven't brought him home to your place?"

"No, Mum," she said, "we went to his flat and let his mother worry."

FANNIES

THE first fanny was made as an afterthought.

God had made Adam and Eve. He looked at his handy-work and thought they looked too much alike. So he split the difference.

* * *

A VAGINA that talks back to you
is called an Answering Cervix.

* * *

AND if Eve wore a fig leaf what did Adam wear?
A hole in it.

* * *

COMPUTERS were already in the Garden of Eden.
Eve had an Apple and Adam had a Wang.

* * *

HE put his head under her skirt and said: "Wow. What a big one. Wow, What a big one."

"Okay," she said self-consciously, "you don't have to repeat it."

"I didn't" he said, "that was an echo."

* * *

CONCERNED that her love-life had quietened down somewhat Miss Lottsabazooma went to the doctor who asked her to strip off.

He noted that she was overweight.

"Why don't you diet?' he said.

She looked down. "What colour do you suggest? she said.

* * *

FRED said to his mate, "Did you know my wife is a wrestler?"

"No, why do you ask?"

"I thought you might have seen her wrestle."

"No. But I've seen her box a few times."

* * *

IT was a first night stand and it wasn't working.

She pushed him back. "It's your organ. It's not big enough."

"Sorry," he said. "It wasn't meant to be played in a cathedral."

*   *   *

AN Irish lad was making a love to a Scottish lass and she wasn't impressed.

"I thought you Irishmen were supposed to be big and thick," she said.

He replied: "I thought you Scots were supposed to be tight."

*   *   *

HE stood beside the blonde at the bar for a while and then said: "Can I smell your fanny?"

"Certainly not," she replied.

"Must be your feet then," he said.

*   *   *

RASTUS and Lulu Belle were walking home across a long low bridge when Lulu desperately needed a leak.

"Rastus, Rastus," she said, "I must do it. There's no-one about so hold me over the rail."

She hitched up her skirt, lowered her drawers and strong Rastus held her over the lake.

Suddenly Lulu looked down and became agitated. "Quick, Rastus, lift me back. There's a man down there in a canoe."

Rastus looked over the rail.

"Silly girl," he said. "That's your darn reflection."

*   *   *

A WOMAN goes in to a sex shop and browses for a while at the dildo counter.

"I'll have that one there, the tartan one with the big white top."

"That's not for sale," said the manager, "That's my thermos flask."

129

FARMERS

TWO wheat farmers finally sold their properties and decided to retire from the land. They surprised each other by buying a four-wheel-drive each and announcing that they intended to drive around Australia.

"What route are you taking?" said one.

"Ar, I think I'll take the missus. She stuck to me through the drought."

* * *

DAVE was courting Mabel who lived on a neighbouring farm.

They were watching a bull humping a cow and Dave took the cue to put the hard word on Mabel.

"I'd sure like to be doing what that bull is doing," he whispered.

"Well why don't you," she whispered back, "it's your cow."

* * *

THE best way to make a bull sweat is to give him a tight jersey.

* * *

WHEN the farmer's daughter responded to a knock on the door she found a neighbouring farmer looking very angry.

"Where's your father?" said the visitor sternly.

"If you've come about the bull it is a hundred dollars, and we have the pedigree papers," she began.

"Miss. I want to see your father," he insisted.

"We have another bull. We don't have papers for him but he is very well bred."

"Young lady. I don't want to talk about any bulls. Your brother Frank has got our daughter pregnant. Where's your father?"

"Oh," she said, "I don't think there is any charge for Frank."

* * *

BREEDING season is a crucial time on the farm so it was

natural that the farmer's son rushed in and said, "Dad, come quick, the bull is fucking the brown cow."

The farmer shook him by the collar. "The vicar is coming this afternoon so watch your language. If it happens again just say the bull is playing one of his dirty tricks, right?" And he gave the boy a clip over the ear for good measure.

Indeed, the vicar was sipping tea with the farmer and his wife that afternoon when the lad rushed in again.

"Dad, the bull has played a dirty trick on the brown cow," he said.

"Really?" said the farmer.

"Yes," said the lad, "he's just fucked the white cow."

* * *

TWO cows were talking in a paddock.

"Aren't you worried about this Crazy Cow disease that's going about?"

"No," said the other, "I'm a goat."

* * *

AT the National Agricultural Conference it was easy to pick the dairy milking champion. He was the bloke who shook hands with everybody, one finger at a time.

* * *

FARMER Snodd called the vet because he though his prize bull was a fairy. "He's not interested in the heiffers," he said. The vet prescribed a special mixture.

A week later Snodd's neighbour commented on the vigour with which the bull was mounting anything that moved.

"What was the mixture the vet prescribed?" he said.

"Don't know," said a very happy Farmer Snodd, "it's brown in colour and tastes like aniseed."

* * *

THE travelling salesman was driving along a country road when he skittled a rooster which ran across the path of his car.

Feeling guilty about killing such a fine bird he approached the farm house and knocked on the door.

A demure young farmer's wife answered.

"Excuse me, missus, I have just killed your rooster, and I would like to replace it."

"Please yourself," said the lady. "The chooks are around the back."

* * *

IT was the night of the school concert and all the kids had their poems, songs and recitations at the ready; except little Charlie had just come down from the country and had started school that day.

"C'mon Charlie," said the teacher. "Surely you can do something for the concert."

It took much cajoling, but finally Charlie agreed to do some farmyard impressions.

The instant applause gave Charlie a boost of confidence and he strode to centre stage."Farmyard noises," he announced.

Then cupping his hands to his face like a megaphone he yelled at the top of his voice: "Get off that f'ckn tractor. Shut that f'ckn gate. Get that f'ckn bull out of that yard .....!"

* * *

THE mayor and mayoress were leading the inspection around the agricultural show when the mayoress stopped beside a prize bull. "My word, what a fine beast," she said.

"Yes, he's a champion," said the lad attending it, "he stood to stud five hundred times last year."

The mayoress was impressed. "Five hundred times you say. Would you mind telling my husband that when he comes along?"

The lad did so. "Very interesting," said the mayor, "five hundred times you say. Always with the same cow of course."

"Oh no sir. Five hundred different cows."

"Would you mind telling that to the mayoress when she comes past?"

FARTS

THE reason farts smell like they do,
    is so that the deaf can enjoy them too.

*   *   *

SHE was delighted when the most eligible bachelor asked her to dance but while they glided around the floor doing the cha-cha-cha the effort caused him to let go a few whoofers.

"Oh what an original way to keep time," she said.

*   *   *

WHAT do you get when you've been eating onions and beans?

Tear Gas.

*   *   *

AT the Galloping Gourmet's annual feast Fred Flabby set a new record of 35 plates of baked beans. However the record was not counted due to a following wind.

*   *   *

PADDY the Irish cook was famous for his bean soup.

"I use exactly 239 beans," he said. "One more and it would be too farty."

*   *   *

STEPPING into the elevator the businessman quickly detected an offensive odour. The only other occupant was a little old lady. "Excuse me," he addressed her, "did you happen to pass wind?"

"Of course I did," she replied. "You don't think I stink like this all the time do you?"

*   *   *

IT was so cold in the mountains that Old Jake woke one morning to find two ice cubes in his sleeping bag.

When he threw them on the fire they went: Phartsst! Pharsst!

* * *

IT is her first date with her supervisor from the office and she is edgy. They are going to a charity concert but she is gripped with nerves and a tightening of the stomach. Just as she hears the doorbell ring she is taken by a great desire to fart.

In great discomfort she stifles it.

Outside in the dark street the young man ushers her into the front seat of the car but does not get in himself. "I'll just nip over to the shop and get some cigarettes," he says.

Immediately she takes the opportunity to let go a rip-snorter of a fart, lifting one cheek of her bum off the seat to let the blast go free. A few seconds later her date returns, settles behind the wheel and says: "Oh, I'm sorry. I forgot to introduce you to my parents," and turning round he indicates the two people sitting in the gloom of the rear seat.

* * *

MADAM was quite the old stager
Who as the result of a wager
Consented to fart the complete oboe part
Of Mozart's Quartet in F major.

* * *

BUT the violinst was just a bit smarter
For he was a magnificent farter
He could play anything, from God Save the King
To Beethoven's Moonlight Sonata.

* * *

AN embarrassed young woman was farting uncontrollably when her date was due to arrive. She was an accomplished pianist so to drown the noise she offered to play the Storm Scene from the William Tell Overture.

She had concluded the piece when she felt another fart attack on its way and quickly asked him if he would like another tune on the piano.

"Well if it is that storm scene again," he said, "can you leave out the bit where the lightning strikes the shithouse?"

* * *

HER marriage into high society was an excuse for Lady Upstart to inveigle princes and diplomats to her candlelit suppers and to put on airs and graces above her station.

It all got up the butler's nose.

But it turned out that on one of these society occasions her stomach was suffering a little internal turbulence and during an unfortunate lull in the conversation she let forth an audible fart.

Without batting an eyelid she turned briskly on the butler and said "Jeeves, stop that."

Jeeves was up to the mark, "Certainly madam, which way did it go?"

* * *

HE sat next to the duchess at tea
    It was just as he feared it would be
    Her rumblings abdominal were simply phenomenal
    And everyone thought it was he.

* * *

AT the Twilight Home old Jake was dozing in his chair. Every time he leaned too far to one side a nurse would gently push him straight. Bert, a new arrival, asked how he liked the rest home just as a nurse pushed Jake up straight again.

"Oh the home is alright," said Jake, leaning to the left again, "It's just that they make it bloody difficult to fart."

* * *

THE sex surrogate had been hired by the rich farmer to teach the son the intracacies of love and she was delighted to find he was a fine strapping lad.

She even skipped some of the basics and advanced to the sophisticated *soixtante-neuf* position.

Unfortunately, she got so excited and carried away she let go a little whoofer.

135

"Crikey, what d'yer call that?" said the country lad.

"Sorry, just an accident," she said. "It's called the 69 position."

They got back to work but again she got so excited another puff of wind escaped her buttocks.

The boy scrambled out from underneath. "That enough," he declared. "Damned if I can stand another 67 of them."

* * *

ELI MUSTAFA was in the Arab bazaar one day when he felt terrible stomach cramps. He couldn't control the thunderous fart which followed. Stall holders and customers alike were startled.

It was so embarrassing for Eli that he ran home, packed his bags on his trusty camel and wandered the Middle East for the rest of his business life.

At last, a weary old man, he yearned to return to the town of his boyhood. He reasoned that most of those who had witnessed his embarrassment would be dead by now. He had grown a long white beard and he was so aged he was sure nobody would recognise him. His heart longed for the old familiar streets of his boyhood.

Once in town he headed for the bazaar and found that the power had been connected and there were bright lights.

He turned to a stallholder and asked when were such improvements carried out.

"Oh that," said the man. "That was done 15 years and 5 months to the day Eli Mustafa farted in the bazaar."

* * *

THERE was a young man from Australia
  Who painted his arse like a dahlia
  The drawing was fine, the colour divine
  But the scent? Ar, that was a failure.

* * *

THE Scot was so mean the only way he would take a bubble bath on Saturday morning was to eat baked beans for his supper on Friday night.

136

TWO old maids were discussing the merits of pantyhose.

"Don't like them at all," said one. "Every time I fart it blows my slippers off."

*   *   *

IT was the season's diplomatic dinner and at the head of the table sat Madam Lottzabazooma, society matron and matriarch of the diplomatic corp. On her right was the British Consul and on her left was the French Consul.

Suddenly, in an unfortunate lull in the conversation the Madam let go a loud and reverberating fart.

The Briton leapt to his feet and apologised profusely to the startled diners. "I crave your indulgence," he said, "a serious war wound makes me particularly susceptible to flatulence and in stimulating conversation such as this, with excitement and laughter, I sometimes lose control. My humblest apologies. I hope you will forgive me." He sat down.

The French consul was puzzled. He knew it was Madam Lottzabazooma who had unleashed the whoofer, yet the Briton had taken the blame.

Twice more the Madam let farts rumble by and twice more the Briton jumped to his feet and apologised.

It was only when the Madam left for the powder room that the Frenchman leaned across and asked for an explanation.

"Well, old chap, we can't let her get embarrassed about it can we. It is my duty as a British gentleman to take the rap. It's a matter of honour," he said.

The conversation was cut short with Madam's return. A few moments later she discharged a rip-snorting fart that shook the chandeliers.

This time both consuls jumped to their feet at the same instant. The Frenchman waggled his finger at the Briton: "Oh, no my friend. The honour of France is at stake. This one is on me."

THE Queen was showing the Archbishop of Canterbury around her new stables when a stallion nearby let go such a resounding fart it rattled the windows and couldn't be ignored.

"Oh dear," said the Queen, blushing, "I'm frightfully sorry about that."

"Think nothing of it, Madam," said the archbishop, "it's a perfectly natural function. Anyway, I thought it was the horse!"

FASHION

HER jeans were so tight she was making a fashion statement without words; you could read her lips.

* * *

MISS Lotzabazooma was very fashion conscious. When she went walking she wore walking clothes. When she went riding she wore riding clothes, and going out for evenings she wore evening clothes.

Which is why her boy friend could hardly wait for her birthday.

* * *

BESSIE was picked up in a singles bar and the following night flounced back to the bar wearing a very expensive fur coat.

"Wow, what an expensive coat," said her friend. "What did you have to do for it?"

"Not much, just shorten the sleeves and raise the hem a little," she said.

FATHERS AND SONS

HIS father was alarmed when he announced that he was going to marry Miss Lottsabazooma.

"But son," he said, "Everybody in town has been to bed with her."

The son thought this over for a moment.

"Yeah, but it's not a very big town is it."

*   *   *

ESTABLISHED at university the son was always writing home for more money. He needed money for football gear, for tennis, for excursions and for an extravagant social life.

Finally he wrote to say he had a part in the college's Gilbert & Sullivan show and he needed money for the costume. Father was annoyed, but mother sent the money.

A month later he wrote home to say thanks for the costume. "Everybody agreed I looked a proper count," he said.

"All that money," said the father "and he still can't spell."

*   *   *

THE farmer decided to send his son into the world to learn about commerce and life. "You are now 18, son. Here is a duck. Go to town and see what you can exchange it for."

The lad soon found the town's knocking shop and wandered in. "It's my 18th birthday. What can I get for my duck?"

The madam said she was sentimental about birthdays and said she would handle the lad herself.

Actually she enjoyed the vigour of the youngster and said: "If you can do it again, I'll give you back the duck."

After the lad had completed his pleasant assignment he was walking home with the duck when a passing truck flattened it. The driver said he was sorry and gave the lad two dollars.

When he got home his father wanted a full report on the day's transactions.

The son said: "I got a fuck for a duck, then a duck for a fuck, then two bucks for a fucked duck."

*   *   *

HE was a young father, wheeling the pram through the gardens while the baby was screaming its head off. "Take it easy Jason," he said calmly. "There's nothing to fuss about."

A middle-aged woman noticed his soothing manner and marvelled at the new breed of young husbands.

When the baby screamed even louder she heard him say: "Cool it, Jason, don't get excited, lad, cool it son."

Touched by his gentle manner the woman leaned into the pram and cooed: "There, there Jason, what's bothering you?"

"Excuse me, lady," said the father, "that's Jeremy, I'm Jason."

* * *

LADY Muck finally confronted the Major and said it was about time their son Cecil was told about the birds and bees.

At the appropriate time that evening the Major did so.

"See here, Cecil," he said. "You remember that time I caught you rooting the maid? Well you mother wants you to know that the birds and bees do it too."

FEMINISTS

THE difference between a clitoris and a pub is simple: Most men know where to find a pub.

* * *

DO you know what you call that useless piece of skin on the end of a penis?

A man!

* * *

THE reason Australian men come so fast is they can't wait to get down the pub and tell their mates about it.

* * *

SHE said her boyfriend wasn't a Sensitive New Age Guy (SNAG). "He's more a Caring Understanding Nineties Type," she said.

* * *

THE feminists were hailing a miracle birth.

The baby had both, a dick AND a brain.

* * *

AUSSIE men don't suffer from piles because they are perfect arseholes.

* * *

MALE Chauvinist Pig's motto:
  Put Womens Libbers behind bras.

* * *

SUPPORT Women's Lib. Get out from under.

* * *

A DISCERNING feminist called Ida
  Said to her bloke as he slipped it insider
  "I'd much rather be
  Underneath as 'ridee'
  Than on top in the role of the rider.

* * *

A MAN wrapped up in himself makes a very small parcel.

* * *

BETTER to have loved and lost than spend your whole damned life with him.

* * *

GERMAN men live by the sweat of their fraus.

* * *

WHEN all that's stiff is his socks,
  take the money and run.

* * *

ONE man's Sunday lunch is one woman's Sunday gone.

* * *

A WOMAN who thinks the way to a man's heart is through his stomach is aiming a little too high.

* * *

IF you want a chick, go buy an egg.

* * *

A WOMAN who calls herself a bird deserves the worms she gets.

* * *

A HARD man is good to find.

NO man has ever stuck his hand up a skirt looking for a tram ticket.

* * *

A MAN who has lost 90 per cent of his brain is called a widower.

* * *

IF a woman does household chores for $300 a week, that's domestic science.

If she does it for nothing, that's marriage.

* * *

SHE said she wouldn't mind having a baby. "But unfortunately," she said, "you have to marry one to get one."

* * *

THERE are three kinds of men in this world; the caring, the sensitive and the majority.

* * *

A WOMAN who strives to be like a man lacks ambition.

* * *

WHEN the boss put the hard word on the lively new employee she had the answer. "No way, Bozo," she said, "you've got the words 'liberated' and 'free' mixed up."

* * *

LOVE is the delusion that one man is different from the rest.

* * *

WHEN a woman makes a fool of a man it is usually an improvement.

* * *

IT is said that the wisest of men can become foolish over woman; and the most foolish of women is wise to man.

* * *

THE only difference between men and pigs is that when pigs drink they don't make men of themselves.

* * *

MEN are like pigeons. They should never be looked up to.

THE only things wives have in common with their husbands is that they were married on the same day.

* * *

SHE wanted a husband and put an advertisement in the Personal Column.

She got a hundred replies saying; "You can have mine."

* * *

WOMEN are called birds because of all the worms they pick up.

* * *

FRED was a window cleaner and he couldn't believe his eyes when he saw a young woman get out of the bath and start drying off right in front of him.

She was a feminist and instead of screaming she stared straight back at him in an effort to shame him.

Their eyes locked in confrontation for an interminable minute. Neither would budge.

Fred finally roared: "What are you staring at? Haven't you ever seen a window cleaner before?"

* * *

THE young couple had a knee-trembler against a paling fence and got so excited they knocked it down. The commotion aroused the householder who grabbed the young man and collected a hundred dollars on the spot for repairs to the fence.

Later the young bloke said, "Listen Mabel. You are a feminist and you are always shouting about equal rights. Here's your chance. You owe me fifty dollars for half the cost of the fence."

"No way," she said, "it was you who did all the pushing."

* * *

"WHERE have you been all my life?" sleazed the middle-aged Casanova.

She looked up and said coyly, "Well, for the first half of it, I wasn't born."

CUCUMBERS are better than men because:
Cucumbers stay hard for weeks.
Cucumbers never suffer performance anxiety.
Cucumbers are there when you want them.
Cucumbers will always respect you next morning.
Cucumbers are eaten only when YOU fancy it.
Cucumbers never need a round of applause.
Cucumbers can stay up all night.
Cucumbers don't mind hiding in the fridge
when mother calls.

FINANCE

WHAT'S the difference between a wanker and a banker?
The wanker knows what he is doing.

* * *

THE Irish call their basic currency the punt,
because it rhymes with bank manager.

* * *

THE Chinese businessman pressed the teller to explain why his interest rate had increased two points from the previous day.
"Fluctuations," said the teller.
"And fluck you too, ya bloody ocker," said the Chinaman.

* * *

MORE often than not, bankruptcy is due to a lack and a lass.

* * *

THE bank manager and his wife were walking down the street when a buxom blonde in a red convertible waved to him as she passed by.
The wife glared and said: "Who the hell was that?"
"Just someone I know professionally," he said.
"Whose profession?" she said sternly. "Yours or hers?"

A FINANCIALLY astute prostitute who works around the stock exchange is known as Cash Flo.

* * *

PADDY fronted the bank teller and whispered gruffly: "This is a cock up."

The startled teller said, "Don't you mean a stick-up?"

"No," said Paddy, "I've left me bloody gun at home."

* * *

TREASURER'S report: "Last year we we were poised on the edge of a precipice. This year we have made a great leap forward!"

* * *

THE wealthy financier took a tumble for a blonde and lost his balance at the bank.

* * *

THE bank manager managed to get his pretty bank teller to bed. As they slid under the sheets he said: "Aren't you going to warn me that there will be a substantial penalty for early withdrawal?"

"That's not likely as your interest begins to peak," she replied.

* * *

A YOUNG woman approached the bank teller with a large bag of cash and said she wanted to open an account.

The teller was surprised at the amount of money she pushed across the counter.

"Did you hoard all this money yourself?"

"Don't be silly, my sister whored half of it."

* * *

THE bank manager noticed the new clerk was adroit at counting money and adding up figures.

"Where did you get your finance education?" he asked.

"Yale," replied the lad.

"And what's your name?" asked the manager.

"Yim Yohnston," he replied.

A BLOKE recently discharged from bankruptcy went down to see the manager of his local bank.

"I'm sorry sir, the manager died last week," said the clerk.

The bloke came in next day and said he would like to see the manager.

"I told you yesterday, sir. He is dead."

When the bloke came in on the third day the clerk said: "How many times do I have to tell you. He is dead, dead, dead."

"I know," said the former bankrupt. "I just like to hear it confirmed."

*　*　*

TIMES were hard so Fred suggested to his wife that every time they went to bed for a nookie he would put a dollar in the jar.

A few months later he happened to empty the jar and found it contained a bunch of dollar notes, mixed with fivers, tens and twenties.

"Where did all this money come from?" he asked his wife. "Each time we screwed I only gave a dollar."

"So?" she said, "Do you think everyone is as miserable as you?"

*　*　*

ANOTHER bloke who put his wife on the streets grabbed her money bag at the end of the week and tipped out the cash. It amounted to $75 dollars and fifty cents.

"What miserable bastard gave you 50 cents?" he said.

"They all did," she replied.

*　*　*

AFTER a political meeting one of the candidates approached the rostrum to announce that he had lost his wallet with $500 in it. "I will pay $50 to anybody who returns it," he said.

"And I'll give $100," said Moishe Isaac.

IT might be the age of the computer and the calculator but some of us can remember the constipated accountant who had to work it out with a pencil.

* * *

PATRICK Whack was promoted to Loan Arranger at the local bank, but the manager made it clear that he would be on trial.

His first customer was an Italian who wanted a loan of $100,000, and of course Paddy asked if he had any collateral.

"I have this miniature elephant carved out of ivory with some precious stones implanted in it?" said the Italian. "It's out in the car."

Patrick didn't think it was good enough, but asked the Italian to bring it in for inspection.

"What did he want, Paddy?" asked the bank manager when he had left.

"Oh, he wanted a loan for $100,000, but all he had for collateral was some knick-knack. He's gone to the car to get it."

The Italian returned with a bundle under his arm and proceeded to unwrap it on Paddy's table. It proved to hold a large ivory carving of an elephant with dazzling diamonds studded all down its back.

The bank manager saw it from his adjoining office and burst in: "What a knick-knack, Paddy Whack, give the wog a loan."

* * *

IN Sydney she was Rhonda
  She was Patsy out in Perth
  In Brisbane she was Brenda,
  The sweetest girl on earth.
  In Wagga she was Wendy
  The pick of all the bunch,
  But down on his expenses
  She was petrol, oil and lunch.

147

AN Indian squaw was elated
She knew she was to be mated
Asked how she knew
That her brave's love was true;
"Because," she said, "the buck is inflated."

*　*　*

TWO female bankers were talking. "My neighbour threatened to take me to court because her husband gets an erection when he sees me sunbathing nude in my yard."

"What did you do?"

"I put up a hedge against inflation," she replied.

FISHERMEN

SHE went out fishing with five blokes and came home with a red snapper.

*　*　*

WE know a nurse who hates fishing.

But she doesn't mind going down on the Docs.

*　*　*

WHEN the boat sank, Gerry knew they were in trouble because Fred couldn't swim.

"Get on my back and we'll do our best," said Gerry as he struck out for the shore.

But after an hour Gerry was getting exhausted. "Try a few strokes," he told Fred.

"But if I take my hands off your shoulders I'll drown," spluttered Fred.

They struggled on and Gerry was encouraged to see Fred making a better effort with his arms.

Eventually they staggered ashore where Gerry collapsed on the beach. "I'm fucked," he said.

"I'm sorry," said Fred, "It was the only way I could hang on."

HE had been away for a dirty weekend with the floozie from the office but had told his wife that he had gone on a fishing trip with the boys.

"How was it?" she enquired when he arrived home.

"Great. But you forgot to pack my shaving gear," he said.

"I put it in your tackle box," she said coldly.

*　*　*

"THERE was a phone call for you while you were out," said the wife to her husband.

"Oh, who was it?"

"It was one of those trouts you were fishing for last week."

*　*　*

O'FLAHERTY was fishing when he hauled up a small stone jar. He looked at it, rubbed it and Whoooosh! Out came a small genie.

"I've been there ten thousand years," it said, "you know the rules, I owe you three wishes," and so saying it disappeared.

O'Flaherty rushed home to tell Brigid. Then they decided to go to town and see what the shops had to wish for.

First Brigid said they would have a quick dinner and she reached for a can of beans but couldn't find the can opener.

"I wish I could find that can opener," she muttered, and Kerzaam! The opener appeared in her hand.

"Christ. You've wasted one wish on that bloody can opener," roared an angry O'Flaherty, "I wish it was up your arse."

It took the third wish to get it out again.

*　*　*

SHE was only a fishermans daughter,
　　but she knew her plaice and to fillet.

FLASHERS

FLASHER'S motto: Grin and bare it.

* * *

FLASHER'S theme song: Whistle while you lurk.

* * *

IT was Fred the Flasher's most humiliating experience.
A woman charged him before the Small Claims Tribunal.

* * *

STANDING in a crowded train the pervert squeezed his
body against the buxom woman and she could feel something like a coke bottle in his pocket pressed against her
thigh.

She said: "I have only three words to say to you; You
Filthy Beast."

Later, as the train approached his station he said: "I have
only three words to say to you; Let Go Now."

* * *

A gent in a long flowing cloak
Unzipped his fly for a joke
An old man gave a shout
A nun almost passed out
And a lady close by had a stroke.

* * *

AS the female conductor came along the train checking
tickets the kinky passenger opened his raincoat with a
flourish and exposed himself.

"I'm sorry," she said, "but you'll have to show me your
ticket, not your stub."

* * *

SHE had a dick-shrivelling approach to flashers.

"Why have you taken that thing out of your trousers?"
she demanded.

"It likes the fresh air," he taunted.

"Yes, it needs some," she said, "It strikes me as being
considerably short of breadth."

150

ON the crowded train she turned to the man behind her.

"For God's sake will you stop pushing that thing at me?"

"It's only my pay packet," he said.

"Well, you must have a good job," she retorted, "You've had three rises since we left Central Station."

* * *

THREE old maids were on a seat in a park when a member of the raincoat brigade flashed at them.

Two had a stroke. The third was too slow.

* * *

HE had a sign hanging on the lowest button of his closed overcoat: "Next session, 4pm".

* * *

AS she walked throught the park at Exeter

Men whistled and craned their necks at her,

But some more depraved,

Went further and waved

The distinguishing mark of their sex at her.

FLOOZIES

A FLOOZIE is a girl who has been tried and found wanton.

* * *

THE richest floozie on Park Avenue wears mink all day and fox all night.

* * *

FLOOZIE failed her driving test.

When the car stalled she got over into the back seat from force of habit.

* * *

THE store attendant said: "I'm, awfully sorry, Miss, this fifty dollar note is counterfeit."

"Damn. Call the police," she said, "I've been raped."

* * *

THE blonde sat at the bar beside Fred and ordered a gin and tonic and swallowed it in one gulp. Then she ordered another and did the same. Fascinated by her capacity to drink Fred watched a third and fourth go down. "Would five make you dizzy?" he asked her.

"The price is alright," she replied, "but the name is Daisy."

* * *

SHE had told the court the defendant had robbed her.

"Yes," said the judge. "You claim this man stole a hundred dollars you had pinned inside your knickers?"

"Yes, judge, that's him."

"But why didn't you put up a fight, scream or kick?"

"Your Honour, at the time I didn't know he was after my money."

* * *

FLOSSIE the floozie said she was off to the Middle East.

She had just read that the favourite pastime for Arabs on Saturday nights was to sit beneath palm trees eating their dates.

* * *

INTERVIEWER: "How many husbands have you had?"

Movie Floozie: "Should I count my own?"

* * *

MANY a starlet trying to make it to the top often wears clothes that don't.

* * *

SHE has an impediment in her speech. She can't say no.

* * *

WHEN he whispered something in her ear she indignantly raised herself to her full height and angrily exclaimed: "Really! Do I look like the sort of girl who would tell a perfect stranger that she lives alone in her own apartment just five minutes from here?"

* * *

A SALESMAN went to a singles bar and fronted the first woman he saw. "I'm only in town for one night and I'm afraid I can't waste time. Do you fuck or don't you?"

152

"Well," she replied shyly, "I don't usually, but you've talked me into it."

* * *

ONE actress complained to her friend that she was tired. "I didn't get to sleep until after three," she said.

"No wonder you are tired," said her friend, "two is all I need."

* * *

SHE sauntered into the singles bar wearing the tightest pair of jeans the regulars had seen. One bloke quickly sat beside her and said: "Heck, honey. How do you get into those pants?"

"A gin and tonic could well be the first move," she said.

* * *

THERE was a young floozie from Kent
    Who said she knew what it meant
    When men asked her to dine
    Gave her cocktails and wine
    She knew what it meant ...But she went.

FOOTBALL

THE football star from the bush was not all he was cracked up to be so the runner was sent out with a message.

"The coach says he will pull you off at half time."

"That's great," replied the country lad. "We only get oranges at Snake Gully."

* * *

THEN the coach got the shock of his life when the team filed on to the ground, dropped their shorts and started wanking.

"But you told us to," said the players. "You said go out and pull yourselves together."

* * *

THE English football team was examined by a medical panel and pronouced fit for FA.

FOOTY FANS

ACCORDING to a survey taken on the state of origin of all football umpires in the Football League, not one of them was born in the state of wedlock.

* * *

TWO factory workers were discussing next Saturday's football match. "I would love to go, but the wife wouldn't let me," said one.

"There's nothing to it," said his mate. "On Saturday morning, buy her a bunch of flowers, then sweep her up in your arms, take her to bed, give her your best and when its finished just tell her your are now going to the footy."

The following Monday the first one said, "What happened? I didn't see you at the game."

His mate said: "Well, I did as you suggested. I bought the flowers, carried her to the bedroom, and flung her onto the bed.

"Then as I dropped my trousers I thought to myself, what the hell, the team hasn't been playing that well lately."

* * *

AT the last grand final the stadium was packed, every seat was sold, except one. It was noticed by the television broadcaster who sent a reporter down to sniff out the story.

"How come this seat is empty?" he asked the man sitting beside it.

"It's my wife's seat," he replied.

"Then why isn't she here?"

"She died," he said, "I'm on my own now."

"Sorry to hear it," said the reporter, "but couldn't you find a friend who could use the seat?"

"No," he replied, "they are all at the funeral."

FRENCH

A FRENCHMAN is a man who kisses other men on cheeks, and girls on all fours.

THERE will never be a French astronaut.

Who ever hears of a Frenchman going up?

* * *

THE French groom was so exhausted by the day's wedding events, the reception, and the celebrations, he went to sleep the moment his feet hit the pillow.

* * *

A FRENCH politician was pleading for legislation giving more equality to women.

"After all," he told the House, "there is very little difference between men and women."

The Chamber rose as a body and shouted: *"Vive la difference!"*

* * *

THE difference between a madam and a mademoiselle, is a monsieur.

* * *

FRENCH kissing is like a toothpick.

You can use it either end.

* * *

FRENCH girls are good at holding their liquor. "First get a good grip of his ears," said Fifi.

* * *

A FRENCH Square Dance is a Go Down Hoedown.

* * *

THE new French Consul was being shown around the city.

"And that is our tallest building," said his guide, "what do you think of it?"

"It reminds me of sex," said the French dignitary.

"That's strange," said his guide, "how can a building remind you of sex?"

"Everything does," replied the Frenchman.

* * *

THE restaurant was not doing so well so the proprietor decided to hire a French chef to stimulate business. But the Frenchman proved to be a hopeless cook, and worse, the proprietor discovered him performing cunnilingus on his wife.

"Look at that," he said. "First he screws up my eating, and now he's eating up my screwing."

* * *

THE difference between French women and those in the rest of the world is simple: All women know what men like, but the French girl doesn't mind.

* * *

IN fact, a French girl went to live in London for a time, but she missed her native tongue.

* * *

A LONDON society couple advertised for help. They had five daughters and desperately wanted advice on how to conceive a son. Advice came from around the world.

Americans suggested apple pie.

An Irishman sent a bottle of whisky.

A German offered a collection of whips.

An Indian suggested yoga.

A Frenchman wrote: "May I be of service?"

* * *

AN angry young man who discovered Pierre had been screwing his fiancee sent a letter challenging Pierre to a duel at an appointed place and time.

Pierre wrote back: "I have received you circular letter. I will be present at the gathering."

* * *

PIERRE passed away at 69
   And we all miss him so
   Pierre passed away at 69
   Boy, what a way to go!

FUNERALS

SOME of the greatest followers of the medical profession are Funeral Directors.

ALL her life she had been a good-time girl.

In fact they had to bury her in a Y-shaped coffin.

* * *

ON an old maid's tombstone:

"Who said you can't take it with you?"

* * *

THE tombstone read: "Here lies the body of Sir Roger Limp, an Englishman and a gentleman."

"Never," said Paddy O'Reilly, "no gentleman would agree to be buried with a Pommie."

* * *

UNCLE Fred died of asbestosis. It took six weeks to cremate the bugger.

* * *

THE Hollywood starlet with the reputation of a steamy sex life had finally died.

"Together at last," said one mourner.

"You mean with her late husbands? asked another.

"I mean her legs," said the first.

* * *

AMONG the funeral and death notices was this little advertisement: For Sale. Second-hand tombstone. Bargain for anybody named McDougal. Owner going abroad."

* * *

ONE mourner said: "I believe Isaac left just on a million dollars."

"No," replied the second mouner, "he didn't leave the money. He was taken from it."

* * *

PADDY O'Flaherty had been ill for some time and he knew he was not long for this world. But one morning the smell of corned beef and cabbage reached his nostrils and quite perked him up.

Feebly, he called his son. "As one of my last requests please fetch me a plate of that lovely corned beef I can smell your mother cooking."

The lad was back in a trice. "Mum says you can't have any. It's for the wake."

* * *

PAT and Mick were working together on the 25th floor when Mick fell to his death. The foreman gave Pat the responsibility of breaking the news to his wife.

"But do it gently," said the foreman.

That afternoon Pat knocked on the door and said, "Does the Widow Gilligan live here?"

"I'm Mrs Gilligan, but I'm certainly no widow."

"That's what you think," said Pat. "Wait till you see what the boys are dragging up the stairs."

* * *

THE Aussie had just laid a wreath of flowers on a work-mate's grave. On the way out of the cemetery he was intrigued to see a Chinese sprinkling rice around a head-stone.

"When do you expect your relative to come and eat the rice," he chuckled.

"The same time your friend pops up to smell the flow-ers," replied the Chinese.

* * *

BENEATH this stone lies Kierly
    They buried him today
    He lived the life of Riley
    While Riley was away.

* * *

IF you don't go to people's funerals...they won't come to yours.

* * *

THE deceased, Frederick, had always been so mean and nasty to her that it was a surprise to relatives and friends when the widow asked for his ashes and carefully cradled the urn on the journey back to their home.

She then took the lid off. "Look at this diamond ring,

Fred," she said, holding the glittering bauble near the ashes, "it's the ring I always wanted."

Then she carried the urn to her wardrobe. "And look at that fur coat, Fred. It's the one I always wanted."

Then she took the ashes over to the window. "And see that Mercedes Sports in the drive-way. It's the one I always wanted."

"And Fred," she said, coming closer to her departed husband's ashes. "You know that blow job you always wanted. Well here it is ...whooosh!"

* * *

BRIDGET took one look of her late husband, laying in his coffin with a smile on his face.

"Look at him now," she said. "He's smiling because he died in his sleep and he doesn't know he's dead yet. He is dreaming he is still alive, so when he wakes up and finds that he is dead, begorrah, the shock will kill him."

* * *

WHEN Isaac's wife died he was told it was the usual thing to place a bereavement notice in the newspaper.

He went down and lodged the notice: "Rachael died."

The clerk pointed out that the minimum charge allowed for five words. So Isaac added three more words: "Holden for sale."

* * *

THE widow placed the death notice in paper but added the line that her husband had died from gonorrhoea.

The family was horrified and quickly pointed out that it was diarrhoea that caused his demise.

The widow said there was no mistake: "I would rather have him remembered as great lover than the great shit he really was."

* * *

AT the funeral service the vicar and the undertaker had never seen a husband so grieved. Fred was sobbing his heart out and beating his breast.

159

He was so distraught that the vicar took him aside in a bid to comfort him.

"It's tough, I know," said the vicar, "but believe me you will eventually get over it. And dare I say it," he paused, "in three or six months you might well meet another woman and ..."

"Yeah!" wailed Fred, "but where will I get a fuck tonight?"

* * *

A GOURMET writer called Brereton
    Took some liver pate and spread it on
    A savoy cracker biscuit
    Then muttered, Ill risk it."
    His tomb bears the date he said it on.

G

GAMBLERS

AN orthodox jew who was worried about his son's gambling sent him a message to remind him of his religious commitments. "And don't forget Yom Kippur starts on Sunday."

"Put $50 on it for me, Pops," replied the son.

* * *

A PUNTER would bank $500 every Monday morning so regularly that finally the bank manager's curiosity got the better of him. Where did he get the money?

"I am a punter," explained the customer, "but I only bet on sure things."

Intrigued, the banker pressed him for an example of a sure thing.

"No worries," said the punter. "I'll bet you $500 that you've got red jocks. That's a sure bet for a start."

The banker could hardly believe his ears, and slapping the money on the counter he said: "You're on."

"Okay, drop your trousers so I can check," said the punter.

"Not here," said the banker, "come into my office."

Once inside the banker said, "there you are, they are definitely not red."

"Not good enough," said the punter, "they look red to me, but I will take an unbiased opinion. Your friend Charlie

Smithers is out in the lobby. Call him in and I'll accept his opinion."

When Charlie came in the punter asked, "what d'yer think, Charlie?" But Charlie had fainted.

"What's up with him?" asked the manager.

"Oh, I bet him $1000 I'd have your trousers off before 10 this morning."

* * *

CHARLIE the conman was usually broke so the barman was wary. "You don't get a drink until I see the money on the bar," he said.

"But I know you to be a sporting man," said Charlie. "I'll bet you the price of a pint that my dick's longer than your cat's tail."

The barman couldn't resist a winning bet and quickly accepted. He also whipped out a measuring rule and checked both items.

"You lose, Charlie, by a good two inches, now beat it."

"Hang on," said the conman, "tell me, from where did you begin measuring the cat's tail?"

"From its arse of course," said the barman.

"Well, would you mind giving me the same courtesy?"

* * *

SHE was an attractive barmaid so he slapped a fiver on the bar and said: "Betcha I can keep an eye on my beer while I go to the loo." She knew the loo was outside and around the corner, so she slapped down a fiver and said. "You're on."

He took out his glass eye, placed it beside the glass and went outside. When he came back he collected the money.

"Betcha I can bite my own ear," he said, thumping another fiver on the bar.

"You're on," she said.

He took out his false teeth, nipped his ear lobe and once again scooped up the money.

He made a circle with the thumb and index finger of his left hand. "Betcha I can poke my head through this."

She looked at the size of hole, shook her head and slammed another fiver on the bar.

With his right index finger he poked his forehead, through the hole made by his left hand, and collected.

"Okay, a chance to get your money back," he said. "Betcha I can make love to you so tenderly that you won't even feel it."

Now that's one thing she did know about. "You're on," she said, and down went another fiver.

He jumped the bar, moved behind her and lifted her skirt.

"I can feel that. I tell you I can feel it," she said.

"Oh well," he mumbled as he shrugged his shoulders and humped away, "win some...lose some."

* * *

A VARIATION on the same joke goes through the glass eye and false teeth routine with the gambler taking the money from, this time, a barman.

"Now I'll give you a chance to win some money back," he says. "Betcha I can pee into the neck of a beer bottle while its rolling along the bar. Betcha a fiver."

The barman could hardly believe the bet but the gambler insisted he could do it, provided the neck of the bottle faced him as it rolled along the bar.

"You're on," said the barman, and laid a bottle on the bar.

"Hang on," said the gambler, "let me get ready," and he lined up opposite the bottle, unzipped his fly, took his weapon in both hands and said, "okay, let it roll."

The barman gave the bottle a push and as it rolled along the bar the gambler shuffled sideways, keeping pace, but with lamentable aim failed to get a single drop in the bottle and ended up piddling along the entire length of the bar.

"Hopeless," said the barman, "the fiver's mine."

"Yes," said the gambler, "five for you, but I collect fifty

each from those three blokes who bet I couldn't piss all over your bar and get away with it."

* * *

PUNTER Pete had won $500 at the trots and went straight to the pub with his mates. He woke next afternoon with a hangover and less than a fiver in his pockets.

He went back to the same pub that evening.

"Tell me," he asked the barman, "was I in here last night?"

"You sure were," he replied. "You shouted drinks all round and we had a hell of a time."

"Thank goodness for that," said Punter Pete, "I thought I'd squandered it."

* * *

THE doctor told the gambler he had some bad news and some good news.

"The bad news is that you have a disease which kills nine out of ten."

"Hell," said the gambler, "then what's the good news?"

"The past nine patients I have treated have all died," said the doc.

* * *

THE big gamblers in the casino had gathered around a rather large dice game. An attractive woman in a long fur coat picked the precise time to flash it open to reveal she was nude, at the same time shouting, "I've won, I've won!"

She scooped up the chips and walked away leaving everybody dumbfounded by this sensational event.

"What was her score?" asked the manager later.

"I don't know," said the croupier, "I wasn't looking at the dice."

* * *

WHEN he got to the tote window a little voice in his ear said: "Put it all on number six."

He did, and it came in at 100 to one.

When he fronted the window for the second race a little voice in his ear said: "Put the lot on number 13."

He did and it romped home by a street.

When he pushed ten thousand over the counter at the tote window for the third race a little voice said: "Put it all on number nine."

He did and it ran stone motherless last, and the little voice in his ear said: "Oh well. Win some, lose some."

GARDENERS

GERALD the gardener was surprised when the lady of the house called him in one morning. He was even more astonished when she took him by the hand up the stairs and into her bedroom where she dropped her housegown and took the startled man to bed.

After a delightful session she took him downstairs, gave him a five dollar note and made him a cup of coffee.

When the shock had eased and Gerald was half way through his coffee he summoned the gumption to ask why.

"Oh, it's Christmas you know," said her ladyship. "I asked my grumpy husband last night what should we give the gardener and he replied: 'Oh fuck him. Give him a fiver.' The coffee was my own idea," she said.

* * *

"ARE you a gardening expert?" asked the small girl when the visiting neighbour was seated in the lounge.

"No Mary I'm not. What makes you think that?"

"Mum says if there is any dirt about you'll dig it up!"

* * *

THE gardener had taken on a new apprentice who was told to mow the lawn. The lad gave a yank on the starter cord and it roared off across the green, through a garden bed and straight into the swimming pool with the lad hanging on like grim death.

The apprentice failed to surface.

After a while the gardener ambled over to the pool and looked in. There was the lad on the bottom pulling at the starter cord over and over again.

"What a fuck-wit," said the gardener, then cupping his hands he shouted at the top of his voice: "More choke! More choke!"

* * *

WHEN the Minister for Prisons visited the low security prison he was impressed by the farm and gardens.

"Oh, that's Old Tom's work." explained the governor. "He's an expert gardener, makes the farm self-sufficient, and his flowers always win first prizes at the horticultural shows."

The Minister was intrigued and sought Tom out. He found him in the gardener's shed which Tom had built himself and which was stocked with books on horticulture, literature and art.

"You really shouldn't be in here, Tom," said the Minister.

"That's what I've been telling them for years," said Tom. He explained that the loss of legal papers concerning his case was the only complication keeping him there.

"First thing on Monday morning I will start the process to get your immediate release," said the Minister. He shook his hand and turned to leave.

That's when he was hit fair square on the back of the head with half a red brick. Tom had thrown it. "You won't forget, will you?" he asked.

GAYS

CECIL said it was true. Your entire life flashes before your eyes when you have gone down on for the third time.

* * *

I'LL be buggered if I'll join the British Conservative Party.

THE definition of an Aussie queer is a bloke who prefers girls to beer.

* * *

AT prison muster one lag said: "I think my cell mate is becoming a queer."

"How can you tell?"

"He shuts his eyes when I kiss him goodnight."

* * *

THEY were leaning on the bar. "Have you ever slept with a gay?"

"Certainly not. But I once slept with a bloke who had."

* * *

PUT the anal back into analysis.

* * *

A HUSBAND and wife were having a rowdy domestic argument in the pub. Observing the disturbance one gay said to his partner, "See. I told you those mixed marriages were no good."

* * *

WITH gay marriages being recognised in America it follows that divorces will be recognised as Gay Abandon.

* * *

GAY pride is a group of homosexual lions.

* * *

CYRIL sauntered into the Interflora shop.

"Is it true that you send flowers abroad?" he asked.

"Yes," was the reply.

"Oh goody, then send me to London, I'm a pansy."

* * *

A CHAP went to the doctor because he had a pain in the bum.

"No wonder," said the doc. "You've got a bunch of roses jammed up there."

"Really?" said the patient excitedly. "Who are they from? Can you read the card?"

DAISIES of the world unite.

You have nothing to lose but your chains.

* * *

AN alligator walked into a menswear shop.

"Do you have any shirts with little faggots on the pocket?" he said.

* * *

A GAY masochist is a sucker for punishment.

* * *

TWO very contented Irish gays were Thomas Fitzpatrick and Patrick Fitzthomas.

* * *

A NEW Gay Club in the Italian quarter of the city is called Innuendo.

* * *

THE new card game at the Gay Club is called camp poker.

Queens are wild and straights don't count.

* * *

OVER the years a lawyer became concerned that his son was doing poorly at university. Each year his marks seemed to be worse so the lawyer eventually rang the dean.

"Well, I have good news and I have bad news," said the dean. "Your son has failed most of his exams because he is a blatant homosexual."

"Good God," said the lawyer, "then what is the good news?"

"He's been voted Queen of the May," said the dean.

* * *

THERE was an airline steward whose colleagues considered him a sexual pervert. He went out with women.

* * *

IF horseracing is the sport of kings,

drag-racing is the sport of queens.

* * *

AS a football coach Cecil was in great demand by teams who wanted to know how to win by coming from behind.

THERE was a gay guy who was so ugly he had to go out with girls.

*   *   *

WHY are there so many queers in the British aristocracy?
    Have you seen their women?

*   *   *

CECIL the ballet star was relating the day's exciting event to his room mate. A society matron had stopped her car, offered him a lift and driven him to her apartment.
    "Then she took all her clothes off and said I could have anything I wanted."
    "How exciting, what did you do?"
    "I took the car. None of her clothes suited me."

*   *   *

OLD fairies never die. They merely blow away.

*   *   *

A JEWISH lawyer looked so despondent that his close friend asked him why. "I have just learned that my son is homosexual," he said. But then he added, "but the situation could be worse. He is in love with a Harley St doctor."

*   *   *

HOW did it feel when you first discovered you were a homosexual?
    It was quite a blow.

*   *   *

DID you hear about the girl whose bloke didn't drink, didn't swear and never made a pass at her?
    He also made his own dresses.

*   *   *

FRED says he loves women so much he thinks he must be a lesbian.

*   *   *

BI-SEXUALS have twice as many friends.
    And it doubles your chance of a date on Saturday night.

WHEN we drink to the Dear Old Queen
   Save a drop for the Queer Old Dean

*   *   *

UP before the court on a charge of sodomy it was mentioned in evidence that the more passive of the partners was a member of town's philharmonic orchestra.

"Case dismissed," said the judge.

"Why?" asked the prosecutor.

"I have heard them play," said the judge "and I can tell you they all need fucking."

*   *   *

WHEN two judges found they were gay they decided to try each other.

*   *   *

HE told his psychiatrist he suffered from anxiety because he thought he was gay.

"What makes you think that?"

"Because my father was a poof."

"Well the condition is not hereditary," said the shrink.

"My brother is a poof," insisted the patient.

"Well that doesn't mean you are."

"And my Uncle Cecil...and my cousin Walter."

"Heck," said the doctor, "doesn't anyone in your family have sexual contact with women?"

"Yes," said the patient, "My sister does."

*   *   *

TWO words that will clear the gent's room, even at the interval break at the theatre.

"N-i-i-ice dick!"

*   *   *

THE old actor said the queers in town were the ugliest he had ever encountered. "But then, buggers can't be choosers," he said.

*   *   *

TWO old boys met at the club after years apart. "How's your son making out in life?" asked one.

170

"Oh he's the top car salesman of a nationwide franchise. Going so well he topped the sales chart and they gave him a brand new Mercedes," said the proud father. "But he gave it away. Can you imagine that, gave it away."

"That's amazing," said the other old chap. "My son's in real estate and development. Clinched the biggest deal on the Gold Coast and they gave him a penthouse, but he gave it away. Can you imagine that?"

Right then a third old boy came in. "How's your son?" they asked him.

"Bit disappointing really," he said. "He's turned out to be a raving poofter. But still, he's managing quite well. One of his best friends gave him a Mercedes last week, and another gave him a penthouse."

* * *

THE publican was considering hiring a barman who had just been sacked from the pub next door. He was fired because he had his hand in the till, was often late and was suspected of being gay.

"I'll take you on," said the publican, "but you had better not be one cent short and never late. Now give me a kiss and get to work."

* * *

THE Odd Couple, Cecil and Cyril, went to Sydney for a holiday and saw all the boats in Circular Quay.

"What are they?" asked Cyril.

"They are ferry boats," he said.

"Gracious. Don't tell me we have our own Navy now?"

* * *

THE Odd Couple, Cecil and Cyril, had lived together for years and were fixed in their ways.

"Has the newsboy come yet?" called Cyril one evening.

"No, but his eyes are glazing over," came the reply.

* * *

THE travelling salesman's car had broken down and he had

staggered for miles to the proverbial farmhouse. He finally stuggled to the porch and knocked on the door.

The farmer said the salesman was welcome to food and water and he could stay the night. "But I must warn you, I don't have any daughters for I am a bachelor," he said.

"Oh gawd," said the salesman, "how far to the next farm?"

* * *

THEN there was the Scottish gay, Ben Doon.

He was found in the bush with nothing but an old Mackintosh on him.

* * *

AND the Greek soldier who re-enlisted because he didn't want to leave his mate's behind.

* * *

IN the days of the Roman Empire many Romans thought that sex was a pain in the arse.

* * *

WHY are there so many gays in Italy?

If you were brought up with so many ugly woman what else could you be?

* * *

TWO fellows in a gay bar had a misunderstanding.

They went outside and exchanged blows.

* * *

DARREN was in the mood for the Gay Mardi Gras.

"I want to eat, drink and be Mary," he said.

* * *

THE Gay Lib recruiting vehicle was seen patrolling the red light district. One couldn't miss it. It was mauve in colour with registration plate: RU 1-2.

* * *

A GAY lad who came from Yeppoon

Took a lesbian up to his room.

They argued a lot
About who would do what
And how and with which and to whom.

GERMANS

NEAR the conclusion of World War 2 Hitler's valet told him that the gossip around the ranks was that he should make an appearance at the front line.

"I have laid out your red tunic," said the valet, "because Napoleon used to wear red in battle so that nobody knew if he was wounded and bleeding."

"Indeed," said Hitler. "In that case get my brown trousers."

*   *   *

HITLER was depressed and consulted his clairvoyant about his future. The mystic studied her crystal ball for some time without a word, for all the prospects were grim.

Finally, she said: "At least you will die on a Jewish holiday."

"Which Jewish holiday?"

"No matter. Any day you die will be a Jewish holiday."

*   *   *

IT is odd that the German police have been unable to catch the Nazis, particularly when they were so efficient when they were the Nazis.

*   *   *

THE Lufthansa flight was about to take off and the captain's voice was heard:

"You vill now fasten your safety belts. And I vant to hear just vun click. Not clickety-clickety click."

GOLF

A WOMAN golfer staggered in to the pro shop to complain she had been stung by a wasp.

The pro looked concerned, "Where?" he asked.

"Between the first and second hole," she said.

"Gawd, you must have a wide stance," he said.

* * *

FRED seemed off his game. He was morose and sulky. By the fifth tee his partner said, "What the hell's the matter with you, Fred?"

"It's Madge, my wife. Ever since she has taken up golf she has cut my sex down to only twice a week."

"Think yourself bloody lucky," said his partner. "I know some blokes she has cut out altogether!"

* * *

THE pro was teaching the young woman the proper stance. He moved behind her and reached around to show her the right grip but the movement of a few practice swings hooked the zipper of his fly to the rear zipper of her skirt. They were stuck fast in a very embarrassing position.

They were moving together towards the clubhouse when a large sheep dog threw a bucket of water over them.

* * *

TWO golfers were enjoying a drink at the 19th when one confided in the other that his wife was making it difficult for him to get to the course every Saturday.

"Nothing to it, old boy," said his mate.

"Every Saturday morning I roll back the bedclothes and say, 'intercourse, or golf course'? It works like a charm."

* * *

THE club officials were called to the fifth tee where three men were fighting. A fourth lay dead in a bunker.

When they quietened them down they got an explanation.

"That's my partner there in the bunker," said one man. "He had a stroke and these two bastards want to add it to my score."

GOLF was invented in Scotland and there are still clubs there that have signs on the course which read: Members will Refrain from Picking Up Lost Balls Until they have Stopped Rolling."

* * *

THE blonde secretary noticed a couple of golf balls on the boss's desk. "What are those things?" she asked.

"They're golf balls," he said.

The following Monday she noticed two more golf balls on his desk.

"Oh I see you shot another golf over the weekend," she said.

* * *

TWO businessmen took time from the office to play a round of golf during their lunch break but were hampered by two women playing ahead and slowing up their game.

Finally one said, "Listen Jack, I"ll go and ask them if they mind if we play through."

He had only gone a hundred metres before he turned and hurried back. He was visibly shaken. "Jack, you won't believe this," he said, "but those two women...one is my wife and the other is my mistress."

Jack was a cool hand. "Listen Reg," he said. "Keep your head down while I approach them and we'll sneak past."

Jack had only gone a hundred metres when he turned back. "Listen Reg, you won't believe this ..." he began.

* * *

HE was a pro with a great ability to teach the game but some argued that he over-corrected faults. Like the young woman who wanted tuition in correcting a terrific slice she had developed. He worked on her for two weeks, now she's the biggest hooker in the club.

* * *

FRED said during his last game of golf he stepped on a rake.

"They were the best two balls I hit all day!"

ONE of the club officials, a stickler for the rules, noted a golfer shaping up to drive off at least half a metre the wrong side of the tee marker.

"Excuse me," he said, "in this club we frown on anyone trying to gain advantage by not driving off from behind the tee marker."

"So do I," said the golfer. "But this is my second shot."

* * *

OLD Ponsonby arrived at the club to find the only person present was a leggy blonde. "I wouldn't mind playing a round with her," he thought (but that's not the joke).

They teamed up together and as he hit the first drive down the fairway she said: "That's terrific, considering your handicap."

"Oh, there's more to it than that, love," said Ponsonby. "I've got a wooden arm."

"Get away, I don't believe it," she said.

And straight away he proved it by rolling up his sleeve and screwing his arm off.

At the next fine drive she said: "That's terrific considering your handicap."

"More to it than that, love," he said. "I've got a wooden leg."

"Get away," she said in disbelief, but to demonstrate, he rolled up his trouser leg and screwed his leg off.

The next driving shot was equally splendid and she said: "That's terrific considering your handicaps."

"There's more to it than that, love," said Ponsonby, "I've got a wooden heart."

She gasped incredulously. "Nobody has a wooden heart," she said.

He began to unbutton his shirt, had second thoughts, then said: "Just come behind this bush and I'll show you."

It was the foursome playing behind who caught up, looked over the bush, and saw Ponsonby screwing his heart out!

176

FUNNY how man blames fate for all accidents, yet claims full responsibility for a hole in one.

* * *

QUESTION on golf etiquette: What do you do when your opponent claims to have found his ball in the rough, and you know he is a liar because you've got it in your pocket?

* * *

THEY called it golf because all the other four-letter words were already taken.

SHE always wears two pair of pants to golf, in case she gets a hole in one.

* * *

HIS drive from the third tee sliced to the left of the fairway and the ball ended in an impossible lie in front of the greenkeeper's tractor shed.

His wife summed up the situation. "No need to take a penalty shot, darling," she said. "Just open the doors of the garage, push the tractor out, open the rear doors, and with a number three wood you could hit straight through the shed."

"Brilliant, darling," he said.

He took a mighty whack but the ball hit the rear of the building, cannoned back and struck his wife stone dead.

The following day he was playing the same hole and by sheer coincidence landed at the same place in front of the shed.

"No need to take a penalty shot," said the caddie, "we can push the tractor out and open both sets of doors. You can hit straight through the shed."

"No way," he said. "I tried that yesterday and ended up with a double bogey."

GORILLAS

A GORILLA left the zoo's reading room quite confused.

He had read the Bible and Charles Darwin's Origin of the Species and didn't know if he was his brother's keeper or his keeper's brother.

*   *   *

SISTER Anastasia wandered away from her party at the zoo to take a second look at the gorilla. Actually, she leant too close to read his name and the brute reached out, grabbed her by the habit, pulled her through the bars and had his wicked way with her.

She was in such a state of shock that it was seven days before the other nuns could visit her in hospital.

"How do you feel?" they asked in chorus.

"How do you think I feel?" she replied. "It's been a week and he hasn't written, he hasn't phoned ..."

*   *   *

AFTER contacting every other zoo in the world Taronga Park realised that it possessed the last of a species; a female gorilla. It called for desperate measures as an international search for a male mate had failed. So as a last resort an advertisement was lodged for a surrogate to do the job for the sum of $5000.

Paddy was the only applicant.

"Oi'll be taking t' job on t'ree conditions," he said.

"Foist, oi be wanting a curtain across the cage for proivacy, loik.

"Second, Oill be wanting any off-spring raised in t' true faith.

"And t'oid, about the money. Can Oi be paying it off in instalments?"

*   *   *

IT was a month after World War 3 had devastated the earth. Not a human being survived. Indeed a battered and dazed chimpanzee had wandered for weeks through what was left of the smouldering jungle without seeing another living thing.

178

One day the chimp saw something move behind the rubble. He was delighted to find it was another chimp, and a female at that.

He rushed up and embraced her, but she pushed him away. "No. Don't let's start all that over again," she said.

GRAFFITI

GRAFFITI should be obscene and not heard.

* * *

AYATOLLAH Khomeini is a Shiite.

* * *

ORAL sex is a matter of taste.

* * *

EUNUCHS Unite! You have nothing to lose.

* * *

YOU can tell the sex of a chromosome by taking down its genes.

* * *

ROSES are red, Violets are blue and Jean isn't wearing any.

* * *

SADO-Masochism means not having to say you are sorry.

* * *

IF you feel strongly about graffiti, sign a partition.

* * *

LIFE is a sexually transmitted disease.

* * *

I CHOKED Linda Lovelace.

* * *

UNTIL I discovered women I thought love was a pain in the arse.

* * *

LOWER the age of puberty.

* * *

WAKE up to insomnia.

GREEKS

WHEN a Greek kid asked his dad what an IQ meant, Nick explained: "When your IQ is over 120 you are very intelligent, when it's around 100 your are average, when it is down below 50 you are bloody stupid. You wouldn't be able to tie your show laces."

"Is this why Australians wear thongs?" asked the kid.

* * *

THE Greek businessman went to his favourite taverna in Carlton and was surprised to be served by a Vietnamese waiter who spoke perfect Greek.

When paying his bill to Con the proprietor he raised the point. "How come the waiter speaks perfect Greek?" he asked Con.

"Ssh! Don't mention it. He thinks it's English."

* * *

THE Greek taverna and the Chinese take-away were side by side and each Friday morning the two owners would sweep the pavement.

Con the Greek would take the opportunity to have his little joke: "What day is it today, Charlie?"

"It's Fliday," the Chinaman would reply, and Con would roll about laughing.

Each week it was the same and Con would even get some friends to come along and listen to Charlie say "Fliday."

It got on Charlie's wick. So he went along for elocution lessons and concentrated on "Friday, Friday, Friday."

Next morning he was waiting for the big showdown, sweeping a clean pavement for ten minutes before Con appeared.

"What day is it today, Charlie," grinned Con.

"It's Friday ... you Gleek plick!"

* * *

WHEN near-sighted Doreen saw Papadopoulos she thought he was a Greek God.

Now that she's had her eyes fixed he lookes like a Goddamned Greek.

* * *

A GREEK truck-driver had just carried a large sack of potatoes up six flights of stairs.

"That will be seven bucks, lady," he said.

Smiling, the woman let her robe slip open. "Wouldn't you like some of this instead?" she said.

"I'll have to see my partner," said the driver, "already this morning we have screwed away ten cases of bananas, 20 kilograms of tomatoes and seven sacks of potatoes."

GYNAECOLOGISTS

THEY called him the conscientious gynaecologist.

Even on his holidays he looked up his old girlfriends.

* * *

THE gallant gynaecologist liked to keep his patients happy: "I'll be at your cervix, madam," he would quip as he invited them to lie on the couch.

And his regular patients would reply: "I am dilated for you to see me."

* * *

THE gynaecologist was also a home handyman. He not only wall-papered the hallway, but he did it through the front door letter box.

* * *

AFTER many years in the practice he described himself as a spreader of old wives' tails.

* * *

AND the deaf gynaeocologist was able to read lips.

H

HEALTH

THERE is a clear difference between cholesterol and fat.

You can hardly wake up in the morning with half a cholesterol.

*   *   *

THE hypochondriac lift driver was a worrier.

He kept thinking he was coming down with something.

*   *   *

SHE asked the doctor: "What's the best thing to take when you are run down?"

"The number of the bastard who hit you," he said.

*   *   *

AT the clinic the nurse asked Lulu, "When did you have your last check-up?"

"Never have," said Lulu. "A Pole and a Ukranian, but never a Czech."

*   *   *

A MAN went to the health clinic with green balls.

The doctor examined the emerald knackers and said, "Have you ever heard of cauliflower ears?"

"Yes," said the patient.

"Well you have got brothel sprouts."

HISTORY

SIR FRANCIS Drake circumcised the world and did it with a hundred-foot clipper.

* * *

NAPOLEON came home tired and weary, wet and wounded, and went straight round to Josephine's flat. He was shocked to find a pair of large gum boots on her front doorstep.

"Josephine! Josephine!" he called out. "What are those rubber boots doing out here?"

"They're not rubber boots," said Josie. "They're Wellington's"

HONEYMOONS

See NEWLY-WEDS

THE new bride was a little embarrassed to bring up the matter of sex, so the groom explained it delicately, yet with authority.

"No need to talk about it, Muriel,"he said. "These are the rules. When you need it just give it a tug three times. When you dont need it just give it a tug 395 times."

* * *

THE morning after their first night he awoke to find his bride crying.

"What's up darling?" he said. "Didn't you enjoy our bridal night?"

"Yes," she sobbed, "but look at it. We've used it all up in one night."

* * *

MISS Fauntleroy-Jones was nearing her use-by date and was finally unloaded from the aristocratic but bankrupt family. On her wedding night she entered the bedroom wearing a sheer nightgown and long white gloves.

"You look lovely dear," said the groom. "but why the white gloves?"

"Because I understand that on these occasions one is expected to handle the filthy thing," she said.

* * *

RUSHING naked from the bathroom to the bedroom, Fred tripped on the rug and pole-vaulted out the window.

* * *

THE honeymoon couple was playing deck quoits on the cruise ship when they suddenly got the urge and rushed to their cabin.

A case of quoitus interruptus.

* * *

THEY began to undress and she got the shock of her life to see he had no toes on his right foot. She thought it was a shocking deformity and grabbed her clothes, jumped in her car and fled home.

In tears she rushed into her mother's kitchen.

"But I told you about the birds and the bees," said her mother. "You knew what to expect. Couldn't he get it up?"

"Oh, it's not that," she sobbed, "when he stripped off he only had half a foot."

Mum chucked the tea towel at her. "That's much better than your father's. Here, you finish the dishes. I'll be back in the morning."

* * *

IT was the first night of their honeymoon and they had booked sleepers on a night train. But somehow they had been assigned top bunks on opposite sides of the corridor.

During the night the bridegoom whispered, "Come on over."

"I can't reach," she said.

"Here, look at this," he said, "poking a very erect donger through the curtains, "grab it and haul yourself over."

A voice from the lower bunk piped up: "And how the hell will she get back?"

HORSES

A HORSE was playing his first cricket match and was slogging sixes all over the ground. Then his partner took the strike, hit a single and dashed up the wicket but the horse just stood there.

"Run," he yelled, "run you bastard," he yelled at the horse.

"If I could run I wouldn't be playing bloody cricket," said the horse, "I'd be at the race track."

*   *   *

THE trainer was giving last minute instructions to the jockey and appeared to slip something in the horse's mouth just as a steward passed by.

"What was that?" inquired the steward.

"Oh, nothing," said the trainer, "just a Mintie." He offered one to the steward. "Here, have one. And I'll have one myself."

After the suspicious steward left the scene the trainer continued with his riding instructions. "Just keep the horse on the rails. You are on a certainty. The only thing that could possibly pass you down the straight is either the steward or me."

HOSPITALS

See DOCTORS

THERE is a sign in the toilet of the Sex Change Clinic.

It reads "We may never piss this way again."

*   *   *

THE young intern said to the nurse, "That bloke in bed 15. He's got WOG tattooed on his penis. True, take a look if you get the chance."

Meeting her later in the day he said "Did you see that tattoo?"

"Yes," said the nurse. "But it's not WOG, it's Woollongong!"

* * *

DID you hear about the clumsy surgeon who was performing a vasectomy? He missed and got the sack.

* * *

TWO nurses were climbing back into the dormitory window, trying to sneak in as quietly as possible when one said, "This makes me feel like a burglar."

"Me too," said the other, "but where would we find two burglars at this time of night?"

* * *

THEN there was the time the nurses' dormitory caught fire. It took the firemen 15 minutes to put the fire out. And it took the nurses three hours to put the firemen out.

* * *

DOCTOR: "How's that man who swallowed the fifty cent piece?"

Nurse: "Still no change."

HOTELS

See PUBS

IT was a small hotel like Fawlty Towers and Fred was half way through his meal when he called the manager.

"Look at this spaghetti," he complained, "there is a hair in it. So I am not paying for it." He left the table.

Later that night the manager found Fred with his head down between the legs of one of the hotel house maids and couldn't resist the jibe: "I see you don't mind a bit of hair now."

Fred lifted his head. "No I don't. But if I find any spaghetti down here I'm not paying for it either."

* * *

ALL hotel rooms have a copy of the Gideon Bible as a comfort to travellers and it was natural for the tub-thumping evangelist to reach for it and thumb through a few pages before going downstairs for a nightcap before retiring.

He soon engaged the barmaid in conversation and was still chatting her up at closing time when she even agreed to come to his room where, after another drink, they adjourned to the cot.

"Should we be doing this?" she giggled as she undressed, "after all, you are a man of the cloth."

"I assure you it is alright. It is written in the Bible," he said, dropping his trousers.

During her post-coitus cigarette, a very reflective time for women, she said to the Bible-basher: "Show me the passage which it says we should have done what we did?"

The evangelist picked up the Bible and turned to the fly-leaf to show her the quote: "The barmaid downstairs is a certainty."

* * *

NEXT at the reception desk was a newly married couple.

"Bridal suite?" he asked discreetly.

"No," she giggled, "I'll just hang on to your ears."

* * *

YOU can tell what kind of a hotel it was.

I left a call for seven in the morning; and woke up with seven blondes in my room.

HUNTERS

EACH day on safari the two hunters pulled on their heavy boots for trekking through the jungle. But there came a day when one bloke pulled on a pair of running shoes.

"What for?" asked his mate in the heavy boots.

"There is a man-eating tiger in these parts."

"But you won't out run a tiger in those."

"Don't have to," said the smartie. "I just have to be faster than you."

A HUNTER had been tracking a huge bear and finally had him in his sights. He fired a shot and then bounded through the bush to where he expected to find the carcase. To his dismay there was no dead bear. To his horror he was tapped on the shoulder by a very live one.

"I am sick of being shot at by you bloody hunters," said the bear. "I'm going to teach you a lesson. So get down on your knees and give me a blow job. Now!"

The terrified hunter did as he was told.

But next day the hunter returned with a bigger gun and spent hours waiting to ambush the bear. Finally he sighted him again, blasted away and dashed forward to where the dead bear should have been. Nothing.

Once more he received the terrifying tap on the shoulder. "You know the ritual," said the bear. "Down you go."

The infuriated hunter returned the following day with yet a bigger and more accurate gun. This time he stalked closer and let go with both barrels.

He ran into the clearing only to find the very alive bear waiting for him once more.

"Okay, let's have the truth," said the bear, "you are not in this for the hunting are you?"

*   *   *

MURPHY knew nothing about the wild when he went on his first hunting trip. He walked into a clearing and was surprised to find a young woman lying there in the nude.

"Pardon me," said Murphy, "are you game?"

She looked him up and down and said, "Yes."

So he shot her.

*   *   *

THE major came home from a hunting trip to spot his wife being humped by a bounder under the oak tree on the front lawn.

In a rage he asked his batman for his rifle and took steady aim.

"Do the sporting thing, sir," said the batman, "shoot him on the rise."

HUSBANDS

A HUSBAND? That's what's left of a lover after the name has been extracted.

* * *

A HUSBAND? That's a gardener who gets to sleep with the boss of the manor.

* * *

USUALLY the husband regards himself as the head of the household, and the pedestrian knows he has the right of way. Both of them are safe until they try to prove it.

* * *

FRED was admitting his great blunder of the previous night. "I must have been legless. So drunk I don't remember leaving here," he confided to Charlie at the bar.

"But I woke up in a bed, with a woman next to me, so I automatically gave her twenty bucks."

"And you don't remember getting your money's worth? Is that why you're sad?" ventured Charlie.

"No," said Fred. "It was my wife and she automatically gave me ten bucks change!"

* * *

TWO blokes were discussing their sex life in the pub.

"We've gone stale on it," said one, "my wife doesn't move and to tell you the truth it has become boring."

His mate gave him some advice. "I went through that stage," he said. "But you have to jazz it up. I buy my wife a bottle of champagne and supply her with some sexy gear then rip it off her every night. Then we screw on the lounge room floor. You ought to try that."

Next week they met again.

"Did you take my advice?"

"Sure did. Sex is great now, and I just love your lounge room carpet."

HYGIENE

WHEN Fred asked for two pies and some dimsims at the local take-away he was impressed to see Luigi using tongs to place the food in the bag.

"Yes, sir," said Luigi responding to Fred's comments, "we are very clean here. Always use tongs. No hands ever touch the food."

As Fred turned to leave he noticed a piece of string hanging from Luigi's fly and asked its purpose.

"All part of the hygiene program," said Luigi. "When I go to the toilet I simply pull it out with the string. Not touched with human hands."

Fred was about to leave when the obvious question prompted him. "How do you get it back?"

"With the tongs," said Luigi.

*   *   *

THE health inspector was aghast to see the pastrycook crimping the edge of the apple pie pastry with his set of false teeth.

"Haven't you got a tool for that?"

"Yes, but I save it for putting holes in the donuts," replied the pastrycook.

I

IMMIGRATION

LUIGI hadn't been long in the country, but urged on by his friends and family he made an application for citizenship and presented himself before the tribunal.

He was nervous. "Yer honor, I not speeka good Eenglish cos I no beena in this country not long. Maybe I no getta my papers because I talka like theese?"

The judge said: Donjoo worry, yousa gonna get yousa papers."

*   *   *

LUIGI was digging a trench by himself on one side of the street while the rest of the road gang worked together on the other.

He finally asked the foreman why he was alone.

"You've got bad breath," was the answer.

"And so would you if you kissed as many politicians' arses as I had to to emmigrate here."

*   *   *

AN enterprising young woman working the docks in New York established her own immigration office in the back seat of her car where she would give newcomers a hand job.

She was officially the Yanker and for $10 her clients became the Yankees.

INDIANS

GENERAL Custer's last words: "I'll never understand these bloody Indians. Just a minute ago they were singing and dancing!"

* * *

THE little Navajo brave asked his father why the members of his tribe had such unusual names like Running Deer, Brown Eagle, Red Wolf and Flying Cloud.

"You see son," began his dad. "We Navajos name our children after the first thing we see after conception. Why do you ask, Broken Rubber?"

* * *

BIG Chief Sitting Bull had a daughter he called Ninety-nine Cents because she was always just under a buck.

* * *

WHILE driving through outback America a woman's car ran out of petrol. However she was delighted when a strong young Indian offered her a lift to the gas station on his horse.

She sat behind him and was intrigued with his habit of letting out a wild yell every so often. Must be one of those Indian whoops, she thought.

When she alighted at the gas station he rode off with yet another "Ya-hoo!"

"What were you two doing?" asked the gas station owner.

"Nothing," she said. "I simply rode behind him with my arms around his sides hanging on to the saddle horn," she said.

"Don't you know Indians ride bareback," he said.

* * *

BIG Chief Running Bear's warriors were soundly defeated by General Custer's army and after the council of war the chief had to report to his tribe.

"Good news and bad news," he said. "The bad news is that the paleface army have routed our warriors, wrecked our camps and destroyed our crops and buffalo herds. We will have nothing to eat through the winter but buffalo turds."

"Hell, what's the good news," piped up one brave.

"We have great stacks of buffalo turds," said the chief.

* * *

IN the same valley lived the Fuk-ar-wee tribe.

They were a tribe of indians with very short legs who persisted in making camp in very tall grass and were noted for doing standing jumps and yelling: "We're the Fuk-ar-wee?"

INFIDELITY
See WARDROBES

"DO you cheat on your wife?"

"Who else?"

* * *

A SAILOR returned home to find his wife had been unfaithful.

"Damn it," he said, "was it Tom?"

"No," she said.

"Was it Dick?" he persisted.

"No."

"Was it my best friend, Harry?"

"No," she yelled, "don't you think I've got any friends of my own?"

* * *

"I WANT to divorce my husband," said the shapely blonde to her lawyer.

"On what grounds?" he asked.

"Infidelity," she said, "I don't think he's the father of my child."

* * *

FRED was relating the amazing experience to his mates at the bar. "Muriel was not too well this morning so I told her that instead of going to work I would stay and care for her.

"So I threw on Muriel's chenille bathrobe and was standing at the stove when the milkman comes in the backdoor behind me, slides his hand under the bathrobe and squeezes my bum.

"Can you imagine the coincidence," said Fred. "The milkman's wife has a chenille bathrobe exactly the same as Muriel's!"

* * *

"THIS suit was a surprise from my wife," said Fred.

"Really?" said his drinking mate.

"Yes, I came home unexpectedly one night and there it was, hanging on the end of the bed."

* * *

WHILE a husband and wife were asleep she had a big smile on her face because of an erotic dream involving another man. It was so real she began to murmer and said: "Look out darling, my husband is coming."

He leapt from the bed and jumped out the window.

* * *

THEY snuggled down in the stalls at the movies, but the woman in front was wearing a large hat which obstructed their view. He tapped her on the shoulder. She turned round and it was his wife.

* * *

AFTER an extremely wild party the hung-over couple were having a late breakfast.

"This is a little embarrassing," he said, "but was it you I made love to in the garden last night?"

"About what time?" she replied.

* * *

The husband came home and found his wife in bed with a strange man. The stranger was exhausted and was sprawled, nude and asleep.

The husband was outraged by the sight and reached into the wardrobe for his gun.

"Wait, darling," she said. "You know the red sports car

I drive? This man gave it to me. You know that brand new set of golf clubs I gave you last week? This man gave me the money. You know we have paid off the mortgage. This man supplied the finance..."

"For Chri'sake woman," said the husband, "cover him up so he doesn't catch cold."

* * *

FRED was trying to console his mate who had just found his wife in bed with another man.

"C'mon, Bert," he said, "it's not the end of the world."

"All right for you to say," said Bert, "but what if you came home one night and caught another man in bed with your wife?"

Fred pondered for a moment. "I'd break his white cane and kick his dog."

* * *

JOCK was in the habit of handing over his sealed pay envelope each week to his wife. But for the last three weeks she noticed that it had been opened and two dollars was missing.

Finally she confronted him: "Right, Jock, tell me straight," she said. "Who's the bit o' skirt you've been taking out these past three weeks?"

* * *

PADDY divulged the sad news to his mates at the bar. He already had eight kids and his sexy wife was once again in the puddin' club. "I swear I'll hang myself if this happens again," he said.

But it was no surprise, one year later, when Paddy announced that his wife was once again pregnant.

"You said you were going to hang yourself," one of his mates reminded him.

"Indeed I did," said Paddy, "indeed I got the rope and threw a loop over the branch of the apple tree. Then I thought, maybe I was hanging the wrong man."

FRED and Joe were talking over their old schooldays with a few drinks. Unfortunately, time got away and Fred had missed the last train.

Joe and his wife insisted he stay the night, but there was no spare bed and Fred would have to bunk in with the married couple.

As soon as Joe was snoring his wife tapped Fred on the shoulder and whispered an invitation.

"No way," said Fred. "Joe would kill me."

"When he has had a few beers like tonight nothing will wake him," the wife insisted.

Fred was still unconvinced.

"Look, pull a hair out of his bum. I'll bet he won't move."

Fred tentatively plucked a hair and, indeed, Joe never stirred.

So Fred threw the leg and enjoyed a quiet screw.

About 15 minutes later the wife tapped him on the shoulder again and whispered the same invitation. And once more Fred was scared about waking the sleeping husband. But again he pulled a hair to test if his old friend was asleep, then did the job.

This went on for much of the night until Joe finally raised himself on one elbow and muttered: "Listen Fred, I don't mind you screwing my wife, but for Chris'sake stop using my arse as a scoreboard."

*   *   *

WHEN Rachel found Isaac had a mistress she demanded to know why, and gave him hell until he explained.

"It's not that I don't love you, my dearest," said Isaac.

"What then?" pressed Rachel.

Finally Isaac admitted that Rachel had always been passive. "This woman moves. She expresses passion. She moans and groans with ecstasy," he said.

With Isaac's fortune in mind Rachel decided to play along. The next evening she enticed him into the cot with a bottle of champagne and new seductive underwear.

While Isaac was humping away she remembered the peculiarity of his mistress and this was the time to start moaning.

"Oh Isaac, vat a day I had today," she moaned, "first the washing machine broke down, then I was short-changed at the supermarket ..."

*   *   *

SHE had her suspicions about her husband, Fred, so when they had an invitation to a fancy dress party at the Smithsons' she conceived a plan to catch him.

When Fred was dressed in his gorilla suit ready to leave she feigned a headache, said she would stay home, but insisted Fred should go on without her.

Later she donned her own disguise and arrived at the party to see him flirting with every floozie at the party.

In her own masked outfit she approached him, whispered a seductive phrase in his ear and was surprised at the immediate response. He rushed her outside and gave her a passionate knee-trembler against a gum tree.

She resisted declaring who she was in an effort to get all the evidence possible.

Just before the unmasking at midnight she left the party and drove home, and next morning was all set to confront Fred with his infidelity.

"How was it at the Smithsons?" she asked at breakfast.

"Dullsville. Boring without you, darling," he said. "When I arrived I saw Ben and the Murphy brothers without partners so we went upstairs and played poker. I lent my gorilla suit to Harry Forbes. He said he had a wow of a time."

*   *   *

BIG Rastus came home early one day to find Lulu Belle lying on the bed. She was naked, except for a small wet towel on her thigh.

"What's going on?" asked Rastus suspiciously.

197

"Nothing," replied Lulu Belle, "just got a fever and lying in bed."

"What's dat towel doing there?"

"I dipped it in water to put on my brow, dat's all," she said.

Rastus pulled out his razor and began stropping it.

"What yo gonna do wit dat razor, honey?" she asked.

"If that towel dries out soft," said Rastus, "I'm gonna shave."

* * *

THE businessman kissed his wife at the usual time, got into his car and headed for the office.

He was half way there when he remembered his wallet and glasses were in his other suit.

He arrived back at his home to find his wife totally nude on the bed and the plumber standing beside the bed, also totally nude.

The plumber promptly went into a squatting position. "I'm glad you are here Mr Fotheringham," he said. "I was just explaining to your wife that if she doesn't pay the outstanding monies on our account I am going to shit on this floor."

* * *

COMING home at a quarter to three
    I caught my wife cheating on me
    I yelled: "Who's this fink?"
    She replied with a wink:
    "I dunno. He's a new one on me."

INSULTS

"OF course there is nobody else," she told her doubting boyfriend, "do you think I'd be sitting here with a dick-head like you if there were?"

* * *

THE sex session was a failure. He said: "You are so

198

unresponsive I wouldn't be surprised if you used cold cream between your legs."

She replied: "I wouldn't be surprised if you used vanishing cream between yours."

* * *

SHE raised herself on one elbow and snapped: "You are the world's most incompetent lover."

"I couldn't be," replied the husband, "that would be just too much of a coincidence."

* * *

McTAVISH was a bad loser. When he was cleaned out in a poker game for particularly high stakes he threw down his hand and stood to leave the table.

He couldn't resist insulting Dapper Dan, the bald gambler who had cleaned him out.

As McTavish walked past he ran his hand over Dan's bald head. "And your noggin feels just like my wife's bum," he said sarcastically.

Dan put his hand to his head. "By crikey, Mac," he said, "you're right, it does."

* * *

THE politician entered the doctor's surgery with a frog on his head.

"That's nasty," said the doctor.

"Bloody oath," said the frog. "It started as a pimple on my bum."

* * *

THE housewife inspected the three small tomatoes and was told by Tony the Fruiterer that they were 55 cents each.

"Well you know what you can do with them," she said. "You can stick them up you know where."

"I can't do that, lady," said Tony. "There is already a three dollar fifty water melon there."

* * *

THE vicar, while pouring the tea

Once asked: "Do you fart when you pee?"

I replied with some wit:

"Do you fart when you shit?"

So the score was one up for me.

* * *

AN indignant lady approached the host of the party and said she was leaving. "Your wife has insulted me," she complained. "She told me I was a woman of the streets."

"Think nothing of it my dear," said the host, "I've been retired from the army for 15 years and she still calls me Colonel."

* * *

SHE said their neighbour must have taken offence at something as she hadn't been over for days.

"Be sure to find out what it was," he said, "and we'll try it on her again."

INSURANCE

FRED was delighted with his new job. He had just sold a life insurance policy for $100,000 and slapped the papers down on the boss's desk.

"Not bad," said the boss, "but you forgot one thing. You forgot the urine specimen for our doctors to examine. That's part of the deal. Remember it next time."

Fred took the rebuke on board and the following week he staggered into the office with two buckets of yellowish fluid.

"I've just sold a big group policy," he beamed.

* * *

MOISHE Leiberwitz was driving along a country road when he came across the scene of an accident. Beside an overturned car was a man covered in blood and groaning.

"Call the ambulance," moaned the injured man.

Moishe quickly surveyed the scene.

"You mean nobody has reported this accident yet?"

"No. It just happened. Get a doctor."

"You mean the police haven't arrived, the insurance people haven't arrived?"

"No."

"Then move over," said Moishe, "let me lie down beside you."

* * *

"DOES this policy have any death benefits?"

"Sure does. When you die you pay no more dues."

* * *

CHARLIE Rippoff had a leg broken in an accident and lodged a claim with the insurance company that he was crippled for life and confined to a wheelchair.

A smart lawyer got him $500,000 compensation.

The insurance company was suspicious. In fact they told Charlie he would not get away with it and that they were assigning an insurance detective to follow his every move.

"Good," said Charlie. "Then he might like to follow us on our world trip."

Charlie said his wife would accompany him and help with the wheelchair on a tour through the United States, then across to Europe and to London, Rome, Paris, "and then to Lourdes where your detective might witness one of the greatest miracles of modern times."

INTERPRETERS

WHAT do you call a brunette with a blonde on either side?

An interpreter.

* * *

WHEN the Godfather in Sicily realised that one of the family bosses in New York was fiddling the books he decided to deal with the matter himself.

As he couldn't speak English he took Luigi as an interpreter.

In New York the first of the suspects was led in and the Godfather put a pistol to his head.

"It wasn't me," he blubbered, "I swear by my mother's heart."

Luigi interpreted: "He says it wasn't him and he swears so by his mother's heart."

The second suspect was confronted with the pistol. He also protested his innocence and invoked the Pope as his witness. Luigi interpreted his denial.

The third suspect was brought in and with the pistol at his temple said: "Okay, I'm sorry. Please be merciful. The million dollars is in a suitcase under my bed upstairs."

"What did he say?" asked the Godfather.

Luigi replied: "He says he did it. He's spent the money and he bets you haven't the balls to pull the trigger!"

* * *

LITTLE Isaac was doing his homework.

"Dad, can you tell me what a vacuum is?" he asks.

"A vacuum, my son is a void."

"I know that," said the lad, "but vat's dat void mean?"

INVENTIONS

* * *

AFTER 15 years of research Dr Schlicker finally presented the Government Scientific Bureau with a cosmetic vaginal deodorant that smelt like oranges.

He received a swift reply: "When you can produce a cosmetic compound that makes oranges smell like fannies, then we're in business."

* * *

MY Ol Dad was an inventor and among his accomplishments were:

Water-proof tea bags.

Peddle wheelchairs.

Parachutes which open on impact.

L-shaped mobile homes.

The one-piece jigsaw puzzle.

An inflatable dartboard for campers.

An index for a dictionary.

Beer glasses with square bases that don't leave rings on the bar or tables.

*　　*　　*

AN innovative young scientist at the sperm bank has packaged their product in an aerosol can and labelled it Heir Spray.

*　　*　　*

THERE is a new patent medicine called Preparation A.

It is for video-game addicts who have asteroids.

*　　*　　*

HE invented a marvellous appliance for speeding up production in factories. He called it a whip.

*　　*　　*

IT was an Irishman who invented the toilet seat.

It was a Scot who figured out how to put a hole in it.

*　　*　　*

THE professor invented the perfect love potion.

It stopped your back from pegging out

and your peg from backing out.

And you had to swallow it quick or you got a stiff neck.

*　　*　　*

IT is not commonly known that the first timepiece was not invented by the Swiss but by the troops fighting for Alexander the Great.

It was back in the days when Alexander was conquering the world and his troops were fighting Persian hordes day after day with no double-time for weekends, definitely no overtime and no holiday pay. Indeed, no holidays.

Finally they got jack of it and formed the first soldiers' trade union.

The delegation fronted Alexander and told him bluntly that eight hours a day was enough sword wielding for anybody.

Alexander saw the point and agreed. But the Swiss had

not yet invented the watch and the problem was how to measure a regular work day.

Alexander himself came up with the answer. If all the troops tied a rag around their wrist and continued to chop away at the enemy, until the rag got damp with sweat, it was time to knock off.

That time-piece became known as Alexander's Rag Time Band.

IRISH

CLEANLINESS is next to Godliness.

But only in an Irish dictionary.

* * *

PADDY thought oral sex was just talking about it.

* * *

THE Irish maiden's prayer: "And now Dear Lord, please have Murphy on me."

* * *

PADDY and Shamus were walking along the pavement when Paddy suddenly grabbed Shamus by the arm.

"Look out," he said. "Mind where you're stepping. It looks like dog shit."

Paddy bent down and pushed it with his finger. "It feels like dog shit," he said.

He put his finger to his lips. "It tastes like dog shit. Shamus my friend I think it is definitely dog shit. Lucky we didn't step in it."

* * *

PADDY entered the bar and approached his mates with a handful of dog shit.

"Look what we nearly trod in," he said.

* * *

HOW do the Irish count bank notes?

One, two, tri, four, foive, another, another, another ...

THERE was a 10pm curfew in Belfast so the sergeant in charge of the patrol got a surprise when he heard a shot ring out at 9.30.

He was alarmed when he discovered Private Murphy had shot a man.

"Why did you do that?" demanded the sergeant.

"But that's O'Flannagan," said Murphy. "I know where he lives. He would never get home by 10pm."

*   *   *

RED Adair's fame in quelling oil rig fires stretches around the globe, so when a well in the middle of the Sahara Desert spewed smoke and flame the alert went out: "Get Red Adair."

But Red had his hands full with a fire crisis on the other side of the world, and nobody can be in two places at the same time.

The Exxon magnates were frantic. Without the famous Red Adair they were in heaps of trouble.

"Why not try Green Adair?" suggested a lackey.

"Who?" But as the flames roared higher in the sky, why not try Green Adair indeed.

Green Adair was contacted in the Limerick Arms in Belfast and offered one million pounds to do the job.

Within a few hours the oil engineers were amazed to see an air transport land in the desert. They gasped as the nose of the aircraft opened and a truck, bearing Green Adair and his crew sped towards the fire. They watched in amazement as the truck approached the wall of flames and disappeared into the very heart of the fire. They could see Green Adair and his men leaping about, jumping and stamping out the flames.

Finally, all charred, singed and blackened they emerged from the smoke to the cheers of their incredulous admirers.

"What will you do with the million pounds?" asked the first reporter on the scene.

"The first thing Ill do," said Green Adair, "will be to get some brakes for that bloody truck!"

* * *

"DO you think if I pour you some gin again,"
   Said Finnegan, "You might care to sin again?"
   Said she with a grin
   If you want it back in
   You must pay me a fin again, Finnegan."

* * *

THERE was a young colleen named Flynn
   Who knew fornication was sin
   But when she was tight
   It seemed quite all right
   So everyone filled her with gin.

ITALIANS

LUIGI considered himself a charmer and had no qualms about heading for the prettiest blonde at the bar.

"Hello, darling,"he said. "Are you Italian?"

"No,"she replied.

"You look Italian," he said.

"Well, Im not."

"Surely you have a bit of Italian in you?"

"No, I dont."

"Would you like some?"

* * *

IS an IQ of 105 considered high?
   Yes!
   For ten Italians?

* * *

WHY does an Italian have a hole in his pocket?
   So he can count to six.

* * *

THE Mafia moll dumped her boyfriend when she learned he was just a finger man.

RECTAL thermometers are banned in Italy.

They found they caused too much brain damage.

* * *

WHEN the Italian girl told her brother the astounding news that she was going to have a baby he replied:

"Well, I'll be a monkey's uncle."

* * *

THE doctor was examining Luigi.

"Have you ever committed sodomy?" he asked.

"No way. One wife is enough for me."

* * *

ITALIAN is an easy language to learn.

All you need to know is one word, *Atsa*. Then you can speak fluently, "atsa car, atsa woman, atsa church, atsa everything."

* * *

THE Italian Don was returning to Italy for a visit and had arranged two appointments, one with the Pope, the other with the Mafia boss.

"Who should I see first?" he asked his lieutenant.

"The Pope first," said his adviser, "you've only got to kiss his hand."

* * *

THE sociologist was taking a survey in the Italian quarter and approached a gentleman in a black suit.

The survey got to sex. "How many times do you do it, sir?"

"Oh, about seven or eight times a year," replied the gent.

"But you are Italian," said the sociologist, "Italians are supposed to be great lovers."

"Well, I'm not doing too badly for a 65-year-old priest without a car."

* * *

WHEN the Italian girl had sex in the back seat of a hire car she said, "Its-a hurts."

207

AFTER a month's holiday in Australia Paddy returned to Ireland where the family wanted to know all about his trip.

He said Australians were the most hospital people he had ever met. "They will share their house, share everything," he said. "It's the white bastards you have to watch."

J

JAIL

THE judge had just made his routine tour of the prison and told the governor he was delighted to hear of the social event planned that evening.

"What do you mean?" said the governor.

"Well one of the prisoners wanted to sell me a ticket for the Wardens' Ball."

"That's not a dance, sir, that's a raffle."

* * *

THE padre was on his regular visit to the jail and came across three lags in the remand yard.

"What are you in for?" he asked the first.

"Murder," was the reply.

"And what did you get for that?"

"Life."

The padre asked the second man what he was in for.

"Fraud," he said. "And I got 15 years.

The padre asked the third what he was in for.

"Pouring petrol over Protestants and setting them alight."

"And what did you get for that?" asked the padre.

"About 15 to the gallon," replied the lag.

* * *

"THIS pen leaks," said the prisoner as the rain came through the roof.

DAD is very popular in prison. He's the lifer of the party.

JAPANESE

WHAT do Japanese men do when they have erections?
  Vote.

* * *

JAPANESE cunnilingus is "constluctive cliticism."

* * *

A JAPANESE orgasm is a Gland Finale.

* * *

A PELVIC examination in Japan is a "nookie lookie."

* * *

THE Japanese call girl call went broke.
  Nobody had a yen for her.

* * *

THE Japanese firm making vibrators is Genital Electric.

* * *

LACKANOOKIE is one of Japan's most dreaded diseases.

* * *

WE know a bloke who is half Japanese and half black.
Every December 7 he attacks Pearl Bailey.

* * *

THE Japanese are beginning to own so much of Queensland that travellers will soon have to leave their shoes at the
NSW border.

* * *

THE Japanese tourist fronted the bank teller and presented
his traveller's cheque. When he counted the cash he said:
"How come I get less money today than yesterday?"
  "Fluctuations," said the clerk.
  "And the bloody same to you," said the tourist.

* * *

THERE was a great lord in Japan
  Whose name on a Monday began
  It carried through Tuesday

Till twilight on Sunday
And sounded like stones in a can.

JEEVES

LORD Ponsonby awoke one morning with a tremendous erection and quickly called for his butler, Jeeves.

"Yes, a magnificent weapon," said Jeeves after close inspection of the member, "shall I rally her Ladyship?"

"No Jeeves," said Ponsonby. "Bring me my baggy golf trousers and I will try to smuggle it down to the village."

* * *

THE lady of the manor was becoming increasingly alarmed at Jeeves' practice of walking in to her bedroom without knocking. Finally she took him to task.

"It could be very embarrassing if I were in a state of undress," she admonished.

"No need to worry about that, m'Lady," said Jeeves. "I always take a peek through the keyhole first!"

* * *

LATER that evening her Ladyship called Jeeves into her bedroom. "Jeeves, please unzip my dress."

With a great deal of embarrassment he did so.

"Now Jeeves," she said. "Take off my stockings."

Jeeves was now in a sweat.

"And now take off my underwear ... and if I ever catch you wearing my gear again you will be instantly dismissed."

* * *

HER Ladyship called Jeeves to her bedroom and he was surprised to find her reclining on the sofa entirely nude.

"Jeeves," she asked. "Are you a good sport?"

"Er, yes, Madam, as a matter of fact I am."

"Good," she said, "and are you a good fuck?"

"Indeed I am, Madam."

"Well fuck off, it's April Fool's Day."

HER Ladyship couldn't remember a thing about her night out with the girls. All she knew when she woke up next morning was that she was totally naked and hung over.

Eventually Jeeves knocked on the door and came in with the breakfast tray.

"Just a moment, Jeeves," she said sleepily. "I can't remember a thing about last night. How did I get into bed?"

"Begging your pardon, your Ladyship, I helped you upstairs and put you to bed."

"But, my dress...?"

"It seemed a shame to crumple it, I took it off and hung it up," said Jeeves.

Looking under the bedclothes she said, "but, my underwear...?"

"I thought the elastic might stop the circulation," explained Jeeves, "I took the liberty of removing them."

"What a night," said her Ladyship, "I must have been tight."

"Only the first time your Ladyship."

* * *

JEEVES was called by Lord Ponsonby. "Jeeves, could you ride down to the village and fetch a bottle of whisky, a box of cigars and a few ounces of snuff. That free-loading bishop will be calling in this afternoon."

Jeeves mounted his trusty bicycle and was off on his errand. It was not until the return trip and he had peddled up the long hill to the manor gates that he realised he had forgotten the snuff.

What to do? It was too hot and too far to ride back down to the village. By chance the problem was solved, right there on the nature strip was some dog shit, three of those white eggs dogs leave in neat little clumps. When dried in the sun and ground back to powder it looks for all the world like snuff.

Did he dare take the chance?

Jeeves quickly bent down, snatched up the three portions and put them in his pocket.

"Did you get the whisky, Jeeves?"

"Yes, M'lord."

"And the cigars, and the snuff?"

"Yes M'lord," said Jeeves as he prepared to leave the room.

"I say, Jeeves," said Lord Ponsonby sniffing the air. "You didn't by any chance stand in something down in the village?"

"No M'lord."

The bishop arrived soon after and headed for the Scotch. "You don't mind if I have a drink, Ponsonby old boy?"

"Not at all, Bishop, go for your life," but Ponsonby was preoccupied with the pervading odour.

"I say Bishop, can you smell dog's doings in here?"

"Can't say as I can dear boy," said the bishop. "I happen to have a heavy head cold."

"In that case, take a pinch of snuff," said Ponsonby.

The bishop responded by taking two pinches and sniffing it up both nostrils.

"My God," he said. "You always get the best snuff. That's cleared my head completely and I can smell that dog's stuff now!"

* * *

EVERY time her Ladyship swoons
  Her boobs would pop out like balloons
  With nary a stare
  Jeeves would always be there
  To lift them back in with warm spoons.

JEWISH

HE was a rabbi who kept a scrapbook of all his clippings.

WHAT do you call an uncircumcised Jewish baby?

A girl.

*   *   *

OF all the pornographic movies Jewish films are the worst. They consist of five minutes of sex and and ninety-five minutes of guilt.

*   *   *

THE Jews have discovered a new disease.

It is Waldheimer's Disease. People who suffer from it forget that they were ever Nazis.

*   *   *

THERE was a Jewish kamikaze pilot. He crashed his plane into his brother's scrap metal yard.

*   *   *

MOISHE and Izzy were out on the harbour when their launch struck a rock and sunk. Moishe was the stronger swimmer and took hold of Izzy with one hand as he paddled towards the shore with the other.

However Moishe soon got exhausted and asked Izzy if he could float alone for a while.

"We're in trouble like this," spluttered Izzy, "and you want to talk business?"

*   *   *

THE Jews are the most confident race in the world.

They cut the end off a dick before they know how long it will grow.

*   *   *

THE Jewish lawyer wore a worried frown. "It's my son," he confided to his rabbi, "he has come out of the closet and declared himself a homosexual. But the situation could be worse," he continued, "at least he is in love with a doctor."

*   *   *

The police sergeant entered the home of Mrs Bernstein to find her at the kitchen table eating her soup.

"Sorry to disturb you," he said, "but I have some terrible news."

"What is it?" she asked, slurping her soup..

"I'm afraid your husband has been killed in an accident," said the cop.

Mrs Bernstein continued to slurp her soup.

"I said," pressed the cop once more, "I said your husband has been killed."

"I know what you said, (slurp, slurp). Believe me, as soon as I finish (slurp) this soup (slurp) I am going to let out one almighty scream."

* * *

THERE was a sound reason why the Israelis did not get involved in the Gulf War. The last time they listened to a Talking Bush they wandered the desert for 40 years.

* * *

TWO Jews were lined up before the Nazi firing squad when the officer asked if they had any last requests.

One said he would like a cigarette. When the Nazi came close enough the condemned man spat in his face.

"Please, Izzie," said his mate, "don't make trouble."

* * *

MOISHE finished his business in Hong Kong early on the Friday and after many enquiries finally found the local synagogue.

Complete with his prayer shawl he attended the service and began to pray, surrounded by Chinese.

He was spotted by the rabbi who introduced himself and asked why he was there.

"Well, whenever I am in a foreign city I like to pray in the synagogue," he said.

"You are a Jew?" asked the rabbi with some surprise.

"Of course," replied Moishe.

"You don't look like a Jew," said the rabbi.

* * *

SAM Goldstein was at the funeral of a good friend when one of the mourners remembered he owed the deceased $10.

"I am a man of my word," he said, placing a ten dollar note in the coffin.

It reminded another of the deceaseds debtors, "I am also a man of my word," and he shuffled forward to place another $10 in the coffin.

"You two have pricked my conscience," said Sam, "for I also owe our dear departed friend $10."

So Sam came forward, wrote a cheque for $30, threw it in the coffin and took $20 change."

* * *

YOUNG Hymie went off to America and after three months he phoned his Momma from Hollywood.

"I'm married, Momma," he said.

"Oh no. You haven't married a goy have you?"

"No Momma."

"Then what's her name?"

"Goldberg, Momma."

"Oh, thank goodness for that. What's her first name?"

"Whoopie, Momma."

* * *

TWO men were standing side by side in the loo when the smaller of the two looked up and said, "You are a Jew?"

"Yes," said the taller.

"And you come from the Greensberg district?"

"Yes."

"And at your circumcision, you were cut by the cock-eyed Rabbi Finklebaum?"

"Yes. How do you know all these things?"

"Because Rabbi Finklebaum always cut with a left bias and you are pissing on my boots."

JOBS

"WHAT do you do for a crust?"

"Simple. I never wash my underpants."

216

HE works at a circus where he circumcises elephants.

The wages are not much, but the tips are enormous.

*   *   *

TWO young women renewed acquaintance after being out of touch since their school days and one asked the other what she worked at.

"I am a receptionist at a hotel and getting half my board."

"Gee," chided the other, "I work at a massage parlour and get my whole board."

*   *   *

FRED had been unemployed for months. One day he was browsing through the newspaper and was startled to read an item which said that men were so scarce in France that women were paying the equivalent of $50 a night to gigolos.

"I might go over there," he said.

His wife wasn't impressed. "How could you live on $50 a week?"

*   *   *

O'FLAHERTY saw a poster outside the police station: "Man Wanted for Armed Robbery in Dublin."

He said to Paddy, "Now if that job was in Donegal, I'd take it."

*   *   *

QUASIMODO, the Hunchback of Notre Dame, told the bishop he needed a holiday after ringing the bells for 15 years so they agreed to put an advertisement in the Bell Ringer's Bugle.

By strange coincidence the only applicants were a pair of identical twins, both with no arms. But they quickly dispelled Quasimodo's doubts that they could do the job.

"Just watch," said one, and he rushed at the bell and butted it with his head. The result was a loud gong.

They both proved they could ring the bells with head butts but Quasi insisted it was a job for one only and the decision was made on the toss of a coin.

Things went well the first week with Armless head-butting the bell each day, but the inevitable happened. While taking his usual run at the bell he tripped on the ropes, missed the bell, and came hurtling down, crash, on the plaza.

The crowd quickly gathered around the body. A gendarme pushed through and said: "Does anybody know his name?"

"No," said a bloke, "but his face rings a bell."

The unfortunate incident caused Quasimodo to send for the bellringer's twin who quickly took over the job.

However, on the third day exactly the same accident occurred. He tripped on the ropes and crashed to his death on the plaza below.

Again the crowd gathered round and a gendarme pushed through. "Does anybody know his name?" he asked.

"No," said a bloke, "but he's a dead ringer for his brother."

JOGGERS

WHEN they heard the back door slam she said: "Quick, that must be my husband." He jumped clean out the window, dashed across the park and merged with a group of joggers.

After he had gone three blocks he knew that he had escaped, but the jogger beside him could contain himself no longer.

"Do you always jog in the nude?" he asked.

"Only in summer," said our Romeo.

"Do you always jog with a condom on?"

"Only when it's raining," he replied.

TWO bachelors were jogging through the park when one said. "I lost my shorts here yesterday?"

"They must have been loose," said his mate.

"No, but the woman I was jogging with was."

*   *   *

A JOGGER picked up a tennis ball while on his regular morning run and having no pockets he put it down the front of his shorts. He was joined by a jogger friend who noticed the bulge.

"What's that?"

"Tennis ball."

"Gee, it must be painful. I had tennis elbow once."

JOKES

THE travelling salesman's car broke down and he wandered across the paddock to the farmhouse and asked if he could sleep the night.

"You're most welcome," said the farmer, "but I must warn you that I don't have daughters, I am a bachelor and you will have to share the only bed with me."

"Oh hell," said the salesman, "I'm in the wrong bloody joke."

*   *   *

FRED was often the butt of office jokes. "Have you heard the story of the dirty window. Fred?" they said.

When he said no, they said: "It's no use telling you. You wouldn't see through it."

Fred could hardly wait until he got home. "Darling," he said. "Have you heard the story of the window you couldn't see through?"

"No," she said.

"Well I can't tell you. It's too dirty."

219

K

KIDS
See SCHOOLS

THE little girl came home from school a bit distressed. In her hand was a computer print-out of her personal data which the teacher had asked her to give to her parents to check.

"And look, Mummy," she said. "Where it has got sex they have put an F and I'm damned if I can remember having one at school."

* * *

LITTLE Johnny happened to look into his big sister's bedroom and was intrigued to see her rubbing her hand between her legs and muttering "I want a man, I want a man."

He was even more surprised to look in next evening to see her in bed with a man.

He rushed to his own room rubbed himself between the legs and muttered: "I want a bike. I want a bike."

* * *

THE barmaid had to look over the bar to see where the voice came from. It was a six-year-old kid.

"Gimme a double Scotch and a packet of cigarettes," he said.

"Do you want to get me into trouble?" she asked.

"Leave the sex out of it," he said, "just get me th[...]
and fags."

* * *

YOUNG Billy brought a note home from school. His Dad read it and announced to his wife: "They want a written excuse for his presence."

* * *

THE little boy in the crowded showgrounds was obviously distressed. "I've lost my Dad," he sobbed when the policeman approached him.

"What's your Dad like?" said the cop.

"Beer, women and the odd bet," said the lad.

* * *

LITTLE Mary stuck her head around the kitchen door, "Hey Mum. Can an eight-year-old girl get pregnant?"

"Of course not," said her mother.

Mary turned round. "It's okay fellas, we can keep playing the game."

* * *

THREE kids are smoking behind the bike shed.

"My dad can blow smoke through his nose," said one.

"Mine can blow smoke through his ears," said the second.

"Mine can blow smoke through his arse," said the third, "I've seen the nicotine stains in his underpants."

* * *

THE English teacher asked young Johnny to give her a sentence using the word "definitely."

Johnny thought for a minute then said, "Miss, does a fart have lumps in it?"

A little shocked but outwardly unperturbed she replied. "No. Not to my knowledge, why do you ask?"

"Well, Miss," said Johnny, "I've definitely shit myself!"

* * *

TWO kids had been sent home with a note from the teacher

booze

...e not to return to school until their language

...s been swearing again?" said the father, and
...o bed without their dinner.

...ing, hoping that they had learned their lesson,
...ked what they would like for breakfast.

...e a plate of those fuckin' cornflakes," said one.

His father immediately started thumping him. Gave him a hell of a hiding and sent him back to bed.

"Now what about you?" he said to the second son. "What will you have for breakfast?"

"Well, I won't be having any of those fuckin' cornflakes, that's for sure."

* * *

THE RSPCA inspector stopped three kids in a billy-cart. It was being pulled by a big mongrel dog they had harnessed to the cart. He accused the kids of cruelty.

"Rubbish," chorused the kids, "Bonzo loves it, he has been doing it for years. He doesn't look unhappy does he?"

The officer had to admit that the big dog seemed to be enjoying himself.

"Okay," he conceded, "but that piece of string hanging from his testicles will have to come off. That could hurt him."

"Arr hell," said one of the kids. "There goes our brakes!"

* * *

FIRST day at school and two eight-year-olds were assessing their new teacher.

"How old d'yer reckon she is," said little Fred.

"Dunno," said his mate. "But if we can get her knickers off we can find out."

"How can that help?"

"Well, on the back of mine it says 8-10 years."

* * *

LITTLE Johnny was having a lot of trouble with his

arithmetic and when teacher asked him what two plus two was he counted on his fingers and said, "four."

"And how much is three and three?"

Again Johnny counted on his fingers and came up with "six."

"Johnny," stormed the teacher, "it is cheating to use your fingers. Now put your hands in your pockets and tell me what is five and five."

There was a fumble and a pause before the answer came up.

"Eleven," he said.

* * *

"MUM," said the little boy, "where did I come from?"

"The stork brought you, dear," was the reply.

"And where did you come from, Mum?"

"The stork brought me too."

"And what about Grandma?"

"The stork brought her too."

"Gee," said the little lad, "doesn't it ever worry you to think that there have been no natural births in our family for three generations?"

* * *

"HEY Mum, where do babies come from?"

"From the stork of course."

"But who roots the stork?"

* * *

LITTLE Tommy, aged eight, marched into the living room with an important announcement for his father.

"Dad," he said with great seriousness, "I'm gonna get married."

His dad grinned indulgently, "Who to, son?"

"My girlfriend, Mary, next door."

Mary was also eight and his Dad decided to carry the joke along.

"Found a place to live yet?" he asked.

"Well, she gets 50 cents pocket money and you give me

a dollar. So if she moves in with me, we can manage," said Tommy seriously.

His Dad nodded. "Well, $1-50 a week is okay for now, but what will you do when the kids start to arrive?"

"Don't worry," said Tommy confidently. "We've been lucky so far."

* * *

ON Sunday morning, while giving little Nigel his breakfast, his mother asked: "Did Daddy look after you last night?"

"Daddy put me to bed," said the boy, "but I couldn't sleep so I got up and opened the door just in time to see Daddy go into the maid's room. He shut the door but I looked through the key hole and saw him get into her bed and ..."

"Don't say any more," said the angry mother. "Here comes your father now and I want you to start again and tell us both what you saw."

The boy began his story again while the wife stared daggers at her husband.

"And what were Daddy and the maid doing?" she gritted through her teeth.

"The same thing you and Uncle Tom were doing last Friday when Dad went to the football."

* * *

"DAD, all the kids at school hit me and call me Pansy."

"That's all right son," said his father. "Next time they do that, whack them over the head with your handbag."

* * *

LITTLE Johnny had just met the new kid at playgroup.

"How old are you?"

"I don't know," said the new kid.

"Do women bother you?"

"No."

"Then you are five."

224

A YOUNG boy was approached by the young housewife who had just moved into the flat next door. "Sonny, I need some bread at the corner store. Do you think you could go for me?"

"No," said the lad, "but I've heard Dad say he could."

*　　*　　*

DAD had just settled down with a book when young Johnny came home from school and asked the question he had dreaded to hear: "Where did I come from, Dad?"

Wiping the sweat from his collar Dad began the lengthy explanation beginning with the birds and the bees right through to sexual intercourse, and after an agonising half hour summed it all up with, "Now, do you understand, son?"

"Not really, Dad," said the lad. "Luigi says he comes from Italy and Ng Van Dong says he comes from Vietnam. Where do I come from?"

*　　*　　*

THE young mother was entertaining her neighbours when her three-year-old son burst into the room, hopping from one foot to the other. "I gotta piss, I gotta piss," he said.

She dragged him off to the toilet by the ear and told him in no uncertain terms, "Next time you want to go, don't use that word. Come in and whisper, right?"

Sure enough, two hours later the youngster interrupted the women again by rushing in, hopping from one foot to the other. "I wanna whisper. I wanna whisper," he said.

At least he was rewarded with a cake for the advance he had made.

That night he jumped out of his bed yet again and ran into his mother's room. She wasn't there, but his dad had just settled down in bed. "What is it son?" he asked.

"I wanna whisper, Daddy, I wanna whisper."

"Okay, son, come and whisper in my ear."

L

LAWYERS

WHAT'S the difference between a prostitute and a lawyer?

Not much. Except the prostitute will stop screwing you once you are dead.

* * *

A BLOKE phoned a lawyer. "I am in deep financial trouble, and I need some advice. I'm down to my last hundred dollars so I want to know if you can answer just two questions for this amount?"

"Certainly, sir," answered the lawyer, "what is the second question?"

* * *

WHAT do you call a hundred lawyers at the bottom of the harbour?

A bloody good start.

* * *

WE know a bloke who buries lawyers in holes fifty feet deep.

Because deep down they are good people.

* * *

WHAT do you call a lawyer with an IQ of 25?

"Your Honour."

* * *

WHAT'S the difference between a lawyer and a football?

You only get six points for kicking a football between the uprights.

* * *

THE lady solicitor dropped her briefs and became a lawyer.

* * *

HE introduced himself as a criminal lawyer.

"Well at least you're up front about describing yourself," said his client.

* * *

FRED knew that a former partner owed him $500 but he was unable to legally prove it. He asked his solicitor what to do about it.

"Easy," replied the legal eagle. "We will send him a letter. We will demand payment of the $1000 within seven days and ..."

"But it is only $500," said Fred.

"And that's exactly what he will reply in his letter, and then we have the proof."

* * *

THE city lawyer received a fax from his partner. It read: "Justice has prevailed."

He faxed back a message immediately: "Appeal at once!"

* * *

McTAVISH was as shrewd as they come and when he sat down with the lawyer he said: "I'm not into throwing money about, but I will certainly pay if you can give me an undertaking that you can win my case."

The lawyer said that was fair enough and told McTavish to outline the story.

McTavish launched into a terrible tale of breach of contract, lying, cheating and fraudulent business practices.

"That's an open and shut case," said the lawyer, "I will cheerfully accept such a brief."

"Oh that's bad news," said McTavish.

"Why?" asked the lawyer.

"That was my opponent's side of the story."

* * *

"YOUNG man, you are accused of stealing a petticoat."

"It was my first slip."

* * *

SHE was seeking maintenance for her baby.

"Do you know who the father is?" asked the solicitor.

"Yes," she sobbed. "It was Tommy."

"But we can't sue Tommy. Don't you know his surname?"

"No. You see I didn't know him personally."

* * *

THE solicitor told Paddy that if he wanted to be defended in court tomorrow he would need money, but Paddy was broke.

"All I've got is an antique gold watch," he said.

Solicitor: "Well that's okay, you can raise cash on that. Now what are you accused of stealing?"

Paddy: "An antique gold watch!"

LESBIANS

HE sat next to her at the singles bar, bought her a beer and began chatting her up.

"Look," she said, "I'd better tell you right from the start. I'm a lesbian."

"What's that?" he asked in all innocence.

"Well," she said, "see that blonde over there. She appeals to me. In fact, I'd love to get her into bed and get into her pants."

"Strewth," he said, "I must be a lesbian too."

* * *

AFTER the examination the gyneocologist said to her patient, "Well, everything's neat and tidy there."

"So it should be," said the lesbian, "I have a woman in twice a week."

LETTERS

JAKE was complaining that he had received a letter from an irate husband who had threatened to shoot his balls off if he didn't stop screwing his wife.

"It's got me worried," he confided to his mate.

"Well, stop screwing her and your worries are over," said his mate.

"That's not the problem," said Jake, "the letter was unsigned."

* * *

HE wanted to write a letter so he went to the post office and got side-tracked for a moment by the voluptuous young blonde behind the counter. He just couldn't help chatting her up.

"By the way, do you keep stationery?" he asked.

"I try to," she said. "Right up until the last few seconds, then I go crazy."

* * *

A SAILOR named Harold had an affair with a geisha girl in Japan. A few months later he received a letter from her:

"Dear Harry. You gone three months. Me gone three months. Should I carry Harry, or hari-kari?"

* * *

HE got a letter from his wife: "Fred, I missed you yesterday. Come home and let me have another shot. ...Beatrice."

* * *

THE university chancellor discovered that one of his professors had been messing about with his wife. So he sent him a letter demanding his presence in the office on Tuesday morning.

The offending professor sent the following reply: "I

received your circular letter. I regret that I cannot attend, but rest assured that I will accept the majority vote."

* * *

A FEW weeks before Christmas the postmaster in a small town received a letter addressed to Santa Claus. He opened it and was touched by its unusually pathetic message.

It read: "Dear Santa. Do you think you could give me fifty dollars for a bike? It is not for myself, but my mother is a widow with five children and we have hit hard times. The bike would help me deliver newspapers and get some medicine for young Johnny ..."

The postmaster was so touched that he took it along to his Masonic Lodge that night and read it aloud. It prompted a quick collection which raised $48. The postmaster slipped the money into a Masonic envelope, addressed it to the boy and posted it.

The following week he noticed another letter to Santa in the same lad's handwriting. He slipped the unopened envelope in his pocket and at the appropriate time stood up at lodge and read it aloud.

It said: "Dear Santa. Thank you for sending the money for the new bike, only next time you do this sort of thing be sure not to sent it through the Masons as the bastards took a two-dollar commission."

* * *

LETTER FROM AN IRISH MOTHER
Dear Son. Just a few lines to let you know I'm still alive. I'm writing this letter slowly because I know you can't read fast. You won't know the house when you get home because we have moved.

About your father. He has a lovely new job. He has 500 men under him; he cuts grass at the cemetery. There was a washing machine in the new house when we moved in but it hasn't been working too good. Last week I put Dad's shirt in, pulled the chain and haven't seen it since.

Your sister Mary had a baby this morning but I haven't found out if it is a boy or a girl yet, so I don't know if you are an auntie or an uncle.

Your Uncle Patrick drowned last week in a vat of whisky at the Dublin Brewery. Some of his workmates tried to save him but he fought them off bravely. They cremated him and it took five days to put out the fire.

I went to the doctor last Thursday and your father came with me. The doctor put a small glass tube in my mouth and told me not to talk for ten minutes. Your father offered to buy it off him.

It only rained twice this week, first for three days and then for four.

We had a letter from the undertaker. He said if the last payment on your grandfather's plot isn't paid within seven days, up he comes.

...Your loving Mother.

PS: I was going to send you $10 but I had already sealed up the envelope.

* * *

WHY I FIRED MY SECRETARY

Two weeks ago it was my 45th birthday. I didn't feel too well that morning, but I knew that when I went to breakfast my wife would be pleasant and say "happy birthday". But she didn't even say good morning.

I thought, that's wives for you. At least the children will remember. But the kids came in for breakfast and didn't say a word, so when I started for the office I was feeling pretty low and despondent.

As I walked into the office, Janet said, "Good morning, Boss. Happy birthday." I immediately felt better because somebody remembered.

About noon she knocked on my door and said that it was such a lovely day we should go out to lunch. It was the best news Id had all day.

We went to lunch. We didn't go where we normally go. Janet said she knew a little private place out in the country. We had two Martinis and enjoyed lunch tremendously.

On the way back to the office she said: "You know, it's such a beautiful day it would be a shame to go back to the office."

When I agreed she said: "Let's go to my apartment and I will fix you another Martini."

We did just that, in fact she fixed two Martinis which put me in a very pleasant mood. Then she said, "Boss, if you don't mind, I think I will go into the bedroom and slip into something more comfortable." I assured her I didn't mind at all.

She went into the bedroom and in about six minutes she came out carrying a big birthday cake followed by my wife and children, all singing Happy Birthday, and there I sat with nothing on except my socks!

*   *   *

CHAIN LETTER FOR WOMEN

Dear Sister. This letter was started by a woman in the hope of bringing relief to other tired and discontented females.

Unlike other chain letters, this one does not cost anything. Just send a copy to five of your friends who are equally tired and discontented, then bundle up your husband or boyfriend. Send him to the woman whose name is at the top of the list and add your name to the bottom of the list.

When your name comes to the top of the list you will receive 16,877 men and one of them is bound to be a heck of a lot better than the one you already have.

Do not break the chain. One woman broke this chain and got her own bastard back.

At this writing a friend of mine has already received 184 men. They buried her yesterday, but it took three undertakers 36 hours to wipe the smile off her face and three days to get her legs together so they could close the coffin. Have faith.

...Liberated Woman

* * *

AUSTRALIAN EXPORT

Mein Tear Herren.

Der last two pecketches ve got from you off coffee vas mitt rattschidtten mixt. Ve did not see any rattschidtten in der samples vich you sent us. It takes much valuable time to pick de ratten durden from der coffee. Ve order der coffee clean but you schipt schidt mixt mit it.

Ve like you schip us der coffee in vun sek, und der rattenschidtten in an udder sek. Und zen ve can mix it to suit der customer. Write please if we should schip der schidt bek und keep der coffee, or should ve chip bek der coffee und keep der shidt, or should ve schip bek der whole schidtten vurks?

We remain at your conwenience...

* * *

DEAR Sir. Please find enclosed $10.50 for one of your razors as advertised. ...Billy Bong.

PS: I forgot to enclose the money, but no doubt a firm of your reputable standing will send the razor anyway.

Dear Mr Bong. Thank you for your order and we have pleasure enclosing the razor as requested.

PS: We forgot to enclose the razor, but no doubt a man with your cheek doesn't need one.

* * *

DEAR Sir. God bless you for the beautiful radio your company donated as a prize at our recent Senior Citizen luncheon. I was the lucky one to win it.

I am 86 years old and live at the Country Home for the Aged. All my people are gone and it was nice to have someone think of me. God bless you for your kindness to an old forgotten lady.

My room mate is 95 and always had her own radio but would never let me listen to it. The other day her radio fell and broke into lots of pieces. It was just awful. She asked if she could listen to my new radio and I told her to get fucked.

Sincerely,
Elsie McEvoy

LIFE

LIFE is a sexually transmitted terminal disease.

* * *

LIFE can be a bed of roses...full of pricks.

* * *

LIFE is like a pubic hair on a toilet seat.
Eventually you get pissed off.

* * *

A WOMAN was walking down the street with her seven-year-old daughter when they couldn't help notice two dogs copulating right on the pavement ahead of them.

"What are those dogs doing, Mummy?" she asked.

The mother was very embarrassed but did some quick thinking to come up with an explanation.

"The dog on top has hurt its leg," she said, "the dog underneath is its friend and is trying to carry the injured one home."

"That's life," said the little girl, "try to help someone and they turn round and fuck you."

LOCAL GOVERNMENT

HE had been Shire President for 15 years and the town's benefactor for 15 before that. Now he was bemoaning the fickle attitude of the town after all those years of dedicated service.

"D'yer see that town square?" he lamented to a fellow

councillor. "I not only designed it, I put thousands of dollars into its construction. I have served this community for nigh on 30 years. Worked on the hospital committee, the sports committee, the town planning committee. Youd think I would have earned a bit of gratitude from the town. But no, fuck just one goat ..."

*　*　*

A TEDDY bear got a job on a council road gang. Monday went well, Tuesday likewise, but on Wednesday when he returned from his lunch break he discovered his pick had been stolen.

He complained to the foreman who was undismayed and had the obvious answer.

"It's Wednesday," he said. "That's the day the teddy bears have their picks nicked!"

*　*　*

A SOCIETY matron was crowing over her husband's re-election on the municipal council. "Yes. my John got elected for his third time and got in unexposed!"

*　*　*

WHEN the municipal council decided to build a fountain outside the town hall they put the project to tender and got three quotes, from contractors in Brisbane, Sydney and Melbourne.

The town clerk interviewed the Brisbane builder and asked his price. "$3000," was the reply.

"And how do you break that down?" asked the clerk.

"That's $1000 for the material, $1000 for the workers and $1000 for me."

The town clerk called in the Sydney contractor who quoted a price of $6000. "And how do you break that down?" asked the clerk.

"That's $2000 for materials, $2000 for the workers and $2000 for me."

The clerk called in the Melbourne bloke, whose price was $9000.

"And how do you break that down?" asked the clerk.

The bloke from Melbourne said, "$3000 for you, $3000 for me, and we give the job to the bloke from Brisbane."

* * *

BANDYWALLOP had never had a woman on the town council before and newly elected Cr Flossie Firebrand intended to make her mark.

The first item on the engineer's agenda was the cost of constructing a urinal.

"What's a urinal?" she asked.

When it was fully explained to her she immediately demanded that the funds be doubled.

"If we are gonna have a urinal I insist that we have an arsenal too."

* * *

THE headline in the local paper's society page jolted a few of the community. It read: "Mayor's Ball Comes Off To-night!"

LOVE

THREE little words, "I love you," can inflate the ego.

Three little words, "Is it in?" can deflate the ego.

* * *

TO go togehter is blessed.

To come together is divine.

M

MAGIC

AN old magician was working the Titanic on its last fateful voyage. He used to put a rabbit in his top hat and pull a hair out of his bum. (No, that's not the joke).

The old-timer had been down on his luck and couldn't afford one of those attractive leggy blonde assistants. On the Titanic he had to make do with a parrot, but to give it credit, the parrot had developed repartee and would squawk to the audience: "It's up his sleeve", or, "It's under his cloak, folks."

They were half way through their act when the Titanic hit the iceberg and sank.

The magician swam all night while the parrot fluttered overhead. He swam all next day and the parrot still fluttered overhead. It was evening of the second day when the parrot finally alighted on the magician's head.

"Okay, I give up. What have you done with the bloody ship?"

* * *

AFTER the leggy blonde had flagged him down on the country road he asked her what she did for a living.

"I'm a magician," she said.

"Get away, prove it then."

And with that she touched him on the dick and turned him into a motel.

237

MARRIAGE

SHE had been married so long she even faked the foreplay.

        *   *   *

THE husband complained: "You never cry out when you have an orgasm."

"How do you know," she replied, "you are never there."

        *   *   *

THEY had been married for 15 years. One night while they were making love he said: "Dear, am I hurting you?"

"No," she replied."Why?"

"I thought you moved," he said.

        *   *   *

SHE: "How is it that I am always catching you rooting the cook?"

He: "It's because you are always wearing sneakers."

        *   *   *

THEY were having another tiff.

"I have never had an affair, never," he said. "Can you say the same?"

"Yes," she said, "but not with such a straight face."

        *   *   *

AFTER 15 years of marriage they finally achieved sexual compatibility.

They both had a headache.

        *   *   *

IN bed the frustrated wife was moaning to her husband: "Why is it taking so long to come up?"

"I'm trying dear, I'm trying," he said. "I just can't think of anyone tonight."

        *   *   *

THE wife said: "This room needs decorating."

The husband said: "The bloke who invented decorating needs fucking."

The wife replied: "Well, you've changed your tune. Last night you said the bloke who invented fucking needs decorating."

THEY had been married for ten years. She looked up from her sewing and said: "Darling, why don't we go out tonight?"

He put his book aside and said: "What a splendid idea. And if I get home before you I will leave the light on."

* * *

PADDY was asked how he managed to get along so well with his wife.

"Cos I always tell her the truth, even if I have to lie a little."

* * *

REMEMBER, Socrates died from an overdose of wedlock.

* * *

MARRIAGE is the price men pay for sex and sex is the price women pay for marriage.

* * *

MARRIAGE has its good side. It teaches you loyalty, forebearance, self-restraint, and many other qualities you wouldn't need if youd stayed single.

* * *

BRIGID had been a devout Catholic so it was a surprise to everybody when she married out of the church. But although married to a Presbyterian she always attended mass.

One Sunday morning she rose as usual and began to dress. She was conscious of her husband watching her as she slipped out of her nightie, pulled on her stockings, and hooked up her bra. She even noticed the bedsheet rising just below his navel.

She took off her bra, her stockings and pants and climbed back in to bed.

"I thought you were going to church," he said.

"The Catholic Church will stand forever," she said, "but how long can you trust a Presbyterian prick?"

239

THE marriage counsellor asked the wife: "Did you shrink from love-making?"

"No," she replied, "I've always been tiny like this."

* * *

DARLING is the wife's maiden name.

* * *

"TELL me dear, before we were married did you say you were oversexed, or over sex?"

* * *

THE reporter wanted to know how his marriage had lasted for fifty years.

"Simple," he said. "We decided right from the start that she would make all the minor decisions while I would decide the major issues.

"So she decided where we would live, what school the kids would attend, what investments we would make, and I made the major decisions like what to do about greenhouse warming, the Middle East and lifting sanctions on South Africa."

* * *

A COUPLE got married and the wife put a wooden box under the bed and told her husband he wasn't allowed to look inside it until after she died.

After 20 years of marriage her husband couldn't resist his curiosity any longer. While his wife was out he opened the box and found three eggs and $25,000.

He looked at it so long in puzzled amazement that his wife caught him.

"Well, what are the eggs for?" asked the husband.

"Every time Ive been unfaithful to you, Ive put an egg in the box," she explained.

The husband said: "Only three times in 20 years, well, that's not bad. I can live with that. But what's the money for?"

The wife replied: "Every time I got a dozen I sold them!"

THE usual scene. The husband comes home and finds a man humping his wife in bed, but she pleads with him for a chance to explain.

"He's been unemployed for months. He knocked on the door and asked for something to eat and I gave him the quiche you didn't want. He had no shoes so I gave him those slippers you threw out yesterday. Then he asked if there was anything else my husband didn't use."

*   *   *

WHEN they checked into the hotel the clerk said the only room available was the bridal suite.

"But we've been married for 25 years, it would be wasted on us," said the husband.

"Look," said the clerk, "if we put you in the ballroom we wouldn't expect you to dance all night."

*   *   *

MADGE fixed her eye on her husband Fred and said: "So, where are you going today?"

"I'm going to the pub."

"Ha, when you tell me you are going to the pub I know that you think that I'll think you are going to the races, but this time I know you are really going to the pub, so why are you lying?"

*   *   *

HARRY stopped off at the pub and was soon chatting up a blonde at the bar. Near closing time she suggested going to her place. They did and after a few more drinks they had a wonderful time.

It was three in the morning when Harry got out of bed and began to dress. And with a worried frown said, "how will I explain this to the wife?"

"No problem," said the blonde. "Tell the truth, and put this bit of chalk behind your ear."

Harry was creeping up the stairs when the light was

flicked on, and there was his fuming wife waiting with folded arms.

"And where the hell have you been?" she demanded.

Harry remembered the blonde's advice and said, "I've been tumbling in bed with a lovely blonde I picked up in the pub."

"Liar!" she roared. "You have been playing billiards all night with those hopeless mates of yours. I can tell by the chalk behind your ear."

* * *

THE old couple sat on the porch, as they had for many years. "I was just thinking," said the old lady, "we've had such a grand life together, but sooner or later one of us will pass on."

"Yes, but don't worry about that now," he said.

"Well I was just thinking," she said, "when it does happen, I'd like to go and live in Queensland."

* * *

REMEMBER that your wife is a romantic and still enjoys chocolates and flowers. So show her that you too remember, by speaking of them occasionally.

* * *

"WHAT'S your husband's average income?"

"About midnight."

* * *

MR and Mrs Offenbloo had been married for 20 years and they were still in love. She with the doctor and he with his secretary.

* * *

A BLOKE came home to find his wife in bed with the next door neighbour.

"What the hell do you think you're doing?" demanded the husband.

The wife said to her bedmate: "There you are, I told you he was stupid."

THE miser was berating his wife over the domestic bills.

"Look at this electricity account," he said. "It's exorbitant."

"And look at these tradesmen's bills."

He held up another document. "And look at this massive gas bill. You and your bungled suicide attempts."

* * *

THE husband was at the bedside of his dying wife. She raised herself on one elbow and in little more than a whisper said she wanted to confess.

"Darling," she said, "I am the one who informed the police about your business activities. Can you forgive me? I am the one who had your mistress deported. And I am the one who stole that $100,000 from your safe and spent it on a sexual affair with your best friend. Will you ever forgive me?"

"Of course, my dear. I am the one who poisoned your mushrooms."

MISTRESSES

FRED has got so many mistresses that when he takes his wife for a drive she has to hide under the dash when they pass a woman in the street.

* * *

THE difference between a missus and a mistress is often a mattress.

MECHANICS

IT was a cold winter's night and they were out on their first date when the car broke down. He said there was nothing to worry about. He was a mechanic and would have it fixed in no time.

After fiddling under the bonnet for a moment he jumped

back into the car and gave her quite a fright when he placed both hands up between her thighs.

"It's so cold," he explained, "I can't get my fingers to work. I just need to warm them for a moment."

After five minutes or so he got out again and continued fiddling with the motor but he was soon back to warm his fingers. Again and again he was jumping back into the car to place his hands between her thighs until finally she said: "Don't your ears ever get cold too?"

* * *

WHEN her date, a young mechanic, arrived to take her out she was surprised to see a set of jumper leads around his neck with the clips holding his trousers up. "My braces broke," he explained.

She gave the jumper leads a dubious look and said: "Well okay. But don't start anything."

* * *

THE mechanic itemized the bill for the woman driver: "$100 repairs to fender, $150 repairs to the tail-light fixture, $50 for not telling your husband and $50 for running over Pete, the petrol pump attendant."

* * *

I ONCE had a dog called Mechanic. If you gave him a kick in the nuts he made a bolt for the door.

MOTHERS-IN-LAW

MY mother-in-law broke up our marriage.

My wife came home early one evening and found me in bed with her.

* * *

MY mother-in-law thinks I'm effeminate.

Compared to her I probably am.

* * *

THE local Peeping Tom knocked on the door the other night

and asked if the mother-in-law would mind closing her bedroom curtains.

*　　*　　*

THE mother-in-law was kidnapped when they returned from their holiday. After three days they got a note from the kidnappers saying that if they didn't send the ransom money immediately, they would send her back.

MOTORING
See CARS

FRED said the local cop was persecuting him. "He pulled me up and walked around my car for ten minutes trying to find some fault. Finally he booked me."

"What for?" said his mates at the pub.

He got me for having a missing hub cap."

"What? That's not an offence," they chorused in protest.

"What was the charge?" they asked.

"Exposing my nuts!" said Fred.

*　　*　　*

WE know a bloke who changed his name by deed poll to CMH-869 so that he could have personalised number plates.

*　　*　　*

THE young Romeo and his girlfriend took the sports car for a test drive. By their flushed faces when they returned the salesman thought he had made a sale.

"It's not bad," said the Romeo, "but we would like something with a bit more headroom under the dashboard."

*　　*　　*

SOCIOLOGISTS have noticed the difference when men and women drivers use self-service fuel pumps.

The men always give the hose a few shakes when they're through.

THE police stopped him because he looked a bit under the weather. He was approached with the breathalyser bag.

"What's that?" he asked.

"It tells if you have had too much to drink," said the cop.

"Amazing. I'm married to one of them."

* * *

FRED drove his car back to the second-hand dealer.

"You remember you sold me this car last week and said its sole previous owner was a little old woman, quiet and reserved and only used the car to go to church on Sundays?"

"Yes," said the salesman a little cautiously.

"Well can you give me her name," said Fred. "I have cleaned out the boot and the glove box and I want to return her cigar butts, two empty gin bottles, a pair of silk garters with spangles on them and a pair of red knickers."

* * *

AFTER the usual Friday night binge at the local Harry took off up High Street, went round the roundabout three times, headed back the way he came, mounted the median strip and finished up against the door of the pub he had left minutes earlier.

"Christ, bloody lucky I didn't bring the car tonight," he said.

MULTI-NATIONALS

See AUSTRALIANS, FRENCH, GERMANS, IRISH, NEW ZEALANDERS, SCOTS, TURKS, WELSH

AT a United Nations function in New York the Norwegian Consul approached a small group of diplomats and made a bid to start small talk. "Pardon me," he said, "what is your opinion of the meat shortage?"

The American looked perplexed: "What's a shortage?"

The Pole scratched his head: "What's meat?"

The Russian shrugged: "What's an opinion?"

The Israeli asked: "What's pardon me?"

FOUR women, one English, one American, one German and one French, were all asked the same question: "What would you do if you were shipwrecked on an island with a regiment of soldiers?"

The Englishwoman said she would hide. The American said she would seek the protection of the commanding officer. The German woman said she would be out marching and it wouldn't bother her.

The French woman thought for a moment: "I understand ze question, but what seems to be ze problem?"

* * *

THE Frenchman, the Italian and the Australian were discussing who was the best lover.

"When I am in bed with my wife I prepare such foreplay and technique that she rises a foot off the bed," said the Frenchman.

Not to be outdone the Italian said he whispered love-talk to his wife and employed such sensuous procedures she moaned and rose two feet off the bed.

"That's nothing," said the Australian, "after I've finished making love to my missus and I wipe my cock on the curtains she hits the roof."

* * *

A SCOT, an Irishman and an Australian were each sentenced to five years in prison and were allowed one request.

The Scot asked for all the great books so he could study and learn.

The Irishman asked if his wife could stay with him so he could start a family.

The Australian did a quick calculation and asked the equivalent of five packets of cigarettes a day for the five years.

At the end of the term the Scot emerged as an erudite scholar. The Irishman emerged from prison with a family of five kids.

The Australian emerged looking a little frustrated. "Anybody got a match?" he asked.

* * *

HELL is multi-cultural.

The Germans are the police force, the Italians the defence force, the Indonesians are in charge of housing, and the Indians run the railways. The Irish make the laws, the English are the cooks and the common language is Dutch.

* * *

LETTER received by the Bureau of Ethnic Affairs:

"Gentlemen. I have always wanted to have an affair with an ethnic. How do I go about it?"

* * *

THE brave Dutch lad stuck his finger in the dyke.

And she punched the bejeezus out of him.

* * *

THE difference between a Jewish woman and an Italian woman is that one has fake orgasms and real diamonds while the other has vice versa.

* * *

"YOU should welcome migrants to your country," said the Jewish gentleman, "you should encourage them to come from everywhere.

"The better the mix the better the population," he continued, "why, in my veins there flows the blood of Poles, Italians, Germans, Norwegians and Greeks."

"Well," said one impressed listener, "all I can say is that your mother must have been a great sport."

* * *

A YOUNG Norwegian couple fronted up to the registry for a marriage licence.

"Name?" asked the clerk.

"Ole Olson,"

"And yours?"

"Inge Olson."

"Any connection?"

Inge blushed. "Only vunce, when he yumped me."

* * *

THREE migrants appeared to be having trouble with the English language.

One was lamenting the fact that he and his wife had no children. "She is unbearable," he explained.

"No, you mean she is inconceivable," said the second.

"You are both wrong," said the third. "He means his wife is impregnable.

* * *

A WELSHMAN and a Pom were arguing politics in the pub.

The left-wing Pommie said: "I think Margaret Thatcher has a face like a sheep's arse."

The Welshman swung his fist and punched him on the nose.

"I didn't know you were a conservative?" said the wounded Pom.

"I'm not," said the Taffy, "I'm a shepherd."

* * *

THREE builders, an Australian, an Englishman and an Irishman were working on a city sky-scraper. The Australian opened his lunch: "Not bloody Vegemite again," he said. "If I get Vegemite sandwiches tomorrow I'll ... I'll jump off this bloody building."

The Englishman opened his lunch. "Not cheese again. If I get cheese sandwiches tomorrow I'll jump off with you."

The Irishman opened his lunch., "Not jam again. If I get jam sandwiches again tomorrow I'll jump with you guys."

Tomorrow came. The Australian took one look at his Vegemite sandwiches and said: "That's it." He immediately jumped off the building.

The Englishman opened his lunch. "Cheese," he roared, and immediately followed suit.

The Irishman tentatively opened his lunch bag. "Oh no. Not jam, again." He also jumped.

At the triple funeral the Australian widow sobbed away: "Oh, if I had only known that he hated Vegemite..."

The English widow was also lamenting: "I didn't know he hated cheese so much."

The Irish widow was also perturbed. "I can't figure it out. Paddy always made his own sandwiches."

* * *

THREE different nationalities were discussing the meaning of *savoir-faire*.

The American said, "It means that if you came home and found your wife in bed with another man and you refrained from killing the son-of-a-bitch, that's *savoire-faire*."

The Englishman said: "Hardly, chaps. If you found your wife in bed with another man and excused yourself for interrupting and invited them to carry on, well that's *savoir-faire*."

The Frenchman had a different view: "If you came home and found your wife in bed with another man and you said 'Please continue, monsieur' and he was able to, then HE'S got *savoir-faire*."

MUSIC

IN a smoke-filled bar in Casablanca the piano player leant across and put his hand on the American's knee.

"Didn't I tell you I could make you forget that girl?"

"Yeah," said the American, "play with it again, Sam."

* * *

GIRLS are like pianos. When they are not upright, they're grand.

* * *

THE hi-fi expert had gone to great trouble to choose the right seductive music for his date. Just as they got down to some heavy fondling he could hear an irritating noise in one of the speakers.

Getting off the sofa he said, "I'll have that Dolby on in a flash."

"Don't worry about it," she said, "I'm on the pill."

* * *

THERE is a new Israeli group called the Fore Skins.

They are backed by Jock Strap and his Elastic Band playing "Stop that Swing."

* * *

THREE music professors were paying homage at Beethoven's grave when one said he thought he heard music. The second said he thought it was the Fifth Symphony being played backwards. The third said he thought it was Beethoven de-composing.

* * *

THE couple were at the opera in a box above the stage and she took the opportunity during interval to give her boyfriend a hand job. After the boyfriend was relieved she flung the handful over the balcony and into the orchestra pit where it hit the second violinst, splat, on his bald pate.

"Hell," he said, "I've just been hit by a flying fuck."

"And so you should be," said the first violinist. "You've been playing like a cunt all night."

* * *

THE old maestro had fallen on hard times, mainly due to tippling the whisky bottle. He had been a concert pianist of great renown in his time and his drinking pals at the Pig and Whistle decided they should be responsible for putting him back on the concert circuit.

They chipped in and bought an old tuxedo from the opportunity shop, not knowing that the trousers that went with it had a split in the crotch.

They booked him for the next benefit concert at the Mechanics' Hall and lined the front row on the opening night. When the maestro came on stage, bowed and sat on his chair at the piano there was a gasp of concern from the front row, and one of his friends was so bold as to leap onto the stage and whisper.

"Do you know your knackers are hanging through the old wicker chair?"

"No," said the maestro thoughtfully, "But if you hum the tune I will soon pick up the melody!"

* * *

A SAILOR who had been six months at sea was hunting the waterfront looking for a bar where he could have a quiet drink. He inspected a few, but the one that took his fancy had a South Sea Island motif, a monkey swinging around the chandelier and a pianist tinkling out a tune in the corner.

He went in and ordered a martini.

As the barman put the drink on the counter the monkey swung down from the rafters, spun around and dunked his nuts in the glass.

Naturally, the sailor reacted with loud abuse at the barman.

"Did you see that!" he roared. "Get me another drink."

The barman dutifully delivered another martini and set it on the bar, but before the sailor could reach for the glass the monkey dropped from the roof again, spun round and once more dunked his vitals in the drink.

The sailor was furious. He gripped the barman by the shirt-front and lifted him across the bar.

"It's not my monkey," protested the barman. "It belongs to the pianist over there."

The sailor dropped the bartender on the floor and strode over to the pianist.

"Do you know your monkey is dunking his balls in my martini,?" he roared.

"No," replied the pianist thoughtfully. "But if you hum the tune I'll soon pick up the melody!"

"LADIES and gentlemen. We have two bands to entertain you tonight. First we have Jock Strap and his 'Lastic Band, to play *Stop That Swing*, followed by the stars of the evening, Phil Landerer and his Oversextette.

* * *

THE flat-warming party had reached the stage where everybody was required to perform their artistic act. Some sang, others recited poems or told their favourite joke.

"What about you, Albert?" they chimed when they realised he was the only one who hadn't performed.

"Well," there is something I can do, but it is a little unusual."

Under more pressure he produced a mouth organ, dropped his dacks, put the instrument behind his bum and played *Britannia Rules the Waves*.

Amazement, wonder and applause was the instant result and Albert was pressed to play an encore.

Particularly astonished was Kevin, a talent scout for Harry M. Miller. He was convinced this act was a commercial winner.

He quickly dialled the entrepreneur who wasn't at all happy about being woken at three in the morning.

"But Harry, listen to this," and he called Albert to come closer to the phone as he played a rendition of *Waltzing Matilda*.

Harry listened for a while and gave Kevin his verdict: "It just sounds like some arse playing the mouth organ!"

* * *

TO the cellist, the lovely Miss Datchet
    Said the conductor, with a voice like a hatchet,
    "You have 'twixt your thighs
    A thing of beauty and size
    Yet you just sit there and scratch it."

253

N

NAMES

THE three Murphy sisters, Sandy, Mandy and Fanny were the prettiest, and tallest girls in town. They also had the largest feet in town.

One night Sandy and Mandy met two fellows at the local dance and when one noticed the size of the girls' shoes he said: "Crickey, you girls have sure got big feet."

"That's nothing," said Mandy, "you should see our Fannys."

* * *

PADDY proudly announced that his sister had just given birth to twins, a boy and a girl.

"What's their names?" asked a friend.

"The girl is called Denise," said Paddy "and the boy is called Da nephew."

* * *

A REPORTER was sent to interview a woman who had 15 children. "What do you call them?" he asked.

"Henry," she said.

"You mean they are all called Henry?" said the surprised reporter.

"Yes."

"But what if you want one in particular?"

"Oh, simple," she said. "They all have different surnames."

IT was all quiet in the stable until the three wise men arrived and one bumped his head on a low beam.

"Jesus Christ," he exclaimed.

"Now that's a better name than Fred," said Mary to Joseph.

*   *   *

THE Cockney family was large. "And the funny thing," said the father, 'Arold, "Orl our kids have names that begin with a haitch. "There's 'Erbert, 'Enry, 'Orace, 'Ubert, 'Ugh, 'Arriet and 'Etty. All except the last one. We called her Halice."

*   *   *

HE said his name was Patrick S. O'Flaherty.

"What's the S stand for?"

"Nothing," said Paddy. "My father dropped some spaghetti on my birth certificate."

*   *   *

THE newly-weds were relaxing after a heavy sex session. He lay back exhausted while she began talking about choosing a name for the baby.

"We don't want babies yet," he mumbled.

"No, but if we do have one we should have a name," she persisted.

With that he pulled off the condom, tied a knot in it and flung it out the window. "If he gets out of that we'll call him Houdini," he said.

NEIGHBOURS

IT was the morning after an all-night party and the bloke next door was raking his front lawn when the guests began leaving.

As one couple left he heard his neighbour call: "Good-bye, and thanks for a lend of your wife. She was terrific in bed. The best hump I've had for years."

This put a stop to the neighbour's raking and he hurried

over to the fence. "I heard that," he said, how could you possible say a thing like that?"

"Oh I had to," said the host. "She's not really that good in bed but I didn't want to hurt their feelings."

* * *

AFTER his business failed and his marriage collapsed he decided to start a new life in hillbilly country. Two lonely nights made him wonder if he had done the right thing but on the third morning he saw the dust of a small truck headed up the valley towards his shack.

"My name's Jake," said the raw-boned visitor extending a friendly hand when he arrived. "Heard you had moved into the district," he continued. "I'm kind of the welcoming committee. D'yer like parties?"

"Yes, I do," said the new settler.

"Well we are having one tomorrow night," said Jake. "It will be in your honour. It's all a bit rugged up here so there'll probably be a bit of drinking, probably a fight or two, but I'll guarantee there will be plenty of sex too."

"Sounds great," said the settler warming to the prospect. "What will I wear?" he asked.

"Oh, come as you are," said Jake. "There'll only be you and me."

* * *

WITH a stern voice the clerk of courts began reading the charge against the man in the dock.

"You are charged that on May 1 you battered your wife to death with a hammer..."

A voice at the back of the court yelled: "You bastard!"

The Clerk continued: "You are further charged that on the same day you battered your mother-in-law to death with a hammer..."

The voice at the rear shouted: "You filthy bastard!"

It was too much for the judge. He ordered a constable to bring the owner of the offensive voice forward.

Hauled before the judge the man explained: "Im his

256

neighbour. "Only a month ago I asked him for a loan of a hammer and the rotten bastard said he didnt have one."

NEWLY-WEDS
See HONEYMOONS

ON their wedding night the groom took off his trousers and told his new wife to try them on.

"They don't fit," she said.

"Then don't forget it," said the husband, "in this house I wear the trousers."

She threw him her knickers. Put them on," she said.

He looked at the skimpy scanties and said, "I can't get into these."

"No," she said, "and if you don't change your bloody attitude you never will."

* * *

THE newly-weds had their first argument and it was the cold shoulder in bed that night. Next day the groom sought the advice of older married men at the office on how to get out of the dog-house.

"Take home some flowers," was the consensus opinion.

That evening he arrived home and presented her with the floral offering.

It worked. She disappeared into the bedroom then called for him to follow.

When he entered the room he found her stretched out on the bed, lying naked with her legs apart.

"This is for the flowers," she said.

"Haven't we got a vase?" he replied.

* * *

THEY had been married a month and while he was reading the paper she came past and gave him a kick in the ankle.

"What's that for?" he complained.

"For being a lousy lover," she replied.

He mulled over this for a while then gave her a cuff over the ear.

"What was that for?" she said.

"For knowing the difference," he said.

* * *

THEY hadn't been married long and one day he came home early to find her on her hands and knees scrubbing the kitchen floor. Her short skirt revealed her tantalising buttocks swinging from side to side.

Without a word he unzipped his trousers, mounted her from behind and they both enjoyed a quickie.

As soon as he recovered he gave her a clip over the ear.

"Is that a nice thing to do after I just gave you so much pleasure?" she said.

"It was for not looking around to see who it was," he said.

* * *

THE vicar got married. On his wedding night he got undressed in the bathroom then entered the bedroom to find his bride already between the sheets.

"I thought I would find you on your knees," he said.

She replied: "Oh I can do it that way too, but tonight I'd like to see your face."

* * *

HENPECKED for years he had always told his son to marry a girl with less intelligence because he believed his smart wife was the reason for his henpecked condition.

"I did the right thing, Dad," said his son on return from his honeymoon.

"Boy is she dumb," he continued. "When we went to bed on our first night she was so stupid she didn't know where to put the pillow. She stuck it under her bum instead of her head."

* * *

THEY had been married a week and one morning while they were lying in bed she was idly fondling his dick and

258

said: "Darling, didn't you say you were the only man with one of these?"

"That's right, love."

"No, you've been telling fibs," she said. "Your brother has one too."

"Oh, that was my spare one. I gave it to him."

"Silly man," she said. "You gave the best one away."

*　　*　　*

AFTER their marriage and bridal night in the town, Jed and his new bride set off for Jed's farm up in the hills in a wooden cart drawn by a donkey.

But the donkey wouldn't move. Jed cajoled, then swore but it wouldn't budge. He then got off the cart picked up a short log and gave the donkey a severe whack over the head.

"That's one," he said, as the beast started to move foward.

An hour later the donkey stopped again. Jed cajoled, then swore at it but it wouldn't budge. He got down from the cart and gave it an almighty biff between the eyes with the short plank.

"That's two," he said as the donkey faltered forward.

When the donkey stopped for the third time and refused to move, despite a series of whacks over the head Jed said, "Well that's three," and he pulled out a shotgun and gave the donkey both barrels between the eyes. It dropped down dead.

It was too much for his new wife who uttered her first protest. "Fancy treating an animal like that," she said, "you beat it unmercifully. You are not only a cruel man you are a stupid one. That donkey was worth a hundred dollars. You are an extravagant fool."

"That's one," he said.

NEWSPAPERS

THE reporter interviewed the oldest lady in the retirement home. Aged 100 she was sprightly and in excellent health.

"Have you ever been bedridden?" he asked.

"Of course, many times, but don't put that in the paper," she said.

*   *   *

WHEN the reporter visited the nudist colony for a story he introduced himself: "I'm Dick Brown, from the Sun."

*   *   *

THREE young businesswomen, former schoolmates, went out on the town for a reunion and ended up in a bar enjoying a few drinks.

One suggested they tell each other something they'd never told anyone else. With a giggle they agreed.

The first beckoned the others to lean forward before she whispered: "I am a lesbian. Always have been, even when I was at school."

After the shock had subsided the second said: "I am having a torrid sex affair with my boss."

The third said: "I am the secret gossip columnist for the *Daily Blab* and if you will excuse me, I must run."

*   *   *

BACK in Egyptian times when newspapers were carved on rock two scribes were chiselling out news of the lusty young Pharaoh who had ascended to the throne. One tapped the other on the shoulder, "How do you spell macho, one testicle or two?"

*   *   *

WHATS the difference between *Cosmopolitan* and *Womens Own*?

Cosmopolitan will teach a woman how to fake an orgasm, *Womens Own* will teach them how to knit one.

NEW ZEALANDERS

WHAT'S long and hard and fucks New Zealanders?
   The third year of primary school.

* * *

A KIWI farmer was counting his sheep:
   "205, 206, 207, hello darling, 209, 210 ..."

* * *

LITTLE Bo Peep has lost her sheep
   And doesn't know where to find them.
   But a search revealed they were in the next field
   With a dirty big Kiwi behind them.

* * *

TOBY had a little lamb ...
   His case comes up next Friday.

* * *

THE New Zealand couple finally worked out a solution to
the eternal triangle.
   They ate the sheep.

* * *

THE farmer's wife gave him a plate of grass for his dinner.
   "What the hell's this?" he exploded.
   "If it's good enough for your girlfriend it's good enough
for you," she said.

* * *

IT was smoko and three shearers sat against a fence when
a flock of sheep walked by.
   "I wish that one was Miss Universe," said one.
   "I wish that one was Mister Universe," said another.
   "I wish it was dark," said the third.

* * *

WHEN a tourist coach passed through a small country town
in New Zealand one of the passengers noticed a sheep tied
to a lamp-post on the corner in the main street.
   "Oh that," said the guide. "That's the Recreation Centre."

A BLOKE went into the fish shop and asked for some "Fish 'n Chups."

"Ar! You're a Kiwi, eh?" said the proprietor.

The Enzedder was sick and tired of this so he spent the next three months at an elocution class.

He finally returned to the shop and asked, in perfect English for some "Fish and Chips."

"Ar, you're a Kiwi, eh?"

"How the hell did you know that?"

"Because this has been a hardware shop for the last two weeks."

* * *

THE potato farmer had recently arrived from Rotorua and had taken up a farm in Gembrook. "You look worried," said his mates in the pub, "what's bothering you?"

"Sex!" he replied.

They gathered around for more information.

"Well," explained the Kiwi, "as you know this is my first harvest here. I've got a wonderful crop of spuds, but not enough sex to put them in."

* * *

THREE couples went into a restaurant in Auckland and asked for a table for sex.

"And three pillows," they added.

NUDISTS

STREAKERS Beware! Your end is in sight.

* * *

TWO nudists stopped dating because they were seeing too much of each other.

* * *

PADDY Murphy caused a sensation by streaking through the nudist camp.

STREAK, or forever hold your piece.

* * *

IN the nudist camp they always sent Jake for the morning tea. He was the only man who could carry two coffees and ten donuts.

* * *

THE midget was asked to leave the nudist colony because he always had his nose in everybody's business.

But then they had a disco night and he was clubbed to death.

* * *

WHEN Jake retired he decided to realise a life-long ambition and join a nudist club. "But I don't know if I'm past it," he explained to the club treasurer.

"Well, make this a probationary day. Come in and see how you go," said the treasurer.

So Jake took a seat on a log by the river bank and, watching the nude women pass by he soon got a roaring horn. Noticing the erection, one woman stopped and gave him the greatest blow job of his life.

When he recovered he went straight into the office and paid his fees.

He was walking back to the log when he dropped his cigar. He bent over to pick it up and was tail-gated by a male member.

He rushed back to the office and demanded his money back.

"I can only manage one horn a month," he said, "but I am always dropping my cigar."

* * *

A NUDIST who picked flowers for smelling
When stung on the dick started yelling
"Doc, get rid of the pain
But let the other remain,
I refer of course to the swelling."

263

NUNS

HELP a nun kick the habit.

* * *

MOTHER Superior was engrossed in a crossword puzzle for some time and muttered that something was wrong.

"What's a four-letter word relating to women that ends in u-n-t?"

"Oh dear," said Sister Priscilla, "I think that would have to be aunt."

"Of course," said Mother Superior. "Do you have an eraser I could borrow."

* * *

THE Queen had a baby and they fired a 21-gun salute.

The nun had a baby and they fired the dirty old Canon.

* * *

THE young novice soon realised that the absence of sex in the convent was a problem. She confessed to mother superior that it was unhealthy and she was restless.

"Comfort yourself with a candle," she was advised.

"I've tried that," she said, "but you get tired of the same thing wick in and wick out."

* * *

BECOME a nun and feel superior.

* * *

THERE was once a monk from Siberia
Whose manners were rather inferior
He did to a nun
What he shouldn't have done
And now she's a Mother Superior

* * *

THE young novice was assigned her first job at the convent: to sweep the steps of the church and keep the entrance clean. But she was having a terrible time with the pigeons. They were flapping, cooing, and shitting all over the steps she had just cleaned.

She would wave her arms and say: "Fuck off. Fuck off."

It annoyed the priest who asked Mother Superior to have a discreet word with the novice.

"Your language is unseemly and entirely unnecessary," Mother Superior told her. "All you have to do is say shoo-shoo, and swipe them with the broom and you will find they will soon fuck off."

* * *

TWO young nuns were assigned to do the shopping and drove to the supermarket in the convent's mini minor. When they couldn't find a parking space one elected to do the shopping while the other drove around the block.

The first nun finally returned to the car park with a loaded trolley and asked a council worker: "Have you seen a nun in a red mini?"

"Not since I stopped drinking," he replied.

* * *

WHEN the novice returned from the presbytery Mother Superior said: "Why were you so long, sister?"

"Father Murphy was showing me how to blow the Horn of Plenty."

"The old villian. He told me it was the Trumpet of Gabriel."

* * *

MOTHER Superior was addressing the graduation ceremony and giving motherly advice. "In the outside world you will meet many temptations," she warned the girls. "You must remember the teachings and ideals you learned here at the convent."

She preached on at length and finally said: "There will be many a wicked man trying to take sexual liberties with you. Resist, and remember that one hour of pleasure could ruin your whole life. Any questions?"

"Yes, sister. How do you make it last an hour?"

THE old priest couldn't help noticing that the new curate sent to replace him had a large stack of luggage which included golf clubs and tennis rackets. And no sooner had the new man settled into his room when he approached the older priest to ask for a loan.

"Can you lend me $25.50?" he asked.

"What for?" asked the priest.

"A nookie," said the curate.

The old priest was puzzled by the request but reluctantly handed over the money.

Later that day, and still bothered by the incident, he met Mother Superior.

"What's a nookie?" he asked.

"$25.50," she replied.

* * *

WALKING into a liquor store Sister Genevieve asked for a bottle of whisky. "Oh it's alright. It's for Mother Superior's constipation."

Later that afternoon the licensee was shocked to see the nun in the park looking the worse for wear.

"I thought you said that whisky was for your superior's constipation," he said.

"Don't worry," slurred Sister Genevieve. "When she sees me she'll shit."

* * *

THE nun began to lecture him on the evils of drink as he tried to enter the pub. "Listen Sister," he said, "how can you knock it if you've never tried it?"

The argument continued along these lines. "If you tasted one drink you would know what you are talking about," he said.

Finally she agreed he had a point. "Just a small ladies drink then," she said, "whatever that is."

He suggested gin.

"Well I don't want to be seen drinking from a hotel glass.

266

Here," she said, hooking a tin mug from her belt, "can you get me some in this?"

So he went up to the bar and asked for a beer, and a gin in the mug.

The barman muttered, "Ar don't tell me that nun is still out there."

* * *

MOTHER Superior had listened to the parish priest ramble on for hours about the increasing number of splinter groups in religion.

Finally she blurted out: "Is that all you can think about, Sects! Sects! Sects!"

* * *

SISTER Priscilla was sent down to get the convent's Peugot from the service station.

"What kind of a car was it, sister?" asked the mechanic.

"Can't remember, but it starts with a P."

"Not here then," said the mechanic. "All ours start with petrol."

* * *

IT was Sister Priscilla's task to drive into town and pick up the mail every morning but she was showing an increasing reluctance to do the job.

"What's wrong?" asked Mother Superior, "I thought you enjoyed the daily excursion away from the convent."

"I do," said Sister Priscilla, "but lately a young policeman has taken to stopping me each morning."

Mother Superior said Priscilla had nothing to fear provided she didn't do anything wrong. She sent her on her way.

She had hardly driven for two minutes along the country lane when the motorcycle policeman signalled her to stop.

"Oh no, not the breathalyser again," muttered Sister Priscilla as the cop approached unzipping his fly.

NYMPHOMANIACS

THE definition of a nymphomaniac is a girl who trips a man and is under him before he hits the floor.

* * *

A NYMPHOMANIAC is a woman who will make love the same day she has her hair done.

* * *

FRED fell in love with the girl dancing on the table as soon as he saw her. "I want to marry her," he said.

"Don't be daft," said his mate. "Don't you know she's a nymphomaniac?"

"I don't care what she steals, I love her," said Fred.

* * *

SHE has a good job in the Nyphomaniacs' Club.

She examines prospective members.

* * *

HE was delighted his brand new girl friend agreed to come home with him so he broke out the whisky and began to pour the drinks.

"Say when," he said.

"Hey," she said, "may I have a drink first?"

* * *

SHE was confiding to the psychiatrist, "Every time I see a handsome muscular man on the beach I get a funny feeling between my toes."

"That's strange," said the doctor. "Which toes?"

"The big ones," she replied.

* * *

THERE was once an English nymphomaniac.

She simply had to have a man every six months.

* * *

A JEWISH nymphomaniac is a woman who allows her husband to make love to her after she has just returned from the beauty parlour.

* * *

IN the singles bar the nympho was checking her list.

"I am seeing Tom at seven, Dick at eight, Harry at nine." She looked around at the remaining men. "Tennish anyone?"

*   *   *

IF it wasn't for orgasms our Noreen wouldn't know when to stop screwing.

*   *   *

THEY called her Elevator, because everybody in the building had been down on her.

*   *   *

HE approached the blonde at the bar and said: "Are you with anyone?"

She smiled and said, "Yes, I'm with anyone."

*   *   *

NYMPHO Noreen said: "I don't know how I will face my mother after being screwed three times by a total stranger?"

"What d'yer mean?" he said. "We've only done it once."

"Yes, but you are not going home yet are you?"

O

OFFICE

THE new blonde in the office is called Virginia. They called her Virgin for short, but not for long.

* * *

HEAR about the office girl who married a William so she could get a Willy of her own?

Her friend married Richard.

* * *

"WHAT do you think of our new boss?"

"He dresses smartly."

"And quickly too!"

* * *

TWO stenographers were comparing experiences after the company's Christmas party.

"Did you get laid?" said one.

"Only twice," was the reply.

"Only twice?"

"Yes, once by the band and again by the despatch department."

* * *

THE new managing director took a fancy to the buxom stenographer and finally summoned up the courage to ask her out.

He took her to the finest restaurant, lavished her with

food and wine on her, took her to the theatre and then to a luxury hotel.

In the morning she had breakfast in bed before he offered to drive her home.

"Oh, you are so kind," she said, "most of you salesmen give me $20 and put me in a taxi."

* * *

TWO businessmen were discussing the managing director's obsession with the new secretary.

"I don't get it," said one, "she's dizzy. There's nothing going on in her top floor."

"That's not the floor he's getting off on," replied his colleague.

* * *

AFTER wining and dining the new secretary all evening the executive finally got around to the moment of truth. "What about dropping around to my flat and listening to some records," he said.

"No ulterior motives, no obligations?" she queried.

"Of course not. We'll just listen to music."

"And what if I don't like the music?"

"Well, you can put your clothes on and go home!"

* * *

HE advertised for a secretary: "Wanted. Young lady assistant who can type. One who has no bad habits and is willing to learn."

* * *

THE partners hired a new secretary and after the first week one of them had taken her out.

"She was terrific," he reported. "I don't mind admitting she was better in the cot than my wife."

Next night the second partner took the secretary out and the following morning he said. "You're right. She is better than your wife."

SOME couldn't spell, others couldn't type, few could do shorthand. The businessman who wanted a private secretary was about to despair when the employment agency phoned to say they were sending round a girl who had a number of things going for her.

She turned out to be a ravishing long-legged blonde, and the business executive was immediately entranced.

"I'll pay you $500 a week, with pleasure," he said.

"With pleasure, will be $1000 a week," she said.

*　*　*

NOTICE in the office: In an effort to spread the work more evenly would all staff take advantage of the stenographers earlier in the day!

*　*　*

EVER fearful of the boss the timid clerk was at his desk with a frightful head cold. "Why don't you take the day off?" said his more forthright workmate.

"The boss wouldn't like it," snuffled the clerk.

"Go on, you won't get caught. He is never here on Wednesdays anyway."

The clerk reluctantly took the advice and went home. But as he passed his bedroom window he saw his boss in bed with his wife.

He rushed back to the office. "You and your advice," he said to his mate, "I nearly got caught."

OLD CODGERS

IT was one of those cruises for the elderly and the sprightly old geezer approached a woman reclining in a deck chair. "Guess how old I am?" he said.

She looked him up and down then put her hand up his shorts and took a firm grip of his family jewels. She felt their weight, moved them gently from side to side and then declared with authority: "You are 73 and five months."

"That's amazing," said the old geezer. "How did you know?"

She replied: "Because you told me yesterday, you silly old bugger."

＊　　＊　　＊

THE old codger staggered into the clinic. "I'm worried, Doc," he said. "I met this nymphomaniac last week and made passionate love to her. Since then my roger has become red and itchy. It has swollen to three times its size and there is a discharge beginning to appear."

The doctor examined his donger.

"You'd better sit down," he said. "You are about to come."

＊　　＊　　＊

AN old gent visited the doctor for his annual check-up.

"Your hearing has got worse," said the doc. "So I want you to cut out smoking, drinking and sex."

"What?" said the old geezer, "just so I can hear better?"

＊　　＊　　＊

WHEN the family learned that Gramps was set to marry a 20-year-old they were horrified. The eldest son took him aside and said: "Frankly, Dad, we're concerned that sex with a young girl like that could be fatal."

"So what," said the old codger, "if she dies, she dies."

＊　　＊　　＊

THEY struck up a romance at the Twilight Retirement Home and he put the hard word on her.

They were quickly in his room where they started to undress. "By the way," she said as she flung off her blouse, "I have acute angina."

"Well I hope it's better than those tits," he replied.

＊　　＊　　＊

THEY had agreed to a secret meeting on the porch of the Twilight Home immediately after supper.

With some excitement they moved their rocking chairs close together.

Then he said: "Fuck you."

She replied: "And fuck you too."

They thought about this for awhile until he said: "I don't think much of that oral sex, do you?"

* * *

GRAMPS went to the pharmacy. "You've got to help me with a potion," he said. "I've scored a date with a lovely young lady and I need something to get it up."

The pharmacist knew Gramps was 82 and past it. Nevertheless he sold him a jar of cream and sent the old man away happy and contented.

The pharmacist wondered if he had done the right thing and later that evening rang Gramps. "Did the potion help?" he asked.

"It was great," said Gramps, "I've managed it three times already."

The pharmacist was surprised, "And what about the girl?" he asked.

"Oh, she's not here yet!"

* * *

JAKE looked a little tired as he took his usual place in the sun lounge. "I'm exhausted," he said to Fred, "I pulled a muscle in the bathroom this morning."

"That shouldn't make you tired," said Fred.

"It does if you pull it 375 times," said Jake.

* * *

WHEN he fronted at the sperm bank counter the matron looked him up and down and asked what he was there for.

"I want to make a donation," he said.

"But you look about 85," she said.

"I am," said the old codger, "but I have been a goer all my life. I can do it okay."

After further pleading the matron decided to give him the benefit of the doubt and handed him a jar. "Use that cubicle there," she said.

After ten minutes of grunting, groaning and heavy

breathing she knocked on the door. "Are you okay?" she said.

He came out with perspiration all over his face. He looked distressed and was out of breath.

"I have tried with my right hand, I have tried with my left," he said. "But I can't get the fucking lid off the jar!"

* * *

"NOT so much sex going on as there was in the old days, eh Bert?"

"Oh yes there is," said Bert. "It's just another crowd doing it."

* * *

OLD Horace complained that he couldn't do it like he used to with his young wife so the doctor advised them to sleep in separate rooms. "You will get better rest and when you go to her room you will give a better performance," said the doc.

He tried it for a month before coming back to the clinic. "Didn't it work?" asked the doc.

"Worked well," said Horace. He told the doc that he got randy twice in April but when he went to her room she said: "What, again? You were here just 15 minutes ago."

"Doc," said Horace, "I think I'm losing my memory."

* * *

OLD Bob had been missing from the senior citizens' club for some time and when he eventually fronted his mate said: "Gee, you look pale, where have you been?"

Bob had to admit he had been three months in jail after being charged with rape.

"But you are 84," said his mate.

"Yeah, that was the trouble," said Bob. "I pleaded guilty and the judge gave me three months for perjury!"

* * *

TWO old ladies at the Twilight Home were talking.

"Did you hear Old Jim Mullins had a massive stroke?"

275

"Always did," said her friend, "that's what made him so popular at our social functions."

* * *

THE old codger came to the doctor with the exciting news that he was going to marry a 20-year-old bride.

"Well, I think at your age you should take things easy. In fact I think you should take in a lodger," said the doctor.

A year later he bumped into the old codger and asked how was married life.

"The wife's pregnant, I am, happy to say," said the old man, and with a wink and a nudge he added, "thanks for that advice about taking in a boarder. She's pregnant too."

* * *

OLD Jake was reminiscing. "I can remember the time I gave up both booze and sex at the same time. Crikey, in all of my life that was the worst half hour I've ever spent!"

* * *

THE old codger wrote to his doctor:

"Dear Doc. For the past sixty years or more, I have awakened in the morning with a roaring Morning Glory, so strong I have never been able to bend it.

But this morning, on applying great pressure, I was able to force a slight bow. Doc, is my dick getting weaker, or my forearm getting stronger?"

* * *

OLD Jake was alone in his hotel room watching television when there was a knock on the door. He opened it and a buxom young girl walked in.

"Oh, I am so sorry," she said, "I must be in the wrong room."

"No love," said Jake. "It's the right room, but you are just 35 years too late."

* * *

OLD Chippendale was a millionaire. He had married a ravishing 20-year-old and it was the same old problem. He was past it.

On good advice he finally went to an audio-hypnotherapist who assured him that a simple audible signal would get it up immediately and the same audible signal repeated, would bring it down again.

"For example," said the doc, "the simple sound 'beeb' will give you a roaring horn, and 'beeb, beeb' will safely bring it down again.

"But I warn you," continued the doc, "at your advanced age three sessions is all your system could stand. Any more and it could kill you."

"Three will see me out," chirped the old man elatedly. "You mean if I go 'beeb' it will ..."

And immediately Chippendale had cracked an enormous erection.

"You can't go home like that," said the doc. "You've got to go 'beeb, beeb." And as soon as the words were uttered the erection subsided.

The old man sat there exhausted, yet delighted that it worked.

But while driving home a Morris Minor overtook him and went 'beeb, then 'beeb, beeb, and he had an erection and a subsidence that caused him to pull over for 20 minutes to recover.

"One final spurt to go," he said to himself as he mounted the stairs to his bedroom, showered and donned his dressing gown.

"Darling," he said to his young bride, "get your clothes off and get on the bed. I'm horny."

She was quick to do so. "About bloody time," she said.

He flashed open the front of his dressing gown, jumped on the bed, yelled 'beep, and presented her with a gigantic throbbing erection.

"Wow," she said. "What a beauty. But what's all this 'beep beep' shit?"

IN his dotage Old Jake had become simple. On his daily walks he would talk to the trees and flowers. Going through the park one day he said, "Hello trees, hello flowers," and when he saw a little ebony idol he said: "Hello little ebony idol."

To his surprise the idol replied: "Oh, please help me. I am, not really a little ebony idol, I am really a beautiful young woman under the spell of a witch. It only needs sexual intercourse with me to break the spell."

"Well, I am a bit beyond that sort of thing," said Jake, "but let me talk to my brother, he's an idle fucking bastard."

* * *

EVEN the parish priest was a welcome visitor for short-sighted Mrs Flanigan.

"But that wasn't the priest," said her daughter after the man had left, "that was the doctor."

"Oh was it?" she exclaimed with relief, "I thought Father O'Reilly was getting rather familiar."

* * *

MRS Flanigan described herself as a sprightly old girl. "Actually I see seven gentlemen a day," she said. "I get out of bed with Will Power, then I go to my John, next it's breakfast with Uncle Toby, followed by Billy T. Then the rest of the day is spent with either Arthur Ritis or Al Zymer until I finally go to bed with Johnny Walker."

* * *

AN old bloke was sitting at the bar sobbing with the odd tear dropping in his beer. "I got married to a lovely young widow last week," he explained to the barman. "She is a great cook, keeps my clothes in great nick and is insatiable in bed," he said.

"Then why the hell are you crying?" said the barman.

"Because I can't remember where I live," sobbed the old codger.

* * *

SHE had always been a lively lady and when she was

finally retired to the nursing home she refused to lead a boring life. She was determined to liven the place up. So she put a large sign on her door: "SEX!" And the small print read: "$20 in bed, $5 on the floor."

Nothing happened for the first few nights, but on Friday there was a timid knock and she opened the door to find Jock standing there. He handed her a $20 note.

"Hang on," she said. "I'll get the bed ready."

"To hell with the bed," said Jock. "I'm here for four on the floor!"

*   *   *

A YOUNG social worker used to call on Old Jake to cut up his steak and help with his meals. She noticed a bowl of almonds beside his tray.

"They were given to me as a present, but I don't want them," he explained. "You can have them."

She said thanks and began to nibble away on them.

"Funny present to give a man with no teeth," she remarked when she had eaten most of them.

"Oh no," he said. "They had chocolate on them then."

*   *   *

THE doctor had examined Old Jake's heart and summed up his advice with "No smoking, no drinking and no sex."

After much protesting by Jake the doctor relented: "Okay, one cigarette only after meals, and no more than two glasses of light beer a day."

"What about sex?" pressed Jake.

"Very occasionally," said the doctor, "and only with your wife because it is important you avoid any excitement."

*   *   *

DID you hear about the 80-year-old man who was acquitted of sexual assault because the evidence wouldn't stand up in court?

*   *   *

AN old chap in his seventies was concerned about his lack of sex drive and consulted his doctor.

"Well, what would you expect at your age?" said the medic.

The old geezer was still worried. "But my next door neighbour is over eighty and he says he gets it every night."

The doc thought for a moment. "Well, why don't you say it too?"

* * *

A COUPLE of old timers were discussing their sexual situation. "You know Jack," said one, "I understand that drinking stout will put lead in your pencil. Why don't we try a bottle?"

"I don't know about you," replied Jack, "but I don't have that many women to write to."

* * *

ON his morning round the doctor stopped beside the little old lady he had been treating for asthma. He checked her over, asked a few questions and listened to her croaky replies.

"What about the wheeze?" he said.

"Oh, fine," she replied. "I went three times last night!"

* * *

TWO old dons were lamenting human nature. "I was the town planner in this village," said one. "Look at all those fine buildings. I was responsible for all that architecture, but do I get any recognition? Eh? No. I donated money to the church all my life, but do I get any acknowledgement, eh? No. But fuck one single goat ..."

P

PARROTS

FRED stands on the edge of a cliff. He places a budgie on the left shoulder and another budgie on the right. Then he takes a great leap into the void and plummets to the rocks below.

"Jeezuz, Kevin," he says, "this budgie jumping is not what it's cracked up to be."

* * *

THE pet shop owner had difficulty selling a parrot. Each time a customer got interested the parrot would say: "Piss off, fuck-face."

Finally the shopkeeper decided that if it could talk so well it could be educated to say phrases other than swearing. He tied a string to each leg of the parrot, repeated a phrase constantly and tugged the string at the same time.

After six months the parrot was for sale again and a customer noticed the strings attached to the parrot's legs.

"Try pulling the one on the left leg," said the shopkeeper to an interested customer. He did and the bird responded with: "Hello, have a nice day."

The customer pulled the string on the other leg and got another pleasant response: "Hello mate, what's new?"

The customer was impressed. "What happens if I pull both strings together?"

The parrot responded: "I'd fall off the fuckin' perch ya stupid bastard."

* * *

AFTER buying a pair of talking parrots Miss Prim wanted to name them but found she couldn't tell Joey from Polly. She phoned the pet shop proprietor for advice.

"Simple," he said. "Wait until you see them mating, then fasten something around the male's neck so that you can identify him."

Miss Prim watched and watched. One day she heard flutters and squawks and dashed in to tie a white ribbon around the male's neck.

A few day's later Miss Prim threw an afternoon tea party for the church. Joey spotted the vicar and said: "Ha, so she caught you fucking around too, eh?"

* * *

THE priest had two parrots and taught them religiously to say the rosary. He even had two sets of rosary beads made and after a year of rigorous training he was delighted to have them perform at fetes and country fairs.

The priest was so pleased he decided to teach another parrot the rosary and bought a new bird from the pet shop.

When he put it into the cage one of the originals said to the other. "Throw away your beads, Fred, our prayers have been answered. It's a sheila!"

* * *

MITZI Lotzabazooma's pet parrot was beginning to embarrass her because it was learning too much and talking too much. Each night when she would bring home a gentleman friend the parrot would screech obscenities and repeatedly say: "Somebody is gonna get it tonight. Somebody is gonna get it tonight!"

Mitzi talked to the bird expert at the pet shop who assured her that the problem would be solved if only the parrot had his own female bird in the cage with him.

He ordered a parrot hen for her, but in the meantime he

offered her the only female bird in the shop, a brown owl, as a stand-in until the other parrot arrived.

That night Mitzi came home with another boyfriend and attempted to creep past the parrot cage, not wanting to interrupt anything the parrot might have going with his new friend.

But suddenly she realised nothing had changed as the parrot screeched: "Somebody is gonna get it tonight. Somebody is gonna get it tonight!"

"Whoo? Whoo?" said the owl.

"Not you, ya round-eyed bag, not you!"

*   *   *

THE young woman got out of bed, slipped on a silk gown, drew back the curtains, switched on the coffee percolator and uncovered the parrot.

Then the phone rang and a man's voice announced he had just arrived on the morning flight and would be there in ten minutes.

The young woman switched off the coffee percolator, covered the parrot, drew the curtains, took off her silk gown and got back into bed.

And the parrot muttered: "Jeez, that must have been the bloody shortest day of the year!"

PEARLY GATES

ST PETER was checking in new arrivals at the gates.

"Name?" he said.

"Lulu Bell," she replied.

"Cause of death?"

"The clap," she said.

"Couldn't be," said Pete, "nobody dies of the clap."

"You do when you give it to Big John."

*   *   *

THREE nuns who died at the same time arrived at the

Pearly Gates simultaneously and intended to go straight in, but St Peter barred their way.

"Just because you are nuns," he said, "doesn't mean you barge straight in without the religious test.

You," he said to the first one. "What was the name of the first man?"

"Er, Adam?" she answered, and the bells clanged and the trumpets blew and in she went.

"You," said St Peter addressing the second. "What was the name of the first woman?"

"Er, Eve?" she ventured, and the bells clanged and the trumpets blew and in she went.

"You," he said to the quaking third nun. "What were the first words Eve said to Adam?"

"Oh, gee. That's a hard one." And the bells clanged and the trumpets blew and in she went.

* * *

WHEN the cardinals' convention was hit by a bomb it sent 50 of them to heaven in one stroke where they all began to shuffle through the Pearly Gates as if they owned the place.

"Hang on. Just a moment," roared St Peter. "You lot have to go through the religious test like anybody else. How many of you have committed sins of the flesh?"

There was an awkward silence before, one after the other, 49 hands went up.

"Right," said St Peter. "You 49 go off to Purgatory, and take this deaf bastard with you."

* * *

NOT too many know that virgins are automatically admitted through the Pearly Gates, provided they pass the inspection test.

A beautiful young brunette presented her papers to St. Peter who checked them with a frown. "It says here that there are seven little dents in your virginity, but you have still passed," he said.

"That's right." she said.

"What's your name?"

"Snow White," she said.

* * *

A BLOKE died and when he regained consciousness he found himself in a big crowd floating on a cloud. There were hundreds of other crowded clouds in a traffic jam at the Pearly Gates. Heaven was closed.

"What's up?" he asked.

A bishop next to him explained that the gates had been shut for a hundred years. "It appears they are adjudicating on a question of doctrine," he said.

They floated about on the clouds for days, weeks and months before a great shout echoed through the skies. People began to jump up and down and slap each other on the back. The gates opened and the clouds began slowly drifting in.

They turned to the bishop for an explanation. "What's up?" they asked.

"Looks like they have made that decision," he said with elation. "Yes, hurrah, we're in. Fucking doesn't count."

* * *

THE Pope dies and arrives at the Pearly Gates on the same cloud as a lawyer. They are both ushered in and St Peter assigns the lawyer to a mansion with a golf course while the Pope is confined to a single room with a radio.

Even the lawyer was surprised. "How come?" he asked.

St Peter replied: "We have near on a hundred popes, but you are the first lawyer."

* * *

WHEN a bus load of nuns went over a cliff they were soon lined up at the Pearly Gates where St Peter produced a large vat of holy water for the nuns' test.

"If any of you have touched a man's genitals you will have to wash your hands before passing the gates," he said.

Three of the nuns came forward, washed their hands and passed through.

Then a fourth approached the holy water, washed her hands then sheepishly opened her habit and washed her breasts before passing through the gates.

A fifth nun approached the holy water, lifted her skirt and splashed some between her legs.

The nun next in line was heard to mutter: "Hey go easy, I've got to gargle that stuff in a minute."

* * *

THE Pope and Casanova arrived at the Pearly Gates on the same cloud. While the Pope hung around the gates meeting and greeting a few friends Casanova went straight in.

When the Pope finally entered he bumped into Casanova at the reception centre and said "I want nothing more than to kneel at the feet of the Virgin Mary. Do you know where I can find her?"

Casanova said, "Yes, but you are just too late, Father."

* * *

A SCOT arrived at the Pearly Gates.

"Name?" asked St Peter.

"Jock McTavish," replied the Scot.

"Piss off," said St. Peter, "we're not making porridge for one."

* * *

WHEN old Abe Goldstein died and fronted the Pearly Gates St Peter checked his clipboard for some time with an ever increasing frown then announced that Abe couldn't come in.

"Why?" said Abe. "I have lived according to the rules."

"That's just it," said St Peter. "You've got a perfect record. Not a blemish. A life of good deeds, always doing good deeds."

"Then what's the problem?" asked the puzzled Abe.

"You're too good," explained St Peter. "We have a score of popes up here with nowhere near your saintly record. It would cause a great stir in the heavenly hierarchy, because you would have to be placed above them."

Abe said he saw the prediciment. "Look," said St Peter, "as you are such an understanding bloke why don't we send you back for another hour. Maybe you could commit a misdemeanour in that time and, with your record, you'd still be in the upper echelon."

Abe reluctantly agreed. "You've got an hour, and no more good deeds," said St Peter.

In a flash Abe found himself slumped in his favourite armchair back in his living room with the clock striking eleven.

"Now what," he thought. "I don't drink, don't gamble, never had sex. How am I going to commit even a venial sin?"

He wasted the first 30 minutes worrying. Finally he thought of Miss Plotkin in the flat next door and the time, 25 years ago, when he momentarily entertained a rude thought about her.

With 25 minutes to go he knocked on her door. "Oh Mr Goldstein," she said, "I thought you were ill. Do come in."

He sat there in silence while he drank her tea and munched on her home-made cookies, ever conscious of the time ticking away.

Suddenly he decided to act.

He threw Miss Plotkin on the sofa, lifted her dress and whipped off her pants, sprang aboard and planted the sausage just as the clock began to strike 12.

As he slipped off the couch and the room began to blur the last thing he remembered was Miss Plotkin's voice: "Oh Mr Goldstein, only God and I will know what a wonderful deed you did for me today."

PHARMACISTS

THE clairvoyant pharmacist prided himself on knowing what each customer was about to ask for. When the blonde came in he said: "Don't tell me, don't tell me. You want a packet of tampons."

"No," she replied. "I want a roll of toilet paper."

"Damn," said the pharmacist, "missed it by a whisker."

* * *

"I'D like some deodorant, please."

"Aerosol?"

"No. It's for under me arms."

* * *

A PRIM young miss asked the pharmacy clerk: "Do you sell condoms in here?"

"Yes," he replied.

"Well wash your hands and get me some cough mixture."

* * *

TWO young lads approached the counter.

"Can we have a packet of tampons, please?"

"Are they for your mother?"

"No."

"Your sister then?"

"No, they're for us."

Asked to explain the kids said: "Well on the TV it says if you've got a packet of tampons you can swim, dive, play tennis and ride horseback."

* * *

THE sweet young thing said: "Do you happen to have multi-coloured sanitary towels?"

"Not during this recession," said the pharmacist, "they were made for brighter periods."

* * *

HE stormed into the store first thing on Monday morning and slammed a receipt on the counter.

"I asked for a gross of condoms, remember? That's 12 dozen. I found one packet only contained 11."

"Sorry sir," said the pharmacist making the cash adjustment. "Sorry to have ruined your weekend."

AN elderly couple toddle into the pharmacy and the gent asks for a packet of condoms. "We are having a weekend away," he says.

The clerk eyes them suspiciously. "You are both over 80, aren't you?" He went on to explain that with the woman well past the menopause she could not become pregnant.

"It's not that," said the old gent. "Emily here just loves the smell of burning rubber."

* * *

THE pharmacist's nurse was constantly getting things back to front and could not be trusted with responsible prescriptions, but when a sportsman came in for a blood test the pharmacist delegated her the job in the belief that it was a simple task.

When more time than was necessary had elapsed he looked in to the back room.

"No, you bimbo," he yelled, "I said prick his finger."

* * *

THE young teenagers met in the back stalls of the theatre and after a hot petting session he wanted to go on with it.

"Not here," she said. "Come around tomorrow. It's Sunday and my parents go to Evensong. We can have the house to ourselves. Oh, and don't forget the condom."

Next evening the lad arrived at the front door just as her father announced that they were off to church.

"I'll come with you," said the lad smartly.

At the first opportunity the young girl whispered, "Why the change of plan and how long have you been religious?"

To which the lad whispered in reply: "How long has your father been a chemist?"

* * *

THE young man agonised outside the pharmacy for an hour before summoning up the courage to enter, only to find a woman behind the counter.

He nervously stammered, "Could I see the pharmacist?"

"I am the pharmacist," said the woman. "My sister and I have run this business for more than 30 years and I can assure you there is no need for embarrassment. We have treated everything."

She finally calmed the young man who said, "Well, I have this insatiable urge to have sex and I suffer from a constant erection. It is driving me insane. What can you do for it?"

"Excuse me a moment," said the woman, "I will consult my sister."

She soon returned and said: "The best we can do is $300 a week, and free board."

* * *

MISS Smythe-Jones was miffed. Her pet miniature chihuahua was consistently second in dog shows throughout the country. One day she decided to tackle the judges.

It was explained to her that the true pedigree chihuahua had smooth hair while her dog, perfect in every other aspect, had a coat that was too shaggy.

"Look at the smooth hair of the champion there," said the judge. A nod is as good as a wink to a keen dog fancier and Miss Smythe-Jones was off to the pharmacy to ask for some hair remover.

The chemist handed her the latest product. "When you slap this on, its best to keep your arms up for two or three minutes," he said.

"Oh, it's not for my arms, it's for my chihuahua," she said.

"In that case," said the chemist, "don't ride a bike for 30 minutes."

PHONES

A COUPLE are in the midst of a steamy session when the phone rings.

She answers it, listens for a moment, hangs up and says to her lover that it was her husband on the phone.

"Jeez, don't tell me he's coming home," says the lover reaching for his clothes.

"Calm down," she says. "He won't be home for ages. He's playing cards with you and two other blokes."

* * *

FLOSSIE was washing her hair when the phone rang. Her room-mate answered it, then called out: "Flossie, it's an obscene phone call for you."

"Get his number. I'll call back," she replied.

* * *

THE atheists have started a Dial-a-Prayer service.

When you phone nobody answers.

* * *

MANY believe that the Pope's phone number is Vat 69.

It's not. It's Et Cum Spirri 2-2-0.

* * *

SHE was in bed with her lover when her phone rang. She reached for it and said: "I'll talk to you later. I have someone on hold."

* * *

TOM, Dick and Harry were in the pub drinking together when a phone rang. "Excuse me fellows," said Tom drawing his right hand from his pocket to take the call. He put his thumb in his ear and spoke into the end of his little finger.

His yuppie mates were impressed. Tom explained that he had a silicon chip inserted into his thumb and another in his finger. "Saves carrying those clumsy mobile phones around," he said.

A month later they were at the same bar and the phone rang. Dick said: "Excuse me," and took the call merely by talking away. When he 'hung up' he explained that he had a chip inserted in his ear and another in his tooth, a vast advancement on the old thumb-and-finger phone.

However, about ten minutes later Dick grimaced and complained of cramps in the stomach. He leant forward, legs slightly apart and put both hands on the bar.

"Are you okay?" asked his mates.

"Yes, I'll be alright. It's just a fax coming through."

* * *

"YOU'VE only been talking an hour," muttered the sarcastic husband, "was it the wrong number?"

* * *

THE phone rang at the motor pool and an authoritative voice demanded to know how many vehicles were operational.

Paddy answered. "We've got twelve trucks, ten utilities, three staff cars and that Bentley the fat-arsed colonel swanks around in."

There was a stony silence for a second or two. "Do you know who you are speaking to?"

"No," said Paddy.

"It is the so-called fat-arsed colonel you so insubordinately referred to."

"Well, do you know who you are talking to?"

"No," roared the colonel.

"Well thank Christ for that," said Paddy as he slammed the phone down.

* * *

"PARDON me, Miss. I am writing a phone book, may I have your number?"

* * *

THE phone rings. "Could I speak to Freddie Fukbrake, please?"

"Don't know anybody by that name, but just a moment and I'll ask. Do we have a Fukbrake here?"

"Hell, we don't even have a coffee break!"

THE Scot was visiting his psychiatrist.

"McAlister, you seem to have lost your stutter."

"Yes, Doc. I've had to phone my brother in New York quite a lot recently."

* * *

MISS Prim, the town's spinster, phoned the police around midnight to complain that two dogs were copulating on her front lawn.

Constable Plod suggested she throw a bucket of water over them.

Ten minutes later the phone rang again. Miss Prim told Constable Plod that the water didn't work. The dogs were still at it.

He told her to get two dustbin lids and clang them together and make as much noise as possible.

Another ten minutes later Miss Prim phoned again. The noise hadn't worked. In fact the dogs were still rooting furiously. "How will I stop them?" she asked the policeman.

"Why don't you tell the dogs that they are wanted on the telephone," said the cop.

"Will that stop them copulating?" she asked.

"It has certainly stopped me," replied Constable Plod.

* * *

A MATHEMATICIAN named Paul
Has a hexahedronical ball
And the cube of its weight
Times his pecker, plus eight
Is his phone number. Give him a call.

PHOTOGRAPHERS

TWO Norwegian beauties were having their picture taken and the photographer was taking some time getting the right angle.

"Vy ees he taking so long?" asked Inga.

"He's got to focus."

"No. You tell him picture first and maybe fokus after."

PIRATES

HE had a wooden leg, a hook on the end of his arm and a black patch over one eye.

"You've been in the wars, matey," said one of the crew.

"Ay, a shark bit my leg off, a cannon shot my hand clean away and a seagull shit in my eye."

"I can understand the shark and the cannon, but how could you lose an eye?"

"It was the day after the hook was attached and I wasn't used to it," said the pirate.

POEMS

THERE was a young playboy called Skinner
   Who took a young lady to dinner
   Around half past nine
   They sat down to dine
   And by quarter to ten it was in her.
   (The dinner, not Skinner).

*   *   *

AND another young fellow called Tupper
   Took the same young lady to supper
   At half past nine
   They sat down to dine
   And by a quarter to ten it was up her.
   (Not Tupper, some bastard called Skinner).

*   *   *

BEWARE of strong drink, my dear
   And only have two, at the most.
   Three, and you're under the table,
   Four and you're under the host.

"DON'T drink nought but water,"
  Was Mum's word to her daughter,
  "Say no to men,
  "Be home by ten,
  "And behave just like you orta!"

*   *   *

"AND what'll you have?"
  Said the waiter,
  Idly picking his nose.
  "I'll have two boiled eggs,
  Ya bastard,
  Ya can't stick yer fingers in those."

*   *   *

SAY it with flowers
  Or say it with sweets,
  Boxes of chocolates
  Or plush theatre seats,
  Say it with diamonds,
  Or say it with mink
  But whatever you do
  Don't say it in ink.

*   *   *

THE limerick packs laughs anatomical
  Into space that is quite economical
  But the good ones I've seen
  So seldom are clean
  And the clean ones are so seldom comical.

*   *   *

ROSES are red
  Pansies are gay
  If it wasn't for women
  We'd all be that way.

*   *   *

A HOT tempered girl from Caracas
  Was to wed an ill-favoured jackass

When he stared to cheat her
With a dark senorita
She kicked him right in the maracas.

*   *   *

THERE was an old gent from Cosham
Who took out his knackers to wash 'em
But his wife said: "Now, Jack
If you don't put them back
I'll jump on the damn things and squash 'em.

*   *   *

FEELING rude in the nude was Miss Prim
When she went down to the river to swim
A man in a punt
Stuck an oar in her eye
And now she wears glasses.

POLICE

SHE rushed into the police station. "I was graped," she said.
"You mean raped?"
"No," she said, "there was a bunch of them."

*   *   *

SHE rushed into the police station. "I've just been sexually molested by a Chinese laundryman."

"Hang on," said the sergeant, "how did you know it was a Chinese laundryman?"

"Because he did the whole thing by hand."

*   *   *

MISS Lottzabazooma was explaining it to the police.

"This guy came up to my apartment with me," she said. "He tore off my clothes and threw me onto the bed. Then when I was naked he ran off with my purse."

"Did you scream?" asked the cop.

"Of course not." she said. "How did I know he was going to rob me?"

THE police raided the house where a steamy orgy was in progress.

"What's the matter with you blokes?" said the hostess, "haven't you ever seen 35 people in love before?"

* * *

THE phone rang at the police station. "I want to report a burglar trapped in an old maid's bedroom."

After getting the address the cop asked: "Who am I talking to?"

"The burglar," replied the frantic voice.

POLITICS

PAUL Keating rang the Queen and said: "Make Australia a kingdom and make me the king."

Her Highness replied: "I'll make it a country and you can be what you are."

* * *

ONE politician said he wouldn't mind a bit if women were in power.

The other said he wouldn't mind a bit and he didn't give a stuff who was in power.

* * *

COME to think of it, there is no difference between politicians and bull sperm. Only one in a thousand actually work.

* * *

AT the political rally the heckler yelled:

"Clinton should be bloody well hung!"

Hillary jumped up: "He is, he is."

* * *

THE romance was off to a shaky start from the beginning because she was conservative while he was traditional labor but they decided to live together on the basis of agreeing to disagree.

It went well for a short time until a television program set off the inevitable political argument.

297

When they retired to bed he remained on the left and she on the extreme right.

Eventually she made an overture: "There is a split in the Tory movement and it is quite likely that if a Labor member stood he could slip in unopposed."

"Too late," he said. "There's been too much stimulation in the private sector and he has blown his deposit."

* * *

WHAT's the difference between a flattened politician and a flattened kangaroo on the road to Canberra?

There are skid marks to the kangaroo.

* * *

PAUL Keating was asked if he had heard the latest political jokes.

"Heard them?" he said. "I work with the bludgers."

* * *

WHILE on safari in cannibal country a traveller came across a cafe in a clearing in the jungle. The sign out front advertised: Fried Missionary $5, Boiled Hunter $4-50, Grilled Safari Guide $5. Stuffed Politician $15.

When the traveller asked why so much for the politician the chef replied, "Have you ever tried to clean one?"

PREGNANCY

BACK from a year at sea the sailor took his wife to the doctor and demanded an explanation for her pregnancy.

"It is a vindictive pregnancy," explained the doctor. "Somebody has had it in for you while you were away."

* * *

THE Japanese sailor demanded to know why his wife presented him with a bouncing baby boy with blue eyes and fair hair.

"Occidents will happen," she said.

AND the Chinese sailor sued for divorce when he was presented with a bundle of joy with blue eyes and blonde hair. The judge agreed: "Two wongs don't make a white," he declared.

* * *

THE State's health system is so run down that the Pregnancy Test Service now has a ten-month waiting list.

* * *

THE young woman looked at the beer gut on the Ocker with disgust. "If that stomach was on a woman, she would be pregnant," she said.

"It was and she is," replied the Ocker.

* * *

TWO women had become friends after meeting each other at various fertility clinics in their quest to become pregnant.

"And now look at you," said one, "you must be six months' gone."

"Yes," said the mother-to-be, "I finally went to a faith healer."

"Oh, we tried that," said the first women, "my husband and I went there for months."

"No," whispered the pregnant one, "You've got to go alone."

* * *

"I'M going to have a little one,"
   Said his girl so pert and frisky
   When he fainted to the floor
   She told him she meant whisky.

* * *

THERE was a young Nellie McStace
   Whose corset got too tight to lace
   Her mother said, "Nellie,
   There's more in your belly
   Than ever went in through your face."

PRIESTS

SUFFERING from depression the priest was advised by his psychiatrist to take a rest from stress with a short break in Paris. "Nobody will know you there," said the shrink.

Indeed, he got to like the sinful city and even went to a strip show. And when a gorgeous blonde danced by he leaned out to touch her.

"Oh, no you don't, Father," said the blonde.

"How did you know I was a priest?"

"Because I'm Sister Priscilla, and we've got the same shrink," she replied.

* * *

THERE once was a young priest from Kew
Who preached with his vestments askew
A lady called Morgan
Caught sight of his organ
And promptly passed out in the pew.

PRIZES

IT was the last day of the Royal Agricultural Show and the crowd had gathered for the drawing of the grand raffle. The minor prizes were to be drawn first and when the mayor reached into the bin and called out the number, 738,562, there was a delighted shriek from a woman at the rear of the crowd.

"Third prize," announced the compere, "is a three-month cruise around the world for you and your family." The woman gave another shriek of delight and the crowd applauded.

The mayor dipped into the barrel again and read out "number 509,677."

This time a gentleman responded, waving the ticket aloft. "Second prize, for you sir," announced the compere, "is a two-tiered fruit cake with white icing and pink piping."

"What?" roared the indignant holder of ticket 509,677. "How come third prize is a trip around the world and I win a bloody fruit cake?"

The compere tried to placate him. "Ah sir, this is not an ordinary fruit cake. This cake was baked by the mayoress."

"Fuck the mayoress," replied the man angrily.

"No, no," said the compere. "That's the first prize!"

PROSTITUTES

A LARGE sign outside the church read: "If you are tired of sin, come in."

Underneath, written in lipstick, was the message: "If not, ring Dulcie on 041-2468."

* * *

HE was a regular client and once again asked for credit.

"No way John," she said. "You're into me for too much already."

* * *

TWO girls were working their regular beat.

"If I'm not in bed by ten o'clock I'm going home," said one.

* * *

THE prayer of the destitute prostitute:

"And now I lay me down too cheap."

* * *

THE call girl wasn't feeling so good. The doctor told her she needed a rest and suggested she stay out of bed for a few days.

* * *

WOMEN can go out and give it away

But they'll be arrested if do it for pay.

* * *

HE was such a loser. He approached a streetwalker one day and she complained of a headache.

THE streetwalker was protesting to the police that she was certainly not selling sex.

"I am selling condoms for a hundred dollars each, and I simply give a free demonstration on how to use them," she said.

* * *

THE overworked prostitute made two appointments for the same time.

She managed to squeeze them both in.

* * *

THE madame heard the commotion in the bedroom and one of her girls came out and slammed the bedroom door.

"I'll never do it that way," she said.

"How did he want you to do it?"

"On tick," said the irate hooker.

* * *

IN a bid to make her services more entertaining a prostitute had the likeness of Mick Jagger tattooed on the cheek of one bum and Elvis Presley tattooed on the other.

She could hardly wait to show her first customer.

When Fred came in, after a few at the pub, she bent over and flipped up her skirt. "Who are they?" she said.

"Easy," said Fred. "That's Mick Jagger on the left, Elvis on the right and Rolf Harris in the middle."

* * *

VINNIE detected that there was something troubling his mate Louie. "C'mon tell me all about it," he said.

A worried Louie began by saying that they had been mates for a long time, "But I've just gotta tell ya," said Louie. "It's your wife, Beryl. I was in the local brothel the other night and there she was. Vinnie, I hate to tell ya but your wife is a prostitute."

"Oh no, you've got it wrong," said Vinnie. "She's a substitute. She's only there on weekends."

A PUNTER approached Big Bessie in Harlem.

"Ah charges ten dollars," she said.

The punter said it was too much. He even refused it at five dollars.

"Okay. My last price," said Bessie. "Yo can have it fo three dollars, but at this price ah'm losing money."

* * *

TWO pros met on the street. "How's business?" said one.

"Slim prickings," said the other.

* * *

A NOTORIOUS hooker named Hurst
In the pleasure of men was well versed
Read a sign overhead
Of her ever-warm bed:
"The customer always comes first!"

* * *

THERE was a young harlot from Kew
Who filled up her fanny with glue
She said with a grin
"If they pay to get in
They'll pay to get out of it too."

* * *

ANOTHER girl who was quite canny
Charged a penny for use of her fanny
But for half of that sum
You could fondle her bum
A source of amusement for many.

PSYCHIATRISTS

ANYBODY who goes to a psychiatrist needs their head read.

A beautiful young woman comes to see the psychiatrist. He says: "Take off your clothes and lie on the couch."

She does so and he jumps on top and makes love to her.

303

When he falls off onto the floor he says: "Now that's my problem solved. What's yours?"

* * *

THE friendly psychiatrist is the one who lies on the couch with you.

* * *

I TOLD my girlfriend the truth, that I was seeing a psychiatrist.

She told me the truth, that she was seeing a psychiatrist, a plumber and two barmen.

* * *

THE patient on the couch said every time he lay down he saw visions of Mickey Mouse and Pluto. If he sat up suddenly he saw visions of Donald Duck and Goofy.

"How long have you had these Disney spells?" said the shrink.

* * *

THE blonde patient on the couch whispered to her psychiatrist, "Kiss me please doctor, kiss me."

"Hardly ethical," said the shrink, "I really shouldn't be screwing you at all."

* * *

"I CAN'T cure you of your premature ejaculation problem," said the psychiatrist. "But I can put you in touch with a woman who has a short attention span."

* * *

"NOW tell me," said the psychiatrist, "have you had any more of those sexually erotic dreams?"

"No," said the patient.

"Tough luck, I've had some beauties."

* * *

"MR BROWN," said the woman psychiatrist, "you have acute paranoia".

"Thanks Doc, and your tits are not bad either!"

THE prostitute had an appointment with her psychiatrist. When she entered at his office he asked her to lie on the couch.

"If you don't mind," she said, "I've been working all say. Do you mind if I stand?"

* * *

ONE intimate question led to another and the prostitute and her psychiatrist ended up on his couch in a very sexy session.

When it was over they lay silent for a moment and then both said simultaneously, "That will be one hundred dollars, thank you."

* * *

THE businessman was on the couch. "The trouble is, Doc," he said, "I've been having an affair with my secretary and I have such a guilty feeling about it that when I am humping her I pretend it is my wife. The problem is, Doc, I am beginning to like it more and more."

* * *

"IF these pills don't stop your kleptomania," said the psychiatrist, "try and get me a video recorder."

* * *

A FEMALE psychiatrist and her nurse took an evening off to go to the movies and early in the film a man seated next to the doctor began groping in his crotch with one hand while skilfully edging his other hand under her skirt and between her thighs.

The nurse observed the activity. "For goodness sake," she said, "why don't you tell that creep he's sick?"

"Why should I?" said the lady shrink. "He's not my patient."

* * *

SHE told her shrink. "I have this constant desire to have sex with every man I meet. What do you call that, Doctor?"

"Good news," he said, carrying her to the couch.

HE told the psychiatrist he thought he was going crazy because he kept dreaming he was having sex with biscuits.

"Are they chocolate biscuits?"

"No Doc."

"Are they those wholemeal biscuits?"

"No Doc."

"Are they those dry biscuits you have with cheese?"

"Yeah, yeah, that's them," said the patient.

"Then you are fucking crackers," said the doc.

* * *

HE told the psychiatrist that before he married his wife she was a nymphomaniac. "She was insatiable," he said. "She would do it anywhere. Now that we are married she is frigid. What do you call that, Doctor?"

"In the trade," said the shrink, "we call it hell freezing over."

* * *

THE psychiatrist told Fred he was going to drop some ink on a blotter and he wanted Fred to explain what the random designs meant to him.

"That's Marilyn Munroe in the nude," said Fred deciphering the first blotch.

"That's Jayne Mansfield taking a bath," he described the second.

He said the third spattering of ink was the Luton Girls Choir all singing in the nude.

"The trouble with you, Fred," said the doctor with some satisfaction, "you are obsessed with sex."

"What, me?" exclaimed Fred. "It's you who's drawing the filthy pictures."

* * *

MOST women in the metropolis
Are opposed to psychoanalysis
Indeed, they're annoyed
By the great Dr Freud
And cling to their long-standing phalluses.

PUBLIC RELATIONS

HE is the biggest bull artist since Picasso.

* * *

A PIMP is a public relations man for a public relations girl.

* * *

SHE got a job as public relations officer in a tampon distribution centre. She would put a get well card in every packet.

PUBS

BLOKE fronted the bar and ordered ten whiskies.

"Oh, and what's the occasion?" asked the barman proceeding to line them up.

"Just had my first blow job," said the customer.

"Celebrating?"

"No," said the customer, "I'm trying to get the taste out of my mouth."

* * *

THE barmaid wondered where the voice came from, before she saw the little lad in short pants with his nose just reaching the bar.

"Hey, you. I said I'll have a glass of beer and a packet of fags," insisted the brat.

The barmaid saw that he was a lad of about 13.

"Do you want to get me into trouble?" she said.

"Forget the sex, just give me the beer and fags," he said.

* * *

THE travelling salesman arrived at the one-pub, three-dog town and fronted the bar. After a couple of drinks he said to the barman: "Is there any night-life hereabouts?"

"You just missed it by a few days. She's gone to the city for a holiday."

* * *

THEY looked an odd trio in the pub; a sailor, an ostrich and a cat.

The ostrich and the sailor would take their turn buying the drinks but the cat appeared to be on the stingy side.

It intrigued the barman. "Why doesn't the cat buy a round?" he said.

"It's a long story," said the sailor. "Suffice to say that when I let the genie out of the bottle on that desert island and he granted me one wish, all I asked for was a long-legged bird with a tight pussy."

* * *

MURPHY had been at sea for five weeks and after settling into his room at his usual waterfront pub he picked up the phone and asked reception to send up a whore.

The publican had married since Murphy was last there and the new landlady was shocked to hear Murphy's request.

She demanded that her husband go up and throw Murphy out. He tried to explain that Murphy was a regular guest but to no avail. "If you are too frightened to throw him out then I'll do it myself," she said.

She was a formidable woman and when she marched up the stairs the publican could hear the sound of furniture being thrown around, thumps, bangs and curses.

Finally Murphy came down, red-faced, puffing, face scratched and shirt torn.

"That was a rugged old bitch you sent up," he said to the publican, "it was more like a wrestle than a screw."

* * *

A KANGAROO hopped up to the bar and ordered a pot of beer. He slapped down a fiver and the barman gave him fifty cents change.

The kangaroo quaffed the beer and put the change in his pocket and was about to leave when the barman's curiosity could be contained no longer.

"Excuse me for mentioning it, but we don't get many kangaroos in here."

"No bloody wonder, at $4-50 a glass," said the kangaroo.

IT is a shabby pub in the red light district. One of the hookers walks in and says: "Gimme a glass of Smirnoff."

The barman does so and she scoffs the lot in one gulp then drops to the floor in a dead faint.

The barman appeals to the only two drinkers to help him carry her into a back room where one of them says: "Hey, let's give her a quickie while she's out."

They do so and an hour later she sits up, scratches her head, says: "Where am I?", gets her bearings and leaves.

Next evening she comes in at the same time and asks for a glass of Smirnoff, drinks it in one gulp and drops to the floor again. The same three carry her to the back room and do it again.

This goes on for a third and fourth night.

On Friday night she comes in and the bartender reaches for the Smirnoff bottle.

"No Pete," she says. "I'll have Bacardi tonight, that Smirnoff makes my cunt sore."

Q

QUESTIONS

WHICH of us is the opposite sex?

* * *

IS a lesbian a pansy without a stalk?

* * *

IS camping loitering within tent?

* * *

IS Red Riding Hood a Russian contraceptive?

* * *

IS Johnny Cash the change from a condom vending machine?

* * *

IS a castrated pig disgruntled?

* * *

DOES the lateral coital position
   mean having a bit on the side?

* * *

WHAT is a Jewish dilemma?
   Free pork.

* * *

WHAT do husbands have in their pants that their wives
don't want on their faces?
   Wrinkles.

* * *

WHAT is pink and wrinkly and hangs out your pants?
   Your grandma.

WHAT'S the difference between blondes and broccoli?
Nobody eats broccoli.

*   *   *

WHY do so many brides start to get crow's feet as soon as they are married?
From squinting and saying: "Suck what?"

*   *   *

WHAT's six inches long, has a bald head and drives Jewish women wild?
A Yankee hundred dollar note.

*   *   *

WHAT'S got 75 balls and screws old ladies?
Bingo.

*   *   *

WHAT does it take to circumcise a whale?
Fore skin divers.

*   *   *

WHY don't rabbits make a noise when they root?
Because they have cotton balls.

*   *   *

WHY is a joke like a pussy?
Neither is any good if you don't get it.

*   *   *

WHAT do light and hard have in common?
You can't sleep with a light on either.

*   *   *

WHAT's the difference between a monkey and a hooker?
One lies on its back for peanuts.
The other lives at the zoo.

*   *   *

WHAT'S the difference between a pothole and a politician?
You would swerve to avoid the pothole.

*   *   *

WHAT'S the difference between a counterfeit note and a very thin prostitute?
One's a phoney buck ...

WHAT'S the difference between a magician's wand and a policeman's truncheon?
The magician's wand is for cunning stunts ...

* * *

WHAT'S difference between a gold fish and a mountain goat?
One mucks around the fountain ...

* * *

WHAT'S the difference between a woman in church and a woman in the bath?
One has a soul full of hope ...

* * *

WHAT'S black and white and eats like a horse?
A zebra.

* * *

WHAT'S the difference between erotic and kinky?
Erotic is when you use a feather.
Kinky is when you use the whole chicken.

* * *

WHY is pubic hair curly?
So it doesn't poke your eyes out.

* * *

WHAT'S the difference between a vitamin and a hormone?
You can't hear a vitamin.

* * *

WHAT'S the difference between a slut and a bitch.
A slut will sleep with anyone.
A bitch will sleep with anyone, but you.

* * *

HOW do you stop a woman giving you head?
Marry her.

* * *

WHAT'S better than a bird in the hand?
A hand in the bush.

312

WHAT'S the difference between a condom and a pork pie?
   You get more meat in a condom.

*   *   *

WHAT'S the difference between a milk-maid and a stripper?
   The milk-maid is fair and buxom ...

*   *   *

WHAT do Christmas trees and vasectomised men have in common?
   They both have balls for decoration.

*   *   *

HOW can you tell the sex of a chromosome?
   Take down its genes.

*   *   *

HOW can you tell if pancakes are male or female?
   Female pancakes are well stacked.

*   *   *

CAN a self-made man pull himself to pieces?

*   *   *

IF a light sleeper sleeps with the light on, does a hard sleeper sleep with the window open?

*   *   *

DO fur covered toilet seats tickle your fancy?

*   *   *

IS a lady barrister without briefs a solicitor?

*   *   *

IS the Pope's wife a Catholic?

*   *   *

DO bears shit in the woods?

R

RADIO ANNOUNCERS

THE disc jockey was driving along the country road when he saw a young nun trying to hitch a ride. He stopped. She explained that she had been a bit naive in trying to walk the distance to church. It was further than she anticipated.

As they drove along she asked why he was up so early in the morning. "I'm a radio announcer on the morning shift at the local regional station," he said.

"Oh," said the nun. "I would do anything to be able to send a cheerio."

The DJ took another look and noticed that she was indeed a comely wench. "Anything?" he repeated.

When she indeed confirmed that it was her major wish in life he drove off the road into a shady glade and whipped out the old John Thomas, as unscrupulous DJs are wont to do.

She bent down, grabbed it with two hands and said: "Hello Mum, Hello Dad, this is Teresa here ..."

*   *   *

THE ABC announcer was delighted to hear the way in which his little son said his prayers, concluding with: "And here again, Dear God, are the headlines."

REAL ESTATE AGENTS

TAKE the Real Estate Agent's advice: Get Lots While You Can."

* * *

THE real estate agent fell on hard times and was selling caravans, changing his status to a wheel estate agent.

* * *

BUSINESS was bad and the real estate agent was unloading his troubles to the blonde he had just met at the bar.

"If I don't sell more homes, I'll lose my arse," he lamented.

"Funny you should say that," she said. "If I don't sell more arse I'll lose my home."

* * *

WHEN Vietnamese Louie rolled a big win at the casino he looked around town for the finest house on the choicest piece of real estate. He found that the Rothschilds, the great financiers, owned the most palatial home. So he began building an identical mansion beside it.

When it was finished Baron Rothschild complimented Vietnamese Louie on his attention to detail. The building was identical in every respect.

"But it's worth more than yours," said Louie.

"How come? I don't see that," said the baron.

"In every way the two places are alike until you try to sell them," explained Louie. "When the prospective buyer asks me about the neighbours I tell them we live next to the famous Rothchilds. But when they ask you about the neighbours you will have to admit it's Vietnamese boat people."

RELIGION

CATHOLIC girls' prayer:
"Oh Blessed Virgin, we believe
That thou without sin did conceive,

Teach us, then, how thus believing,
We can sin without conceiving.

*   *   *

AN international conference on family planning was organised by the world's church leaders.

Unfortunately, the Catholic representative had to pull out at the last moment.

*   *   *

MURPHY lived next to McTavish, one a Catholic the other a Protestant, but they were good neighbours.

One day McTavish, looking at his five kids, said to Murphy: "You Catholics don't use birth control, yet you've got no kids and I've got five."

"We use the Safe Period," explained Murphy.

"Never heard of it," said McTavish. "What's the Safe Period?"

"Every second Tuesday when you go to Lodge," said Murphy.

*   *   *

THE vicar said to the young lad: "Tell me, who went to Mount Olive?"

"Popeye," was the quick reply.

*   *   *

ONE priest said to the other. "Do you think the Pope will ever allow priests to marry?"

"Not in our time", mused his colleague, "maybe in our children's."

*   *   *

ONE priest confided in another. "I don't know what to do to repress these feelings of sexual desire."

"Take a cold shower," said his colleague.

"But I've taken so many cold showers that when it rains I now get an erection."

*   *   *

THE priest spoke to the villagers: "You must not use the pill."

The young signorina replied: "You no play the game, you no make the rules."

* * *

TERESA Murphy had married out of her faith, nevertheless she still went to mass regularly.

One Sunday morning she was getting dressed and while fixing her stockings she noticed her husband watching with a lustful eye. She also noticed his morning glory had made a little tent of the bedsheet. She paused for a moment and then began taking her clothes off.

"I thought you were going to church?" said her husband.

Now naked, Teresa hopped back into bed and said: "The Catholic Church will stand forever, but how long can you trust a Protestant prick?"

* * *

FATHER O'Grady was preaching on the difference between knowledge and faith.

"In the front row we have Teresa and Shamus with their six children," he said. "Teresa knows they are her children. That's knowledge. Shamus believes they are his children. That's faith."

* * *

MONKS do it out of habit

While nuns were once novices at it.

* * *

FROM the pulpit the vicar announced that one of his flock, Miss Helen Hunt, had found a purse containing money, a variety of personal items and what he believed to be a small packet of white balloons.

"So whoever has lost this purse, can go to Helen Hunt for it!"

* * *

"GIRLS," said the mother superior, addressing the class which was about to graduate and leave the convent.

"You are about to go into the sinful world. I must warn you against certain men who will whisper rude suggestions

317

to you, buy you drinks, take you to their rooms, undress you and offer you money to do rude things."

"Excuse me, Mother," piped up a rather buxom girl, "did you say these wicked men would give us money?"

"Yes, child, why do you ask?"

"Father Flanagan only gives us lollies."

* * *

AN elderly couple were watching a TV evangelist ranting away and when he said he was about to transmit some spiritual healing through the telly set he urged his listeners to place one hand on their heart and the other on the organ which needed healing.

The old lady put one hand on her heart and the other on her arthritic hip.

The old man had one hand on his heart, the other on his genitals.

"For goodness sake, Jake," said the old woman, "he aims to heal the sick, not raise the dead."

* * *

AS the proud father handed the baby to the vicar at the christening font the cleric said: "And what will we call this little chap?"

"It's a girl," whispered the father. "You've got hold of my thumb!"

* * *

A PRIEST and a nun partnered up for a game of golf. As the priest swung the first drive he missed and sent a large divot flying through the air.

"Shit, I missed," he said.

The nun was shocked.

Several holes later he missed a vital putt.

"Shit, I missed," muttered the priest.

This time the nun could not contain herself. "Father, you must watch your language."

The priest apologised. "May God strike me dead if I swear again," he said.

But on the 18th he chipped the ball into a bunker.

"Ah shit, missed again," he said.

Suddenly a bolt of lightening flashed down from a black cloud and struck the nun dead.

And a thunderous voice from above boomed: "Ah, shit, missed again."

* * *

THERE was a young lady called Alice

Who peed in the presbytery's chalice

The padre agreed

'Twas done out of need

And not out of Protestant malice.

* * *

THE notice board outside the church declared the stern warning: "What would you do if Christ returned this week?"

The graffiti scrawled underneath said: "Move McNally to full foward and have Christ at centre half."

* * *

THE priest called on the village belle Mary O'Shaunessy who was in hospital after falling off the stage during her dance act for the church fete. "I prayed for you last night," he said.

"No need," she replied, "I'm in the phone book."

* * *

WHEN the diocese finally sent an assistant to Father O'Sullivan, the old priest had some misgivings when the young curate arrived with luggage that included a bag of golf clubs and two tennis racquets.

And he had no sooner settled in when he asked Fr O'Sullivan for an advance until pay day. "Can you spare $25.50?" he asked.

"What for?" asked the old priest.

"For a nookie," replied the younger man frankly.

Not wanting to appear ignorant, the priest handed over

the money, but he pondered over it for the rest of the day until he chanced to meet Mother Superior.

"What's a nookie?" he asked her.

"$25.50" she replied.

* * *

THREE young priests had been driving interstate when they stopped at a country pub for a drink. At the bar was a pretty barmaid with a shapely set of breasts set off by a deep cleavage.

One young priest approached the bar. "Could I have three pots of titters?" he stammered.

"Cheeky lad," she said as the priest retreated.

"I'll get the drinks," said the second priest, but as he approached the bar he couldn't keep his eyes off them.

"We'll have three tits of potters," he blurted.

The third priest had to take the issue in hand. He approached the bar with confidence. "Three pots of bitter please, Miss. And you should dress more modestly, young woman, or St Finger is going to point his Peter at you."

* * *

WHAT do you get when cross a Jehovah's Witness with a bikie?

Somebody who knocks on your door and tells YOU to piss off!"

* * *

AN old archaeologist named Tossel
  Discovered a marvellous fossil
  He knew from its bend
  And the knob on the end
  'Twas the peter of Paul the Apostle.

* * *

THE Archbishop of Canterbury had found a quiet corner for his usual morning fondle and got so carried away he didn't hear a tourist approach. It was the flash of a camera that jolted himback to reality from his self amusement.

"I'll buy the film," he said. "In fact, I'll buy the camera," he insisted.

Later the Dean noticed the Archbishop's new camera. "How much did you pay for that?"

The Archbishop replied: "One thousand pounds."

"My God," said the Dean. "Somebody saw you coming?"

REPARTEE

FRED was selling raffle tickets for the Society of Retired Seafarers and knocked on the door of old Mrs Billingham.

"Would you care to support the Society for Retired Seafarers?" he asked.

"What's that?" said Mrs Billingham, "I'm hard of hearing."

"Would you care to buy a ticket?" repeated Fred.

"What's that," she answered, cupping her hand round her ear.

In disgust Fred turned and walked away.

"Don't forget to shut the gate," said Mrs Billingham.

"Fuck the gate," muttered Fred.

"And fuck the Society for Retired Seafarers," said Mrs Billingham.

* * *

WHEN Doreen wore her new bikini it brought a quick response from the lifeguards.

"Hey there," called one. "You're the best thing I've seen all day. Why don't you stop so I can look a little longer?"

"No need to," said Doreen. "You look a little longer already."

* * *

AT a wild party Fred had noticed a prim and pretty girl sitting apart from the revellers. She didn't seem to be enjoying herself. He approached her and said: "You don't appear to be having a good time. Would you like me to take you home?"

"Alright," said the girl, "where do you live?"

RESTAURANTS

THERE is a Mongolian-Jewish restaurant. It's called Genghis Cohen.

* * *

THE health inspector made one of his surprise visits to the restaurant kitchen to find the pastrycook crimping the edge of the apple pies with a set of false teeth.

"Haven't you got a tool for that?"

"Yes, but I save it for putting holes in the doughnuts!"

* * *

THE editor wanted to know why the restaurant writer had never given Fred's Diner on Main St a favourable write-up. "Don't you like the food?" he said.

"Never eaten there," said the writer."But I did notice the alley cat out back shoving its paws down its throat."

* * *

WHILE touring Madrid, Bruce the Ocker touro discovered a tavern which served the biggest rissoles he had ever seen, for a mere fifty pesetas.

After the splendid meal he asked Manuel the waiter how come the meal was so cheap.

"Two leetle secrets," said Manuel. "As you see, we are right beside the bull-ring. We gets the meat cheep. And second, seez rissoles are really the bull's testicles, sauted in beef sauce."

That was a bit of a shock to our ocker, but nevertheless, the meal was tasty and most el cheapo.

Boasting about his find to Kevin they both returned the following night and ordered the same dish. When Manuel returned with two plates bearing one small rissole on each, Bruce predictably began moaning.

"Hey, Manuel, what the hell's this?"

"Eet is the same dish senor," said Manuel with a shrug of the shoulders. "Sometimes the bull wins!"

* * *

THE discovery of a fly in the soup can mean different responses to different diners in different countries.

In Australia the soup is sent back to the kitchen and the diner has an argument with the manager.

In England the fly is quietly and daintily removed and hidden under a serviette.

In France the soup is eaten and the fly is left high and dry on the side of the plate.

In the Orient the fly is eaten first and washed down by the soup.

In Scotland the fly is wrung out and then the soup is consumed.

And there are places where the diner stares at the fly and says: "Waiter, what's this? Only one fly?"

* * *

TWO crayfish were in the restaurant's aquarium. It seemed this would be their last night so the male cray put the hard word on the female.

She said: "Okay, but will you still respect me in the mornay?"

* * *

A RESTAURANT boasted that it could provide any dish the customer could order, no matter how alien or rare. If the chef couldn't produce the dish, then an alternative meal was on the house.

Consequently they did good business with smart alecs ordering filleted bee's dick marinated in port sauce, or roast goanna tails in curry, surrounded by Tibetan cabbage on rice.

But one evening the order was for braised elephant's balls on toast. A simple demand, but as ten minutes stretched to twenty the chef finally came out to apologise.

Due to an earlier rush on crocodile knuckle sandwiches they were completely out of bread.

ROYALS

ONE day the king took a fancy to the court jester, and from then on he was at his wit's end.

* * *

THE lecherous monarch was giving the princess the option. "Which would you prefer, my dear," he said. "A crowned head or a royal shafting?"

* * *

THE king was wandering around the palace gardens when he saw the gardener's wife with seven kids.

"Are these all yours?" he asked.

"Yes, Your Majesty, and we have another seven at home."

"Good God, your husband deserves a knightood,"

"He's got one Sir, but he never uses it," she replied.

* * *

WHEN King Arthur rode off in search of the Holy Grail he didn't trust the motley crew of courtiers he left behind, so he devised an ingenious chastity belt for his Queen Guinevere. It contained a little guillotine.

When he came back a year later he commanded the courtiers to drop their dacks and sure enough there was hardly a dick in sight. They had all been cut off, except Sir Lancelot's.

"You are the only one to remain loyal," said the king to Sir Lancelot. "What will we do with these traitors? These blackguards? What will their punishment be? Speak up, Sir Lancelot, or have you lost your tongue?"

* * *

RICHARD the Lion Heart was about to set out on yet another Crusade. He summoned his brother, Sir Arthur, and confided that he had a premonition that this time he could be killed.

"Arthur, if I do not return by this time three years hence, I want you to take this key and release the chastity belt and give the queen her freedom to take another knight."

Arthur accepted the key and said he would do as his lord bid.

At dawn next morning the column of armored knights set forth across the drawbridge and the army began its long march east.

They had stopped for morning tea when they noted a lone horseman creating a cloud of dust as he rode furiously to catch Sir Richard's battalion. He galloped to the head of the column where he was recognised as Sir Arthur.

"Richard," he said, "thank goodness I caught you." He reached into his pocket, "you have given me the wrong key."

* * *

SIR Lancelot led his war weary troop back in to Camelot and reported to King Arthur: "I have raped and pillaged all the Saxons to the south."

"You idiot," exclaimed the king, "I told you to rape and pillage the Saxons in the north. I don't have any enemies in the south."

"You do now," said Sir Lancelot.

* * *

THE Prince of Wales looked resplendent in his naval uniform while delivering a stirring speech at the opening of the Oodnadatta Flower Show. But one astute reporter had noted he was wearing a fur hat with a tail hanging down his back.

Waiting for the right moment the journo siddled up to him and said: "Er, excuse me yer Highness. The uniform looks great, but what's with the fur hat?"

"Oh that!" said the Prince. "I was tawking to Mummy

last night. When I told her I was going to Oodnadatta she said wear the fok's 'at!"

*   *   *

A KNIGHT of the realm asked the royal alchemist if he had discovered something to alleviate the knight's constant erection.

"No, M'Lord," said the alchemist, "but I mentioned it to the King and he has a new post for you."

"What's that?"

"You have been named His Majesty's Sundial."

*   *   *

AS the young man was ushered into Queen Elizabeth's presence he explained: "I'm the Royal photographer."

"How remarkable," said the Queen. "My brother-in-law is a photographer."

"How odd," said the photographer. "My brother-in-law is a queen."

*   *   *

OF the Edwards 'tis thought that the First,
   Although bad, was by no means the worst
   The Third one is reckoned
   Much worse than the Second
And the Second much worse than the First.

*   *   *

ONE day the Queen and the Princess were driving through the Royal Estate in the regal landrover when a gang of IRA bandits jumped out from behind the trees.

"It's just yer jewels we want. Hand 'em over," said the gang leader.

It was a quick and audacious robbery and the gang soon made off with their loot.

"What a terrible loss," said the Queen. "How will we explain it?"

"Well, I saved all my jewels," said the Princess, "I stuffed them up my you-know-what."

"Oh I wish I could think as quickly. I could have saved the crown."

* * *

QUEEN Victoria lay in bed next to Prince Albert exhausted and delighted on their first night of love.

"Oh, Albert, that was wonderful," she said, "is there a name for it?"

"Yes," he murmured, "it is called intercourse."

She sighed: "Well it is far too good for the common people. Let's prohibit it."

RUSSIANS

THE sole occupants of a compartment on the Trans Siberian Railway were a man and a woman.

On the first day he said: "Do you come from Minsk?"

She replied, "Nyet."

On the second he tried: "Do you come from Vladisvostok?"

She replied, "Nyet."

On the third day he said: "Enough of this love talk. Down with your pants."

* * *

WALKING into the empty store the Russian women said to the shopkeeper, "I see you have no vegetables today."

"No," he said. "This is a bread shop. It's bread we haven't got. The shop with no vegetables is around the corner."

* * *

SHE saw a man with one shoe walking down a Moscow street.

"Excuse me," she said, "do you realise you have lost a shoe?"

"You are mistaken," he said. "I just found one."

327

STUNG by world criticism that Soviet agents were behind an assassination attempt on the Pope the KGB said they would take the suspects in hand and investigate the matter.

After extensive interviews and countless viewings of video tapes it became clear that the Pope opened fire first.

*   *   *

WHAT do you call an attractive woman in Russia?

A tourist.

S

SALES

WHEN you knock on her door and her husband opens it...Sell something. For Chris'sake sell something.

* * *

SHOE salesman: "Can I interest you in a casual pump?"
  Floozie: "Why not? I can look at shoes later."

* * *

THE salesman said quietly: "Is it in?"
  "Yes," she replied.
  "Does it hurt?"
  "No," she said. "It feels wonderful."
  "Shall I wrap your old shoes?"

* * *

THE car salesman divorced his wife.
  She was giving too many demonstration rides.

* * *

THE salesman with his foot in the door had been observing the curvaceous shape of the housewife.
  "I can arrange easy credit terms, Madam," he said.
  "How easy?" she asked.
  "Nothing down but your pants," he said.

* * *

IZZI Goldstein had just returned from his monthly sales schedule and had an incredible story to tell his wife, Rachel.
  When he got to Sydney there was an airport strike and

he was delayed overnight. All the hotels were booked so he had to ask Schmidst, one of his customers, if he could put him up for the night.

Schmidst gladly offered to share his double bed and even offered Izzi a fine meal with wine.

In the middle of the night Goldstein felt a hand on his privates. Possibly his companion was dreaming. But there was no mistake when he felt an erect penis pushed against his bum.

"What did you do?" said Rachel with alarm.

"What could I do," said Goldstein, "Schmidst is my best Sydney account."

* * *

THE salesman was travelling late at night when his car blew a tyre and he realised he didn't have a jack. It was miles from anywhere, but across the field he could see a farmhouse in silhouette against the rising moon.

"He could lend me a jack," mused the salesman as he set off towards the farm.

As he stumbled across the paddocks in the dark he wondered if farmers still had the hospitality for which they were renowned.

"It's late," he thought. "He probably won't be too pleased about being woken up. He has probably had a hard day in the field and was looking forward to a bit of rest."

He approached the farmhouse and knocked on the door.

While he waited his thoughts continued: "The poor bloke is most likely getting out of bed now. His wife could be nagging him. He will be upset. He could even put the dogs onto me."

When the farmer opened the door the traveller said: "You can stick the jack up your arse!"

* * *

AN attractive salesgirl approached a young man in a department store and said: "What would you like, Sir?"

"What would I like?" he repeated. "Why I would like to

330

take you out of here, take you to my pad, mix a nice cocktail, take you in my arms, rip your pants off and make passionate love to you. That's what I'd like...but what I need is a pair of socks."

* * *

SID was told if he didn't sell more toothbrushes he would be fired. One month later his sales record had soared and the manager called him in to explain the dramatic turnaround.

Sid explained that he got sick of calling on pharmacies. He said he set up a little table at Flinders St Station with some dry biscuits and a new dip.

"Try my dip," he would say, and a constant stream of people did so. When they enquired about the ingredients of the dip Sid told them: "Garlic and chook shit!"

They would go "Aaaargh!" and spit it out.

Then Sid would say: "Would you like to buy a toothbrush?"

* * *

IT was the old story of a salesman finding himself stranded in the country and knocking on the door of the only pub in town.

"Well, we don't have a spare room," said the proprietor, "but you are welcome to share with the little red-headed school teacher if you like."

The salesman could hardly contain his excitement. "Oh thanks. I will be a real gentleman."

"That's good," said the publican. "So's the little red-headed school teacher!"

* * *

ONCE again the salesman found himself knocking on a farmhouse door seeking a bed for the night.

"Sure," said the farmer, "but we only have one spare bed and you will have to share that with Cecil, my son."

The salesman turned and headed for his car. "Crikey, how did I get into the wrong joke?"

331

"THERE'S a salesman outside with a young lady."

"Tell him I'll take one."

* * *

THE travelling salesman sent a telegram to his wife: "Coming home Friday."

When he arrived home he was alarmed to find a man in bed with his wife. He went berserk, but was restrained by his mother-in-law. She urged him to keep calm and not to commit any violent and hasty action he would, in time, regret. "Leave it to me," she said, "there must be an explanation."

Next day she explained it all to her son-in-law. "I have gone into the matter thoroughly, and like I told you, there is a reason for your wife's behaviour. There was a postal strike on Friday and she didn't get the telegram!"

SCHOOLS
See TEACHERS

THE little bush school had the reputation of being the toughest in the region so it was with a great deal of trepidation that the new mistress took her first class.

"Give me a word beginning with A," she said.

"Arsehole!" said little Johnny as quick as a flash.

She covered her shock and moved on to B.

"Bastard," came the answer from little Mick.

She thought she would give C a miss and moved on to D.

"Dwarf," said little Fred.

And with a sigh of relief she asked Fred to explain what a dwarf was.

"A little cunt about this big," said Fred.

* * *

WHEN I was a kid I went to an immoral school. It had no principal and it had no class.

IT was show and tell at school and little Johnny stood up and said his Dad had two dicks.

Miss Prim the teacher said she couldn't believe it.

"Yes," said Johnny, "a little one he wears in the shower and a big one he cleans Mum's teeth with."

* * *

THE new teacher at the boys' school was Miss Franny and she was disturbed to find that even the headmaster made a mistake when he welcomed her as Miss Fanny.

"The name is Franny," she said coldly.

"Sorry," said the headmaster who made a mental note not to forget the "r".

He escorted her to her new class. "Good morning boys," he said,"I would like to introduce you to Miss Crunt."

* * *

IN order to get the kids to study the teacher devised a plan. She would ask a questions early each Friday afternoon and those who could answer could go home.

"Can anyone tell me the square root of seven?" she said.

Nobody knew the answer so they remained at their desks.

Next week she said "Can anyone tell me the capital of Pakistan?" Again no answer so no escape.

Little Ronnie came up with a plan for the following Friday. He arrived with some black marbles and to the amusment of the other kids he rolled them with a clatter along the floor.

"Okay," said the teacher. "Who's the comedian with the black balls?"

"Bill Cosbie," shouted Ronnie. "See yer Monday."

* * *

IT was the geography class and little Lulu was asked to point out Tasmania on the map. She did so.

"Now Frankie," she said, "Tell us who discovered Tasmania?"

"Lulu did," said Frankie.

WHEN the school council decided to teach a sex education program there was a deputation from the parents' association.. "We want no graphic demonstrations," said one dissenting parent, "so just make sure it's oral."

* * *

POINTING at young Fred the teacher asked him to spell 'weather.

Fred made a valiant attempt: "W-O-T-H-E-R?"

In despair the teacher said: "That's the worst spell of weather we've had in quite a time."

* * *

Sex educator Miss Best
    Told Johnny his work had regressed
    "But since learning's a tool
    If you stay after school
    I'll help you bone up for the test."

SCIENCE

DURING the next lunar eclipse get out under the stars. Face south and bend your body at the waist to form a 90 degree angle. Bend the knees at a 45 degree angle. Then get a shaving mirror and hold it between your knees. With a bit of luck, and if all the angles are correct, you should see Uranus.

* * *

ARTIFICIAL insemination is so reliable because there is no chance of a cock-up.

* * *

AT an international medical conference the Russian doctor told how they transplanted a new heart into a man and he was working within one month.

"That's nothing," said the American. "We put a heart, lungs and a new liver into a man and within one month he was up looking for work."

"That's bugger-all," said the Australian. "We put a fart

in Canberra and in no time at all he put half the population out of work."

SCOTS

THE reason Scots have blisters on their dicks is because they are such tight-fisted wankers.

* * *

WHAT do Scotsmen do with their old condoms?
    They keep rooting with them.

* * *

JOCK McPerv was so mean he used to reverse charge his obscene telephone calls.

* * *

WHEN Jock had a vasectomy he asked the doctor if he was entitled to severance pay.

* * *

HOW does a Scot take a bubble bath?
    He has baked beans for supper the night before.

* * *

WE have all heard about the Scotsman who found a crutch.
    So he broke his wife's leg.

* * *

A SCOTTISH gentleman is one who gets out of the bath to piss in the sink.

* * *

JOCK's fiancee peered at her engagement ring.
    "Oh Jock, is it a real diamond?"
    "Och, if it isnae, I've been done out of a fiver," he replied.

* * *

McTAVISH stopped a young man in the street. "Aren't you the chap who hauled my son from the lake yesterday?"
    "Yes," said the life saver, "but think nothing of it. It was nothing."

"Nothing indeed?" roared McTavish. "Where's the lad's bloody cap then?"

* * *

TWO Scottish migrants met in Sydney. They hadn't seen each other since they migrated from Scotland together 25 years ago. They hugged and slapped each other on the shoulder.

"Let's have a drink, like we did in the old times in Glasgow," said one.

"Aye, and don't forget, it's your shout," said the other.

* * *

A SCOT, a Jew and an Englishman were dining together in a restaurant. When the waiter cleared away the coffee the Scot was heard to ask for the bill.

Next day the newspaper headlines declared: JEWISH VENTRILOQUIST SHOT IN RESTAURANT.

* * *

WHAT is the difference between a Scotsman and a canoe?

A canoe sometimes tips.

* * *

A SCOT met a doctor on the street and hoping for some free advice asked: "What should I do for a sprained ankle?"

The doctor, also a Scot, replied: "Limp."

* * *

SERGEANT McTavish of the Highland Regiment swaggered into a pharmacy. He placed a battered condom on the counter and asked the chemist how much would it cost to repair it.

The chemist held the damaged item up to the light. "I could launder it and disinfect it, vulcanise a patch on the holes and tears on the side and insert new elastic around the top, but if you take my advice it would be almost as cheap to buy a new one."

McTavish could recognise sales talk when he heard it and said he would think it over.

He returned next morning. "You've persuaded us," he declared, "the regiment has decided to invest in a new one."

* * *

A TRUE Scot never sends his pyjamas to the laundry unless he has a pair of socks stuffed in the pocket.

* * *

McTAVISH heard about a doctor who charged $20 for the first consultation, but only $5 for subsequent visits.

So when he entered the clinic he said: "Well, here I am again, Doc."

"Good. Keep up the treatment I prescribed the first time," said the doctor who was also a Scot.

* * *

WHEN the Scot went to the clinic for a check-up the doctor told him he had too much sugar in his water.

Next morning he pissed on his porridge.

* * *

A SCOT went to London for two weeks' holiday. He took a shirt and a five pound note. When he returned he hadn't changed either of them.

* * *

McTAVISH donates a lot of money to charity but he likes to do it anonymously.

In fact, he doesn't even sign the cheques.

* * *

THE Scots even enjoy being constipated.

They hate to part with anything.

* * *

DO you know what McTavish did with his first fifty cent piece?

Married her.

* * *

DID you hear about the Scotsmen who started a squash club?

Ten of them pooled their finances and bought their own bottle.

JOCK was due for his annual medical check-up and as usual arrived with a liberal specimen in a very large bottle. After the test the doctor announced that Jock was fine. There was nothing abnormal in the specimen.

Jock happily returned home to relay the good news. "Agnes," he said, "you and I, the kids and grandpa are all in good health."

* * *

AN Englishman, a Scot and an Irishman were on the Titanic when she struck the iceberg.

As she started to sink the purser shouted: "We are about to meet our maker. We'd better do something religious."

The Englishman said a prayer. The Irishman sung a hymn. The Scot took up a collection.

* * *

IN his later years Sandy began to be a little deaf but was too mean to buy a hearing aid.

So he scrounged some thin wire and put one end in his top pocket and hooked the other end behind his ear.

It made no difference to his deafness, but it prompted people to speak to him more loudly.

* * *

JOCK walked into the fish shop and ordered two pieces of fish, two pickled onions, plenty of vinegar and salt, "and wrap the lot up in today's newspaper."

* * *

McTAVISH had kept vigil beside his dying wife for two days. Finally he had to keep an appointment at the local inn. "I'll be away for a while," he said. "I'll be back as soon as I can, however, if you feel yourself slipping away while I'm gone would you mind blowing out the candle."

* * *

THE rich Sultan of Istanbul was dying from a disease that baffled the medical world for months before they discovered that only a blood transfusion would save him. It was a rare blood group and a search throughout the globe revealed that there was only one man who could match the sultan's blood group. It was Jock McTavish from the Highlands.

Jock donated the blood. It saved the sultan's life and shortly afterwards Jock received a gift of $5000.

Two years later the sultan had a replapse and Jock was asked to supply more of his unique blood. Again the sultan recovered and soon after Jock received a gift of $2000.

When the sultan fell ill for the third time Jock once again came to the rescue with more Celtic blood. The sultan recovered and sent Jock a thank-you note.

* * *

JOCK was walking down the street in his kilt when a curious woman asked if there was anything worn under the tartan.

"Nothing's worn," he replied, "everything's in perfect working order."

* * *

THE Scotsman gave the waiter a tip.

It didn't even run a place.

* * *

THE chaps in the bar invited Jock to a small bore shooting club. When he got there they stood him on a box and started firing at him.

* * *

WHEN a Scottish millionaire in his eighties decided to marry an eighteen year old chorus girl the vicar protested.

"I don't believe in marrying for money," he said.

"Good," replied the millionaire, "then I won't insult you by offering you a fee for performing the ceremony."

* * *

HAVE you heard about the Scotsman who gave an Englishman, a Welshman and an Irishman ten pounds each?

Neither has anyone else.

339

THEN there's the Scot who drinks Scotch and Horlicks. When it is his turn to shout he is fast asleep.

* * *

A SCOT pushes his way to the bar. "I've had an attack of the yaws," he says to the barman.

"What's yaws?" says the barman.

"Double whisky," says the canny Scot.

* * *

A SCOT ordered a pot of beer and as the barman handed it over he said, "D'yer think yer canna fit a nip o whisky in it too?"

"Certainly," said the barman.

"Then fill it ta the top wi beer."

* * *

THREE Scots were in church one Sunday when the collection plate came their way. One fainted and the other two carried him out.

* * *

THE young Scotsman's delight was obvious as the train pulled in to Victoria Station.

"First time in London?" enquired the passenger opposite.

"Aye," said Scotty, "and not only that, I am on my honeymoon."

The passenger looked surprised. "Then where is your wife?"

"Oh, she's been here before," said Scotty.

* * *

LETTER to the Editor: "If you don't stop making jokes at the expense of Scotsmen I shall discontinue borrowing your newspaper."

* * *

A SCOTTISH music lover married a woman because he was charmed by her voice. So charmed that he didn't realise how ugly she was until the first morning of the honeymoon when he sat in bed looking at her without her make-up.

He stared at her for some time, then grabbed her by the shoulders and roared: "Sing ya bugger, sing. Fer Chrissake sing."

* * *

DOWN at the Edinburgh Arms the worst drunk at the bar is always Duncan Disorderly.

* * *

A SCOTTISH hotel is an establishment where they pinch the towels off the guests.

* * *

McTAVISH took all his money out of the bank for a holiday. After it rested in his pocket for a week he put it all back.

* * *

WHEN the police put a price on Jock's head he turned himself in.

* * *

SHE said she would never go to a restaurant with Jock again. "He reads the menu from right to left," she said.

SEDUCTION

OVER their fifth drink the young man asked the girl to come to his apartment to see his etchings.

She thought the excuse was so corny and so sweet she agreed.

When she got there and he opened the door and snapped on the light she was surprised to see thousands of etchings covering the walls. Not a stick of furniture, not a lounge nor a bed.

Boy was she floored.

* * *

BEING seduced is a matter of perfect timing.

The woman has to give in, just before the man gives up.

"MRS Robinson, don't you think it is wrong to have an 18-year-old boy in your flat for hours every night?"

"I assure you it's only platonic. It's play for him and its a tonic for me!"

*   *   *

HE asked her for a dance and while he held her close he whispered: "Would you like to have breakfast with me tomorrow morning?"

She replied tentatively: "Sounds nice."

"Will I phone you, or nudge you?" he said.

*   *   *

THE rich old rogue was delighted that his delightful and voluptuous young niece from the country had agreed to have dinner with him. Hed had his eye on her for some time.

But he was a little surprised that when the waiter arrived she ordered big serves of the most expensive dishes.

"Do you always eat like this at home?" he asked.

"No," she said. "Only when someone wants to get into my pants."

*   *   *

AN Australian had been wandering the Outback for months. He finally came to a farm where a pretty girl met him at the gate.

"D'yer root?" he said.

"No," she replied, "but you have talked me into it, you silver-tongued bastard."

*   *   *

IN the morning was beautiful Molly
    Bemoaning her nocturnal folly
    She had gone with this bloke
    Just for a joke
    But the joke was on Molly by golly.

SHOPKEEPERS

THE shopkeeper was giving his female assistant a knee-trembler against the counter. He was right on the gravy stroke when the front door clanger signalled a customer coming in.

There was a panic for a place to hide. She dived under the counter and he stuck his donger in the till.

The customer said: "You look pleased with yourself today, Mr Johnston."

"Yes," he said. "I've just come into money."

* * *

A MAN went into jewellers shop and when the beautiful blonde assistant said: "Can I help you?" he flopped his donger on the counter.

Unperturbed, she looked him in the eye and said: "This is not a cock shop. It's a clock shop."

Just as cool he replied, "Well, can you put two hands on it?"

* * *

SHE walked into the delicatessen and selected a chicken. She prodded and poked it. She lifted one wing and sniffed underneath. Lifted the other wing and did the same. Finally she looked at the chicken's rear end and gave it another sniff.

"This chicken is not fresh," she declared.

"Lady," said the shopkeeper, "do you think you could pass the same test?"

SHOWBIZ

HE didn't have $50 to see the Broadway musical, *Cats*, so he settled for some off-Broadway pussy for $25.

* * *

"I NEVER have sex in the morning," said the pop star. "It is bad for the voice, it's bad for the health, and besides, you never know who you might meet in the afternoon."

THE young starlet wore black scanties with the label:
   "Made in Hollywood, by almost everyone."
* * *
STARRING in Hamlet, actress Amelia Hubb
   Learned her lines while immersed in her tub
   Using Method a bit,
   She fingered her clit
   To memorise, with passion, "Ah, there's the rub."
* * *
A YOUNG porno star called Sue
   Was a hit when it came to a screw
   Her climactic fame spread
   With promotions that said:
   "Coming Soon, to a Theatre Near You."
* * *
MALE porno stars get it easy.
   They can get away with muffing their lines.
* * *
GOING backstage after the ballet the devoted theatre fan realised his lifelong dream.
   He kissed every ballerina in the joint.
* * *
THE chorus girl scored a date with the star of mime.
   "He is one of those silent actors who relies on gestures and facial expressions," she said. "It was a mime blowing experience."
* * *
THE old actor's agent had a good spiel on his casting couch:
"Come to bed with me and I will make you a star, and then you can sleep with the biggest names in Hollywood."
* * *
THE director took the young starlet aside.
   "In this first scene you are supposed to look virginal."
   "What do you think I am," she replied, "a character actress?"

SID the shady director heard that one of the chorus girls doubled as a hooker and was generous with her favours. He put the hard word on her and was soon invited to her room. After the steamy session he was about to leave, then reached into his pocket and gave her two tickets for Saturday's gala performance.

The woman looked at them with disdain. "Do you expect me to buy bread with these?"

"If you are looking for bread," said Sid, "you should have fucked a baker."

*   *   *

THERE was a drum roll and the spotlight hit the Great Alfonso as he approached the growling lion. He cracked the whip and the lion opened its jaws wide. The Great Alphonso stepped closer, unzipped his fly and to the amazement of the audience, flopped it between the gaping jaws.

When he stepped back after a terrifying ten seconds there was resounding applause and the ringmaster proclaimed it the bravest act in circus history. "Indeed, anyone who can emulate that feat right here and now will readily receive the sum of one hundred thousand dollars." roared the ringmaster. "Do we have any volunteers?"

There was a timid voice of acceptance in the back row and the spotlight picked out a reluctant hero being pushed to the front of the crowd.

He finally reached the ringmaster and said: "I don't think I can open my mouth as wide as the lion, but I'm willing to give it a try!"

*   *   *

STAR of film and screen, Harry Glitter, wanted a stunt man and took advantage of the achievements in medical technology to have a clone made of himself so that he wouldn't have to play the dangerous scenes.

The amazing likeness of the actor was delivered to his

345

penthouse where Harry soon discovered that one of his characteristics had been developed too far.

The clone stripped off, went out on the balcony and began exposing himself to the crowd below.

Harry was shocked. In the struggle to hustle the clone inside they fell against the railing and the clone overbalanced and fell to his death.

The police were quickly on the scene to charge Harry Glitter with murder.

"Murder! Of course it's not murder," said the star.

"No doubt about it," said the sergeant. "It was you who made the obscene clone fall."

* * *

A YOUNG trapeze artist well stacked
    Is faced by a very sad fact
    Imagine the pain
    When time and again
    He catches his wife in the act.

* * *

THERE was a young actor named Bates
    Who danced the fandango on skates
    But he fell on his cutlass
    Which rendered him nutless
    And practically useless on dates.

* * *

WHEN the much married actress finally died her friends clubbed together for a fitting funeral and a tombstone with the fitting epitaph: "At last she sleeps alone."

* * *

HE was only six years old, but he decided to take his girl-friend to the movies.

"How much is it?" he asked at the box office.

"Well, Sonny, for grown ups in long pants it is eight dollars, but as you are only wearing short pants it is four dollars."

"Well in that case," piped up his girlfriend, "I should get in for nothing!"

* * *

GEORGE had taken his wife to the theatre, but half way through the first act he was busting for a leak. Then at interval he had a difficult time pushing through the crowd trying to find the Gents down one passage and around the next until he was somewhere backstage.

He was desperate, and when he discovered a fountain, surrounded by foliage, the effect of the tinkling water was the last straw. Nobody was about so he took out his willy and pissed into the fountain. It was a great relief.

He took some time finding his way back to his seat and when he sat next to his wife again he whispered, "Have I missed much of this second act?"

"Missed it?" she said. "You were the star."

* * *

IT was halfway through the movie when a woman dashed up the aisle and complained that she had been "interfered with" in the front stalls.

The manager quietened her down and ushered her to another seat, but no more than a minute passed and another woman complained to him that she had been "interfered with" in the front stalls.

This was too much, so the manager went down to the front and shone his torch along the second row. He was surprised to see a bald man crawling along on his hands and knees.

"What are you doing?" asked the manager.

The bald man looked up. "Oh, I've lost my toupee. It fell off in the dark. I had my hand on it twice but it got away!"

* * *

IT happened some time ago, when a young man walked into a theatrical agency and said he could sing and dance.

He backed it up with such a convincing demonstration that the agent knew he had a future star.

"You are great," he said. "What's your name?"

"Penis van Lesbian," answered the young hopeful.

"That's a shocker. We'll have to change that for a start," said the agent scratching his head. "I've got it. We'll call you Dick Van Dyke."

SMOKING

THEY were surprised to find the anti-smoking crusader had married a chain smoker.

"Yes, but I am forcing her to give it up," he said. "By strictly limiting her to an after coitus cigarette only she is down to a pack a week."

* * *

AN elderly couple killed in a car accident arrived in Heaven. St Peter took them on a tour of the facilities and showed them into their ocean-view apartment.

"Here are the buttons to press if you need food, wine, movies, trips, new cars, massage, etc. It's all there."

When St Peter had gone the husband turned to the wife and snarled: "Shit Mabel, we could have been here years ago if you hadn't made us give up smoking."

SOCIALITES

THE YOUNG socialite's Porsche was weaving from one side of the road to the other as she wended her way home from a party. She was stopped by a young traffic cop and given a breathalyser test.

The young cop studied the result and said: "Well, Miss, you've had a few stiff ones tonight."

"Gracious," replied the girl, "can it tell that as well?"

* * *

KNOWN for his ranting against the evils of drink the vicar

attended a village council meeting held at the Ponsonby Manor. After the business was over Jeeves began to pour everyone a glass of whisky. The vicar placed his hand over his glass.

"None of the evils of drink for me thank you, I'd rather commit adultery."

Fred began pouring his drink back into the neck of the bottle.

"I didn't realise we had a choice," he said.

SOCIETY

LADY Ponsonby received a letter from her son in boarding school which finished with the sentence, "Last night I had my first naughty."

She was aghast and quickly wrote back berating him and instructing him not to have another one.

Eventually she got a reply. "No mother, I haven't had one since. The first one hurt too much."

* * *

WHEN the plain daughter of a tenant farmer came home pregnant he reached for his shotgun. "But father," she said, "it was the squire of the manor."

With his shotgun cocked he headed for the manor in a rage.

"Hold on Murphy," said the squire, "I'll do the right thing by your daughter. If it's a boy I will settle $5000 for you. If it's a girl, then $3000."

"And what if it's twins?" snarled Murphy.

"Double of course," said the squire.

Murphy pondered for a moment. "And if she has a miscarriage, can she have another go?"

* * *

THE squire took his son to the library for a heart-to-heart. "Look here Cecil," he said, "you are 35 now and your mother thinks it is high time you were married. What about marrying Lady Genevieve?"

"I don't love Lady Genevieve," he said.

"Well what about Lady Cynthia?"

"I don't love Lady Cynthia. Actually I love Lord Ponsonby."

"Well you can't marry him. He's a Catholic."

SONGS

MARY had a little lamb
So her father shot the shepherd.

* * *

I'LL be seizing you, in all the old familiar places.

* * *

IF you were the only girl in the world, well okay, but as you're not, forget it.

* * *

I CAN'T get over a girl like you,
So answer the phone yourself.

SPINSTERS

AUNT Maud dreamt she was married.

But when she woke up she found there was nothing in it.

* * *

AN elderly spinster sniffed with disdain when asked why she didn't marry.

"I have a dog that growls, a parrot that swears, a fireplace that smokes and a cat that stays out all night. Why should I want a husband?"

* * *

THE spinster was coming home from evensong when a man jumped from behind a tree and said: "Don't move, this is a stick-up."

"I haven't got any money," she said, showing him her empty handbag.

"I'll see for myself," he said, and with that he began searching her. He felt around her waist, felt inside her bra, ran his hands up and down her legs and even searched her knickers.

Not finding a brass cent he turned to walk away.

"Don't stop searching," she said. "I can write you a cheque."

* * *

THE spinster approached the salesman in the furniture store. "I can't decide between the armchair or the sofa," she said.

"Believe me, Madam," said the salesman, "you won't make a mistake on the armchair."

"Right, then I'll take the sofa," she said.

* * *

MURGATROYD had noticed the spinster at the next table giving him a dirty look but he persisted with his meal. Nevertheless he was surprised when the waiter delivered a note from her. It read: "Young man, maybe you don't know it but your fly is unzipped. You should be ashamed of yourself. Exposing your person in a public place is disgusting. It's indecent. PS: I love you."

* * *

STELLA the spinster had heard that men with big feet have big pricks so when a tramp knocked on her door asking for a hand-out she was quick to notice his very large shoes stretched across the entire width of the step.

She invited him in, gave him a hearty meal, a bottle of beer and took him to bed.

When he woke alone next morning he found $50 and a brief note.

It said: "Buy yourself a pair of shoes that fit."

THE spinster had just settled into the seaside resort when she noticed the sign on the wall: "If the electric blanket doesn't work switch it off and call in a man."

* * *

SHE called at the police station to complain about the young man next door. "It's not safe to go out on the street," she said. "He's always sitting on his front porch whistling dirty songs!"

* * *

MISS Prim complained to the police that the men on the building site were using foul language.

The cop told her that builders' labourers tended to call a spade a spade.

"No they don't," she said. "They've been calling it a fucking shovel."

* * *

OLD Spinster's Prayer:
And now I lay me down to sleep
I wish I had a man to keep
If there's a man beneath the bed
I hope he heard each word I said.

* * *

YOUNG Spinster's Prayer:
Oh Lord, I ask nothing for myself, but would you please send my dear mother a son-in-law?

* * *

SPINSTER'S advice:
Dear girls. Be wary of Cupid
And hark to the lines of this verse
To let a fool kiss you is stupid
To let a kiss fool you is worse.

SPORT

"I'M a little stiff from Badminton."

"I don't care where you come from."

NEVER fall in love with a tennis player.

To them love means nothing.

* * *

THE annual university boat race resulted in an exciting finish, but there was a dramatic moment when a blonde rushed through the crowd and kissed the cox of the winning crew.

* * *

SPIV and Nick were a little cheesed off when the gates of the sports ground were slammed shut. It was full to capacity for the grand final.

The ground was so crowded the toilet facilities could not cope and at half time many fans were forced to head for the perimeter fence and find a knot hole.

Spiv and Nick were still outside mutttering about their bad luck when Spiv noticed the odd dick being poked through the fence.

"Here's a chance to make some money," he said. He grabbed a dick and shouted: "Throw a fiver over or I'll cutcha cock off."

They were delighted to see a note flutter over the fence.

"We're on to something here," said Spiv, "you go that way and I'll meet you back here when we go right around the ground."

Ten minutes later they met. "I've got near on fifty dollars," said Spiv. "How did you go?"

"Not so good," said Nick, "I got forty-five dollars. But I've got three cocks!"

* * *

AN AUSTRALIAN girl phoned her boyfriend.

"Trevor, I've just been to the doctor and he tells me I'm up the duff. Trevor, if you don't marry me I will drown myself."

"Well, Sheryl, that's bloody decent of you. Not only are you a good fuck, you're a good sport too."

SQUELCH

THE blonde was having a quiet drink when Larry Loud-mouth sat beside her. "Hi babe," he said. "I'd love to get into your pants."

"Why?" she replied. "There's already one arsehole there."

* * *

AS he arrived home from the pub he noticed his wife ironing her bra and couldn't refrain from commenting, "I don't know why you bother with that, dear, you've nothing to put in it."

She continued ironing and casually remarked, "I often think the same thing when I'm ironing your underpants."

* * *

THE drunk boarded the train and plonked himself down beside a priest and began to read the paper.

He looked up after a bit and said: "Tell me Father, what causes arthritis?"

It was just the opening the priest wanted. "I will tell you what causes arthritis my man," he said with passion. "It's immoral living, too much drinking and smoking and no doubt sins of the flesh. How long have you had it?"

"Oh it's not me, Father," said the drunk. "It says here the Pope's got it."

* * *

AFTER 25 years of marriage a couple decided on an amicable divorce. To celebrate the granting of the decree they had dinner together.

After the third glass of champagne the husband said: "There's something I have always wanted to ask you, but I didn't have the nerve. Now it can't possibly worry me."

"What's that?" said his ex-wife.

"Why is it that five out of our six children have black hair and Tommy is so blonde."

She didn't answer.

"Come on, you can tell me now," he insisted. "Whose child is Tommy?"

Finally she acquiesced. "Well, if you really want to know, Tommy is your child."

*   *   *

HE believed in the direct approach and even on their first date asked if she wanted to hear his sexual philosophy.

"I suppose so." she replied.

"Well, it's Get-It-Up, Get-It-In, Get-It-Off, and Get-It-Out," he said, "What do you think about that?"

"I think that's the Four-Get-It approach," she said coolly.

STATISTICS

ON the question of girls legs 19% of men said they liked fat legs, 27% said they liked slender legs and the rest said they liked something in between.

T

TAXIDERMISTS

AN old lady had two pet monkeys. They had been with her for years until one died and the second died out of sympathy.

She took them to a taxidermist.

"Do you want them mounted?" he asked.

"No, just shaking hands will do," she replied.

* * *

WE knew he was elderly because he looked much older than the blonde at the table with him.

We knew he was rich because of the amount of food and wine he was lavishing on the girl.

We knew that he was a taxidermist because he was obviously stuffing the bird before mounting her.

TAXIS

THE prostitute hailed a cab and gave directions to take her home. When the cab stopped she said:

"Oh goodness. I've forgotten my purse."

"Well how are you going to pay for the ride?" demanded the driver.

She lifted her skirt. "With this," she said.

"Haven't you got anything smaller?" he said.

THE taxi screeched to a halt.

"What's the idea of stopping here?" said the bloke in the back.

"But I heard a woman say stop," said the cabbie.

"Yes, but she wasn't talking to you. Keep going."

* * *

AFTER travelling a few blocks Miss Lottsabazooma realised she had no money and immediately informed the driver. "Youd better stop. I can't pay you and it's ten dollars already," she said.

The driver checked her out in the rear-vision mirror. "That's okay," he said. "I'll turn down the first dark street, get in the back seat and take off your knickers."

"You'd be cheating yourself," she replied. "These knickers are only worth a fiver."

* * *

THE canny Scot took a taxi to the bankruptcy court, then invited the driver inside as one of the creditors.

* * *

HE lay under the cab tinkering with the motor and groping for spanners and tools when his attractive fare said: "Do you want a screwdriver?"

"Not now, Miss, but try me as soon as I fix this motor."

* * *

LEAVING the wedding reception the honeymoon couple hailed a cab to take them to their romantic boutique hotel in the hills. The driver wasn't too sure how to get there and said he would ask directions when they got closer. Meanwhile, the lovers couldn't wait and got down to it on the back seat.

Seeing a fork in the road the driver said: "I take the next turn, right?"

"No way, get your own," said the groom, "this one's all mine."

357

SCOT McTavish was lugging a heavy suitcase. He hailed a cab. "How much to the train station?"

"Five dollars," said the driver.

"How much for my suitcase?"

"Nothing."

McTavish opened the door, slung his case in and said: "Here, take it to the station then."

* * *

A DRUNK in the back seat of the cab says to the driver: "Exchooze me. Do you have room in the front for a crayfish and half a dozen bottles?"

"Yes," said the cabbie.

The drunk leans over and throws up. (Action joke).

* * *

MOISHE had a little scheme which always seemed to work. When the taxi delivered him to his address he would fumble in his waistcoat for the money and then search around the floor of the cab claiming to have dropped a fifty dollar note.

"Stay here while I get some matches from that tobacconist's stall so I can strike a light to find it," he would say.

As soon as Moishe got out of the cab it would invariably drive away.

* * *

WHEN the taxi company lowered its rates from two dollars flagfall to a single dollar there was a protest meeting at the Celtic Club. The Scots were annoyed that in most cases they were saving around five dollars a night by walking home, now they would only save around $2-50.

* * *

TWO teenage layabouts decided to share a taxi.

One took the hub caps the other took the radio.

358

TAXMAN

THERE is a major difference between cheating on your wife and cheating on the taxman.

When you get caught the taxman will still want to screw you.

* * *

PADDY was walking down the street when he stumbled on a fat and unopened pay envelope.

"That's a lucky find," said his mate Shamus.

"Lucky nothing," said Paddy. "Look at the bloody tax I'm paying."

* * *

FORTUNATELY the penis is still exempt from taxation. This is because it is usually hanging around unemployed.

The rest of the time it is either hard up, pissed off or in a hole. It also has two dependants and they are both nuts.

* * *

FRED consulted his lawyer. "I've been receiving threatening letters," he said.

"That's terrible," said the legal eagle. "We'll put a stop to that. Who are they from?"

"The Taxation Department," said Fred.

* * *

THE rabbi was surprised to receive a call from the tax inspector. "The synagogue is exempt from taxes," explained the rabbi.

"Oh, it's not you we are enquiring about," said the taxman, "it's one of your community, Isaac Goldstein."

The taxman explained that on his tax return Goldstein indicated that he donated $50,000 to the synagogue.

"Is this true?" asked the taxman.

"The money hasn't arrived yet but I am sure it will be here as soon as I remind dear Isaac."

TEACHERS

THE English teacher was seeking an example of the word 'contagious' and little Billy's hand went up like a rocket.

"Only last Sunday," he said, "a big truck full of oranges nearly forced Dad's car off the road. And as it swerved around the next bend the truck lost its load and my Dad said it would take that contagious to pick up all those oranges."

* * *

A STRAPPING young farmhand was sent to the station to pick up the new school teacher who turned out to be an attractive young woman.

On the way back to the farm she noticed a stallion mounting a mare. "How do they know when to do that?" she enquired.

The young man explained that it was a sense of smell.

In the very next paddock a bull was enjoying himself on a cow.

"Again, it is a sense of smell," explained the country boy. "Just like that ram and ewe over there."

He unloaded her luggage at the farmhouse and turned to go. "See you later," he said.

"Thanks," she replied. "And do come over when your cold gets better."

* * *

SHE was a teacher in her mid-forties and a spinster until she finally allowed herself to be seduced by the school inspector.

She sat up in bed and started crying. "Oh the shame," she sobbed. "How can I stand up in front of those children tomorrow and pretend to be worthy when I've been sinful so often."

"What do you mean, often?" said the school inspector, "I thought this was the first time."

"It is," she said, "but you are going to do it again, aren't you?"

TIME

THEY are thinking of putting a clock on the Leaning Tower of Pisa. It's for those who have the inclination but not the time.

*   *   *

TIME is nature's way of preventing everything happening at once.

*   *   *

MURPHY had been in the bar for a while when his mate arrived.

"Hey Murph, what time is it?"

"Don't know," replied Murphy, "Except that it ain't foive o'clock."

"How come?"

"Because I told my missus I'd be home by foive, and here I am still here."

*   *   *

MY brother hates daylight saving.

He gets his early morning erection on the 8-30 train to the office.

TOASTS

"FORNICATION," roared the MC, "Fornication like this we need champagne for the toast...

*   *   *

HERE'S to the kisses you've snatched,
   and vice versa.

*   *   *

MAY all your ups and downs be in a bed..

*   *   *

HERE'S to your genitalia
   May it never land you in jailiya

*   *   *

MAY you live as long as you want to
   And want to, as long as your live.

MAY we kiss who we please
  And please who we kiss.

*   *   *

IF I'm asleep when you want me. Wake me.
  And if I don't want to. Make me.

*   *   *

IF I am sleeping
  and you want to wake me
  don't shake me
  just take me.

*   *   *

MAY the fleas of a thousand camels infest the underpants
of our enemies.

*   *   *

MAY your chooks turn into emus and kick down your
dunny door.

*   *   *

HERE'S to the bloke down the lane
  He courted a girl, all in vain
  She swore when he kissed her
  So he slept with her sister
  Again and again and again.

*   *   *

MUSICIANS' TOAST: May your organ never quit while
you are half way through your favourite piece.

*   *   *

MAY we all get to heaven half an hour before the devil
knows we're dead.

*   *   *

MAY the skin of your bum never cover a drum.

*   *   *

MAY you live as long as you want, and may you never want
as long as you live.

*   *   *

MAY you live a hundred years, and another month to
repent.

MAY we never put our finger in another man's pie.

*   *   *

MAY you never have to eat your hat.

*   *   *

MAY the frost never afflict your spuds.

*   *   *

MAY the Blue Bird of Happiness crap down your chimney.

*   *   *

MAY we drink to the thirst which is yet to come.

*   *   *

MAY we all be alive this time, twelve months.

*   *   *

MAY you slide down the bannister of life, with nary a splinter.

*   *   *

MAY your luck be like the capital of Ireland, always Dublin!

*   *   *

HERE'S to the wowsers, whose abstinence gives us all the more to drink.

*   *   *

THERE'S many a toast, if I could think of it Damned if I can, so let's drink to it.

*   *   *

TO our wives and sweethearts. May they never meet.

*   *   *

LET'S drink to the soup. May it be seen and not heard.

*   *   *

HERE'S to the girl who lives on the hill
    She won't be in it, but her sister will
    Here's to her sister, then.

*   *   *

HERE'S to the happiest days of my life,
    Spent in the arms of another man's wife,
    My mother's.

HERE'S to your eyes, and mine
   Here's to your lips, and mine
   The former have met
   The latter not yet
   So here's to that moment, sublime.

          *   *   *

HERE'S to us
   May we live a long life
   And heres mud in your eye
   While I wink at your wife.

          *   *   *

HERE'S to Miss Prim
   For her life held no terrors
   Born a virgin, died a virgin
   No hits, no runs, no errors.

          *   *   *

I DRINK to your health when I'm with you
   I drink to your health when alone
   I drink to your health so often
   I'm becoming concerned at my own.

          *   *   *

LONG live centenarians

TRADESMEN

TWO builders' labourers were walking home from a party.

One said: "Basil, as soon as I get home I am going to rip the wife's knickers off."

"Why's that, Trevor?"

"'Cos the bloody elastic is killing me," he said.

          *   *   *

SHE had the decorators refurbishing the house and was proudly showing her husband the new colour of the bedroom walls when the clumsy bugger lent on the door and smudged the new paintwork.

Next day she interrupted the painter as he was doing some work in the kitchen.

"Excuse me, Mr Painter," she said. "Can you come up to the bedroom? I'd like to show you where my husband put his hand last night."

"If it's all the same, m'am," he replied, "I'd rather a cup of tea and a cake."

*　　*　　*

IZZI came home early one day and caught Rachel screwing with the baker.

"I'm ashamed of you," he shrieked. "Why are you screwing the baker when its to the butcher we owe money?"

*　　*　　*

PADDY was new to the carpentry game so when he called at the timber yard to pick up some two-by-fours he was corrected by the timber merchant.

"You mean four-by-twos?"

"Okay, if you say so," said Paddy.

"And how long do you want them?"

"A long time," said Paddy, "I'm building a bloody house."

*　　*　　*

PADDY was a builders' labourer and found he had been overpaid a fiver. He didn't say anything about it.

However, the following week he was underpaid a fiver and he went straight to the boss to complain about being short-changed.

"But you didn't complain last week when you were overpaid," said the boss.

"One mistake is one thing," said Paddy, "but to make two mistakes in successive weeks is very sloppy administration."

*　　*　　*

A PLUMBER knocked at the door with toolbox in hand. "I've come to fix your leaking cistern," he said to the woman who answered the door.

"But we haven't got a leaking cistern."

"Aren't you Mrs Snodsbody?"

"No. They moved away six months ago."

"Bloody typical," said the plumber. "They ring for a plumber saying it's an emergency, then piss off to another address."

* * *

A PLUMBER one night feeling free
Was plumbing his girl by the sea
Said the maid: "Quick stop plumbing
I fear someone's coming
Said the plumber, still plumbing,
"It's me!"

TRAINS

THE Vatican has taken over the railways and called it the Transportus Coitus Interuptus.

Everybody gets off one stop before their destination.

* * *

WHEN the train conductor saw the young couple screwing away in the compartment he used his radio to notify the police who boarded at the next station.

The girl was let off with a warning, but the bloke was charged with mounting and dismounting while the train was in motion and for having a first class ride while holding a second class ticket.

* * *

FOUR people were in the same compartment on a long train journey; a young woman, a priest, a businessman and a drunk.

All had been quiet for an hour or two until the young woman suddenly began to sob. The priest bent over to console her. "Tell me why you are crying," he said.

The girl sniffed and said: "I have just learnt that I am illegitimate."

The priest replied, "That's no sin. As a matter of fact I am illegitimate myself."

Then the businessman spoke up. "Excuse me, I couldn't help overhearing, but I must tell you that I am a self-made man. I own several businesses, in fact I am a millionaire, yet I am illegitimate too."

The drunk took out a cigarette and asked: "Any of you bastards got a light?"

TRAVEL

IT was their honeymoon and they told the travel agent they wanted to fly United.

She said the other passengers might object.

* * *

TWO women were side by side in deckchairs aboard the Queen Mary as it crossed the Atlantic.

"I'm so lucky to have this trip," said one. "My husband worked so hard to scrape the money together."

The other neighbour was unimpressed.

"First trip is it?" she said haughtily. "This is my 20th crossing. My husband works for Cunard."

"Well I told you mine does too," said the first woman, "but I don't swear about it."

* * *

A YOUNG man was enjoying his first night in Rome drinking cappucino at a pavement cafe when a pretty girl sat beside him.

"Hello," he said. "Do you understand English?"

"Only a little," she answered.

"How much?" he asked.

"Fifty dollars," she replied.

* * *

THERE is an American Express card holder who insists on early morning sex. He never leaves home without it.

PADDY, the left-handed barman had been pulling beers for 25 years in the same pub. "Why don't you travel and broaden your mind?" he was told repeatedly.

Finally he took the advice, and a week's holiday on the Canary Islands.

When he returned he was a changed and knowledgeable man. "Well what did you learn?" asked the regulars.

"I can tell you this," he said as they all leaned forward for his pearl of wisdom. "There are no canaries in the Canary Islands."

A year passed and Paddy once more took his annual leave abroad. This time his travel agent suggested the Virgin Islands.

"Well what did you learn this time, Paddy?" asked the regulars when he returned from his second world odyssey.

"I can tell you this," he said as they all leaned forward. "There are no canaries on the Virgin Islands, either!"

* * *

SHE was on the phone from the Gold Coast. "The holiday is wonderful darling, I feel like a new woman."

"So do I. Stay there another week."

* * *

A YOUNG chap boarded the Ansett flight at Cairns and the hostess noticed a newspaper parcel under his arm. "Mudcrabs," he explained. "I'm taking them back to Melbourne for a gourmet meal tonight."

"Then in that case they would be best placed in the fridge," said the hostess, stowing them away appropriately.

The flight landed on time and as the aircraft taxied across the tarmac the passengers were welcomed to Melbourne, and told to remain seated until the aircraft came to a halt ..."And would the gentleman who gave me the crabs in Cairns please identify himself?"

* * *

AN Australian football team took an end-of-season trip to

London where they hired a double-decker bus to see the sights. Half went upstairs.

Those down below were cheering, shouting and enjoying themselves but there was not a sound from those upstairs. The coach went up to check the reason and found them all gripping the seats with white knuckles.

"It's all right for you lot down below," one said, "you've got a driver."

*　*　*

DEAR diary. This is day one of my first holiday on a cruise ship.

Day two. While the cruise is nice there are an awful lot of men, including the stewards, making passes at me.

Day three. I have been invited to sit at the captain's table.

Day four. The captain made an improper suggestion last night. I refused.

Day five. The captain says that unless I agree, he will sink the ship.

Day six. Last night I saved the lives of 2,765 people.

*　*　*

UNCLE Fred had heard about the massage parlours in Bangkok and when he booked into his hotel was surprised to find this service offered as part of the hotel facilities.

He was on the phone in a flash.

When the girl had finished working on his back she asked him to roll over and it was evident by the state of his Onkaparinga that the rub had done him the world of good.

The girl noticed it. "Oh," she said, "by the look of that you might like wanky-wanky?"

Fred gave an eager nod.

"Okay, I'll come back as soon as you've finished," she said.

*　*　*

A TRAVEL agent looked up from his desk to notice an old lady and an old gent peering in the shop window at the posters showing the glamorous destinations around the world.

The agent had had a good week and the dejected couple looking in the window gave him a rare feeling of generosity.

He called them in. "I know that on your pension you could never hope to have a holiday, so I am sending you off to Queensland at my expense, and I won't take no for an answer," he said.

He took them inside and asked his secretary to write two flight tickets and book a room on the Gold Coast. They gladly accepted and were off.

About a month later the little old lady came into his shop. "And how did you like the holiday?" he asked eagerly.

"The flight was exciting and the room was lovely," she said. "I've come to thank you. But one thing has puzzled me. Who was that old bloke I had to share the room with?"

* * *

THE pilot had just given the passengers the usual announcement about the estimated time of arrival and weather conditions, then forgot to switch off the public address system.

"And as soon as we get settled into our hotel I am going to have a stiff whisky and put the hard word on that curvey red-haired hostess," he said to his co-pilot.

The hostess concerned was aghast that the PA system was still turned on. She hurried towards the flight deck but tripped over a small bag which had been left in the aisle.

A little old lady leant down to help her up and said: "No need to hurry, lass. He said he was going to have a whisky first!"

* * *

LETTER from a travel agent: "Dear Sir, In reference to your proposed trip to London, the flight you requested is completely full, but we will keep in contact and inform you immediately somebody falls out, as is often the case."

A BUSLOAD of tourists stopped for the night in Kakadu. The tour leader sent his offsider down to the billabong for water. A few minutes later the offsider came running back to say hed confronted a large crocodile in the shallows.

"Never mind about the croc," said the leader. "He's more frightened of you than you are of him."

"Well in that case," said the offsider, "the water in the billabong isn't fit to drink."

* * *

THE tourists all trooped off the bus when it stopped in Kakadu, except for one little old lady. "Don't you want to see the Aboriginal carving?"

"Nup," she replied. "I've lived on a farm all my life and I've seen plenty of cows calving, so I don't suppose it would be much different."

* * *

THE coach was travelling through Dublin when the guide announced: "We are now passing the biggest pub in Ireland."

An Aussie voice at the back of the bus said: "Why?"

* * *

YOUNG Aussie tourist, first time abroad, dashed into the Gents in Trinidad and lined up beside a tall Jamaican. He could hardly fail to notice the huge donger the Jamaican held with both hands, but got the shock of his life when he saw the name 'Wendy tattooed along its length.

"Look," he said excitedly, "Me too. Our girl friends have got the same name."

"Sorry man," said the Jamaican. "Mine really says: "Welcome to Trinidad. Have a nice day!"

TRUCKIES

EVER since the hitch-hiker had climbed aboard hed noticed the lack of conversation and that the truckie was the silent type. It eventually prompted him to ask the truckie if he had a radio.

"Nup," was the stern reply.

After another long silence the hiker said: "Well what do you do to help the time pass?"

There was yet another pause before the truckie finally answered: "Well I've got my little mate," and with that he snapped his fingers and a monkey jumped from behind the cabin and landed on the driver's lap.

It sat there for ten minutes or so until the hiker said: "Well you can't talk to a monkey. What's the use of that."

"Watch this," said the truckie. He gave the monkey a belt on the head and it opened the truckie's fly and gave him a head job.

Yet another poignant silence and the relieved driver said: "What do you think of that?"

"Not bad. I'm impressed," said the hiker.

"Would you like to try one yourself?" asked the truckie.

"Well I would, if you don't mind, provided you don't hit me on the head as hard as you hit the monkey."

* * *

THE truckie couldn't believe his eyes. There in the middle of the desert was a flashing neon sign: 'Mama's Desert Diner. He had crossed this desolate stretch many times and never seen it before.

"No, we are new," said Mama. "What will ya have luv?"

"Two hamburgers and a hot dog," he ordered.

He saw Mama go the fridge, reach for two rissoles and whack them up under her armpits.

"What for?" roared the truckie.

"Everything is deep frozen out here luv," she explained, "that's the only way I can thaw them out."

"Well okay," said the reluctant diner, "but cancel the hot dog."

372

THE hitch-hiker lay back in the cabin and lifted her skirt. "So it's true," she said as the truckie went down on her, "you truck drivers sure know the best places to eat."

TURKS

WHEN the sultan entered his harem unexpectedly his wives let out a terrified sheik.

*　*　*

THE sultan had ten wives.
Nine of them had it pretty soft.

*　*　*

IN the harem, a lonely girl calls
But the guard takes no notice at alls
When asked if he cheats
On the sultan, he bleats,
"Oh I would, but I ain't got the balls."

U

UNDERTAKERS

IT is an unusual profession, but somebody has to do it and the money is good. Which is why old Marmaduke assigned his son as an apprentice to the great funeral director, Turner Sod.

Each evening the proud father would ask young Marmaduke what he learned in his profession.

"Well Dad," said the lad. "We had an unusual job today. We got a phone call from the Ritz to say that a man and woman had died in the hotel. They had died side by side, lying naked on a double bed."

"Well, what happened?" pressed the father. "I am sure the great Turner Sod could handle it."

"Indeed he did, Father. We donned our mourning coats and top hats and went around in style to the hotel. We met the manager and went up to the room in dignity and silence."

"And what happened then?" said his father.

"Well we came to the room and Turner Sod pushed the door open with his brolly and we entered quietly in a solemn manner befitting the occasion, and there, on the bed was this naked couple lying on their backs.

"Mr Turner's practised eye saw what I thought would be a problem. The man had a gigantic erection. But it was no problem to the experienced Mr Turner Sod who simply turned his brolly around and gave it a mighty whack with the handle."

"And what happened then, Son?"

"A hell of a commotion, Dad. We had entered the wrong room!"

*   *   *

DYING aboard ship can also have its complications.

The captain told his first mate, an Irishman, that a passenger had died in cabin 23 and he wanted the mate to arrange the burial at sea.

An hour later the mate returned to report that the matter concerning cabin 25 had been attended to.

"What?" exclaimed the captain, "I said cabin 23. Who the hell was in cabin 25?"

"An Englishman, sir."

"Was he dead?"

"Well, he said he wasn't, but you know what bloody liars those Pommies are!"

*   *   *

WHEN Widow Bloom saw how the undertaker had laid out her dear departed Horace in his coffin she was mortified to see he was in his grey suit.

"No," she cried. "I promised him I would lay him to rest in his black suit. That's the way he wanted to go."

The undertaker said it was a problem because *rigor mortis* had set in and it would be one hell of a job to change suits.

"We don't care about the cost, just do it," ordered the widow.

Next day she returned to the mortuary to find her husband laid out in his best black suit as he had wished.

"Wasn't so hard was it," she said.

"Not really as it turned out," said the undertaker. "Actually we had another widow insisting her husband should be buried in a grey suit. So we just swapped heads!"

375

RON Sup was a Chinese funeral director.

On the front of his parlor was his business sign: 'People Buried. R Sup.

* * *

ALL her life she had been a good-time girl.

In fact they had to bury her in a Y-shaped coffin.

UNIONS

THE police came to the factory and asked for a suspect called Harry Fukbrake.

The foreman said he didn't know him but turned and shouted: "Do we have a Fukbrake here?"

The union steward replied: "Christ, we've just managed to get a tea brake."

* * *

UNION shop steward telling his kid a bedtime story:

"One upon a time and a half ..."

* * *

THE sign in the factory read: 'Any Italian who wishes to attend the funeral of a relative must tell the foreman on the day of the game.

* * *

A SHOP steward noticed a sign outside the local church. It said: JESUS LIVES

He hurried to the union office. "Does this mean no Easter holidays?" he asked.

* * *

JAKE the plumber was on a house job and noted that the lady of the house was quite a woman. By mid afternoon they were having a tumble in the bedroom when the phone rang.

"That's my husband," she said. "He is coming home now because he has a meeting tonight. Why don't you come back and we can continue where we left off."

"What?" said the plumber. "On my own time?"

V

VETS

FARMER McTavish had groomed the prize bull for the annual show and was confident of winning a blue ribbon, but on the very eve of the big event he was aghast to find the bull had gone cock-eyed.

He made a panic call to the vet who was quickly on the scene and summed up the problem in a professional and composed manner. He simply picked up a length of plastic pipe from the barn floor, inserted one end in the bull's rectum and blew forcefully on the other.

The bull's eyes popped straight ahead.

But next day, as McTavish unloaded the bull into his stall at the show, he was distraught to find the cock-eyed affliction had returned.

He shoved the pipe up the bull's bum and blew for all he was worth, but to no avail. In desperation he made another panic call to the vet, who once again arrived in his usual calm manner.

"I did what you did," said McTavish. "But it doesn't work."

"Show me," said the vet.

Once again McTavish shoved the pipe in and blew his best.

"No, no," said the vet. He pulled the pipe out, turned it

round, and plunged the opposite end into the beast. He gave one puff and the bull's eyes popped straight.

"Oh, so I was using the wrong end of the pipe?" said McTavish.

"No," said the vet. "It makes no difference."

"Then why did you turn it around?"

"You don't think I would use the same end you've had in your mouth do you?" said the vet.

VIETNAMESE

HUNG Le, Australia's Vietnamese comic asks: "How do you know when a Vietnamese has robbed your house?"

He says because the dog is missing and your homework's done.

* * *

A VIETNAMESE migrant got excited when he saw a hot dog stall. "You beauty," he said, until he took a closer look.

"That's disgusting," he said. "In my country we don't eat that part of the dog."

* * *

SIGN on a Vietnamese restaurant door: DOGS NOT AL-LOWED...OUT

* * *

HUNG LE said he came to Australia aboard a very leaky prawn boat. "It was so leaky even the prawns were wearing life jackets," he said.

VIRGINS

"OOPS," he said, "I think I felt something break."

"Oh, it's okay," she replied."It's only my promise to my mother."

* * *

A VIRGIN is a nice girl who whispers sweet nothing-doings in your ear.

HE said: "Do you know what virgins eat for breakfast?"

"No," she said.

"I didn't think so," he said.

* * *

THE old hillbilly wanted to know why his son had suddenly cancelled his wedding when so much preparation for a wing-ding party had taken place.

"Well, Pa," drawled the son, "I got to feeling in Betsy-Lou's pants and I found out she's a virgin. That's why I decided not to marry her."

"Quite right, son," said the old man, "if she ain't good enough fer her kinfolks, then she ain't good enough for ours neither."

* * *

GERALD had always been intent on marrying a virgin and purposely selected a bride who had attended convent school all her life.

In the lobby of the hotel in which they were to spend their wedding night they passed the bar and the bride was surprised to see so many single women in there.

"I am afraid they are prostitutes," said her husband.

Gerald was delighted to hear her next question. "What's a prostitute?" she asked.

"A prostitute," said Gerald with disdain, "is a woman who will go to bed with any man for money."

"Really," said the bride in amazement, "the priests only gave us lollies."

* * *

FARMER Brown and his wife had sacrificed all to send their daughter to a convent school for a good education and when she came home for Christmas he drove in to the railway station.

"I've got a confession to make, Dad." she said while driving back to the farm. "I ain't a virgin anymore."

"What will your mother say?" he said, "after all that money spent on your education and you still say ain't."

NO longer a virgin, but wise
   She managed a marriage disguise
   More verbal than surgical art
   She mentally refurbished the part
   By constructing a tissue of lies.

WAITERS

"WAITER, are you sure this lobster is fresh?"

"Yes Sir, it walked here from the beach this morning."

The customer gave it another sniff. "Well I think it must have trodden in something on the way!"

* * *

"WAITER, why have you got your thumb in my soup?"

"It's bruised, sir, the doctor told me to keep it warm."

"He should have told you to stick it up your arse."

"That's what I do in the kitchen, sir."

* * *

MOISHE settled down in his favourite kosher restaurant. "Oi waiter, do you have matzo balls?"

"No," he said, "I always walk like this!"

WANKERS

HE was a whimsical masturbator, with an offbeat sense of humour.

* * *

HE was a disfunctional male patient and the sex therapist was advising him on the release that could be obtained through masturbation.

"Oh but I do get pleasure from my organ," he replied. "I frequently grasp my penis and hold it tight. It's a habit with me."

"Well, it's a habit you'll have to shake," said the therapist.

*   *   *

THERE is a big difference between an egg and a wank.

You can beat an egg, but you can't beat a wank.

*   *   *

THERE is a big difference between wanking and clogs.

You can hear yourself coming in clogs.

*   *   *

HE was such a conceited wanker he would call out his own name and come.

*   *   *

WHY is masturbation better than intercourse?

Because you know who you are dealing with.

Because you don't have to buy flowers.

Because you know when you've had enough.

Because you don't have to be polite.

Because you don't have to make conversation.

Because you don't have to look your best.

Because you meet a better class of person.

*   *   *

A SHAKESPEARIAN actor was being interviewed by the press.

"Did you ever have a really embarrassing experience?"

"Well, yes. One experience I will never forget was when my mother caught me playing with myself."

"Oh we all did that when we were kids."

"Yes, but this was last night."

*   *   *

WANKING is very much like playing Bridge.

If you've got a good hand you don't need a partner.

*   *   *

LOVERS may celebrate Valentine's Day, but wankers celebrate Palm Sunday.

THE leading manufacturer of imported vibrators is a Japanese firm called Genital Electric.

* * *

FRED had been stranded on the desert island for three years and now had blisters on his hands. One day he grabbed his old binoculars and scanned the horizon.

"My God, a ship," he muttered to himself. And there, on the mast, a naked blonde, beautiful breasts, and look at those hips, wow, she is headed this way."

By now he had a roaring erection.

Suddenly he flung the binoculars away and grabbed his donk.

"Gotcha again, ya bastard. There is no bloody ship."

* * *

IT was the Yuppies turn to host the bridge club evening and although they packed their 12 year-old son off to bed early, Junior was constantly coming downstairs and interrupting the game asking for drinks of water, wanting to go to the toilet, and had one excuse after another.

Finally one of the guests, Miss Lottzabazooma, said she could sort the matter out and took the youngster upstairs.

When she returned the game ran smoothly and there wasn't another sound from the lad all night.

As the guests were leaving the young mother asked Miss Lottzabazooma what her secret was.

"Nothing really," she said, "I just taught him to masturbate."

* * *

OLD Beryl and Dave struck up a relationship in the nursing home. They would meet in the television room after the evening meal, spread a rug across their adjacent chairs and Beryl would quietly give Dave a hand job.

Then one night Beryl was alarmed to see another woman sitting next to Dave, the rug spread across their knees and tell-tale movement beneath it.

"How could you, Dave?" said Beryl.

"I'm sorry," said Dave, "but she's got Parkinson's."

* * *

GOING down to the workshed one day a father surprised his 15 year-old son masturbating. In an understanding manner the father explained that what the boy had been doing was natural enough because the urge for release was strong.

"But you must save all that energy and not waste it," he said. "That sperm is your life essence. Save it until you are a man and can use it in the normal manner."

The boy promised and the years slipped by.

He was given a great party on his 21st birthday and when the guests had left he thanked his dad. "I never forgot what you told me in shed years ago," he said. "And I saved my seed like you told me to. But now I am a man and I have three barrels full. Heck Dad, what the hell will I do with it?"

* * *

BASIL was still pulling his pud and by his 30th birthday his father took him aside and said he would have to get married.

So Basil found himself a nice girl, got married and brought her home. Yet less than a month after the wedding the father found him whacking off in the shed again.

"What's this?" he said, "I thought this would stop once you got married."

"But Dad, the poor girl's not used to it. Her little arms get so tired."

* * *

THE American tourist got the shock of his life when the Mexican, brandishing a six-shooter, jumped out from behind a cactus.

"Take my money, my car, but don't kill me," said the tourist.

"I no kill you if you do what I say," said the Mexican. "Just unzip your pants and start masturbating," he ordered.

Although shocked the traveller did what he was told.

"Right, now do it again," said the Mexican.

The Yank protested but with the gun against his nose he managed again.

"And yet again, Gringo, or I shoot you dead."

With sweat running down his brow the Yank managed a final effort and fell exhausted.

"Good," said the Mexican, "now you can give my sister a ride to the next village."

*   *   *

"ACCORDING to the latest survey," said the sex therapist to the reporter, "only half the population sing in the shower. The other half masturbate. And do you know what the singers sing?"

"No," said the reporter.

"No, I didn't think you did."

*   *   *

THE single girl told her psychiatrist: "I sometimes have 20 or so consecutive orgasms during my clitoris stimulation sessions."

"That's amazing," said the normally unflappable shrink.

"Oh, I don't know," shrugged the woman, "after 16 or so I run out of fantasies and from then on it's not much fun."

WARDROBES

THE husband came home to find his wife in bed. Then he opened the wardrobe door to discover a naked woman.

"Well," he said to the stranger in the wardrobe, "fancy finding a nice girl like you in the old proverbial situation like this?"

*   *   *

THE car was heard to stop in the driveway. "Jeez, that's my husband," she said. Her lover grabbed a gun from his coat and jumped into the wardrobe.

The husband came in, saw his wife in bed and yelled: "I know there is a man in here. Just wait till I find him."

He looked out on the window ledge. "He's not here," he said.

He looked under the bed. "He's not here," he said.

He looked in the wardrobe where he saw the lover with the gun. "And he's not here either."

*   *   *

A BUSINESSMAN arrived home unexpectedly in the afternoon to find his wife in bed and the milkman standing naked in the middle of the room.

"I'm glad you arrived Mr Sullivan," said the milkman, squatting down on his haunches. "I was just explaining to your wife that if the milk bill is not paid immediately I am going to shit on this carpet!"

*   *   *

THE back door slammed. "Hell, it's my husband," she cried, "quick, hide in that wardrobe."

He gathered up his clothes and dived from the bed to the wardrobe in a flash. After a few moments another voice in the wardrobe said: "It's bloody dark in here isn't it?"

The man, shivering in the nude, was shocked. "Who is it?" he whispered. It was a little boy's voice and it said: "I know who you are and it will cost you. Promise to give me $50 and I won't yell for my dad."

He was in no position to argue, he grudgingly paid up, and when the crisis was over made a quick exit from the bedroom window.

Next day the little boy and his mother were down town and he said he was going to buy a brand new skateboad. "What with?" asked his mother.

"I've got $50" said the boy.

"Where did you get that kind of money?" asked his mother, but the lad refused to tell.

"You must have done something wrong," she persisted

386

and after slapping him about shoved him into the nearby church.

"Confession is the thing for you, my lad. If you won't tell me, then you will have to tell the parish priest," and she shoved him into the confessional box and shut the door.

"It's bloody dark in here," said the boy.

"Now don't you start that again," said the priest.

WEATHER

COLD as the depths of a polar bear's pool,
Cold as the tip of an Icelander's tool.

*   *   *

IT was so cold that Old Jake woke to find two ice cubes in his sleeping bag. When he threw them on the fire they went "Fartzzz!"

*   *   *

FATHER Murphy was sent to a small Eskimo village in the northern wastes of Alaska. After a year the bishop paid him a visit.

"How do you stand the weather, my son?" asked the bishop.

"Oh I don't care how cold it gets," said Father Murphy, "I have my Rosary and my vodka."

"That's good," said the bishop. "Come to mention it, I wouldn't mind a vodka right now."

"No problem," said the priest. "Hey Rosary, bring two vodkas, pronto."

*   *   *

IT was so cold in London last week that the local flasher on the Thames Embankment was spotted describing himself to a group of women.

*   *   *

IT was so cold it would freeze the walls off a bark humpy.

*   *   *

IT was dry as a Pommie's towel.

WHEN Mrs Lottsabazooma got caught in the rain after buying a brand new hat for the Easter Parade she hoisted her dress up over her hat and dashed for cover.

It brought a comment from a taxi driver: "Hey Missus," he said. "Your arse is sticking out in the rain."

"Don't I know it," said our heroine. "But that arse is 45 years old and this hat is brand new."

* * *

THE wind blew so hard...

it blew three dogs off their chains...

a chook facing east laid the same egg three times...

it blew the pricks off a barbed wire fence.

WEDDINGS

THE priest was partial to the whisky bottle and when the young couple stood before the altar to be married the bride noticed he was slurring the wrong words.

"Father," she said, "you are reading the burial service."

"Doesn't matter," he whispered back, "you'll be under the sod tonight either way."

* * *

THE couple at the altar had almost the same thought.

He: "All I have to do is say 'I do' and I can have sex whenever I want."

She: "All I have to do is say 'I do' and I never have to have sex again."

* * *

IT was a typical Outback wedding and the celebrations had been raging for two days before Ned finally arrived at the shearing shed with his present. It was there he encountered his mate Joe leaving the party.

"Don't go in," warned Joe. "There's bound to be strife. They've run out of beer and the best man has just rooted the bride."

Indeed that meant trouble and Ned turned back towards

his car. They were about to leave when another guest came out of the hall and shouted: "Don't go you blokes. No problems. There's another keg on the way and the best man has apologised."

*   *   *

THERE was a little man
  And he had a little gun
  And his bullets were made of lead
  He stood close by
  With a fatherly eye
  While me and my girl were wed.

WELSH

WHY are the Welsh always singing?
  Because they don't have doors on their dunnies.

WIDOWS

THE pretty widow went into the hardware shop. She wanted a hinge for her back door. She selected one and asked if it would do the job.

"You will need a screw," said the shopkeeper.

"You men are all the same," she replied, "but I'll give you a blow job for that toaster on the top shelf."

*   *   *

PRETTY Widow Winkle had been in hospital three days before the vicar learned that his favourite parishioner was ill.

"But I prayed for you last night," he said as he paid his first visit.

"Silly man," she pouted. "You know I'm on the phone."

*   *   *

THE lawyer informed the widow: "I'm sorry to tell you, but Fred left all he had to the Twilight Home for Destitute Women."

389

"But what about me?"

"You're all he had."

* * *

SID Skinflint had been as mean as a junk yard dog all his life, and had been particularly stingy to his wife. So it was with some surprise to mortuary officials when she insisted on taking his ashes home in a box.

Back at the house she placed the box on the table and began walking around the room talking aloud.

"Sid, you know the red sports car I always wanted and you would never give me? Well, there it is in the driveway."

"And Sid," she said. "You know the diamond rings I always wanted and you would never buy me? Well, here they are, all from your insurance," and she displayed some dazzlers on three fingers.

"And here are the pearls I've always wanted."

"And Sid. You know that blow job you always wanted? Well, here it is," and with that she blew his ashes to buggery.

WOMEN

WOMEN have only themselves to blame for all the lying men do.

They ask so many damned questions.

* * *

THERE is hardly a woman in this country who hasn't been asked to marry at least twice.

Once by her mother and once by her father.

* * *

A WISE woman is one who makes her husband feel as if he is master of the house, when in reality he is only chairman of the entertainment committee.

* * *

HE was a bit old to be chasing young girls so one of the neighbours alerted his wife to his disgusting habit.

"It doesn't worry me," said the wife. "He can chase girls

if he wants to. After all, dogs chase cars. I've never seen a dog catch one and I doubt if they could drive one if they did."

WOMEN'S TALK

"HOW was your blind date?" asked one girl of her flatmate.

"Boring," she replied. "He was so boring I finally agreed to sit on his face just to stop him from talking."

* * *

"WHEN I met him in the singles bar I told him I was Libra on the cusp of Scorpio. He replied that he was Taurus with penis rising."

* * *

"GOING out with Trevor is like playing draughts," she said, "I make one move and he jumps me."

* * *

"FIRST I faked chastity," she said, "then I faked orgasm. And now I fake fidelity."

* * *

"I'LL never forget the night my husband discovered my great love," she said.

"What happened?"

"He beat the shit out of him."

* * *

"WHY did you divorce that big strong bikie?"

"Beats me."

* * *

"WHAT do women desire most in a man?" she asked, "brains, wealth or appearance?"

"Appearance," was the quick reply, "and the sooner the better."

* * *

"DID you sleep with my husband last night?"

"Not a wink."

"IT was a wonderful night. I had three orgasms," she said.
"Oh, I had 50," said her friend.
"He must have been a marvellous lover,"
"Oh, you mean with just one bloke!"

* * *

"MY boyfriend has just graduated as a doctor. So he is going to practice for a few years before we get married."

* * *

"DID Noreen discover the cause of those green marks on the inside of her thighs?"
"Yes. It appears her boyfriend's earrings are not gold after all."

* * *

"WHEN my sugar daddy dies I inherit the lot. It is in his last will and testicles."
"You mean testament."
"No. I've got him by the balls."

WORDS

CUNNILINGUS is a real tongue twister.

* * *

WHAT a lot of cunning linguists you are.

* * *

'CONTAGIOUS was the word the students had to use in a sentence and little Johnny's hand was up like a rocket.
"My dad doesn't like the fruiterer next door so when he knocked over his case of oranges he said it would take that con-tages to pick them all up."

* * *

"DO you know the difference between a popular girl and an unpopular girl?"
"Yes and no."

* * *

A GIRL from the country called at the hospital.
"I'd like to see an out-turn, please," she said.

"You mean an intern?" said the nurse.

"Whatever you call him, I want a contamination," she insisted.

"You mean an examination," said the nurse.

"Yes, I need to see the fraternity ward."

"You mean the maternity ward."

"Call it what you will," said the girl with annoyance. "But I certainly know I haven't demonstrated for two months and I think I'm stagnant."

* * *

THE professor was teaching an African tribe English and took the chief through the jungle pointing out various objects and relating their names, like 'Tree, monkey, bush, river.

They came across a nude couple screwing away on the river bank.

"What's dat?" said the chief.

The embarrassed professor said, "Bike."

The chief stabbed his spear into the rider's arse.

"Why did you do that?" said the professor.

"My bike," said the chief.

* * *

WHEN it came to writing up the log book Captain Squiggs was a stickler for accuracy, so when the first mate received news that he was the father of twins and celebrated in his cabin the captain noted in the logbook: 'The first mate was drunk last night.

When the mate saw it he argued that it should be struck from the record but the pedantic captain was resolute. "You were drunk last night. I can't change that fact, so it must stay in the log."

Next day the mate was on watch and it was his duty to keep the log.

In the morning the captain was aghast to read: "The captain was sober last night."

WORDS were the big topic of the million dollar television quiz show where Professor Geewhizz challenged the audience to stump him with a word he couldn't put into a sentence.

"Garn!" shouted a bloke in the third row.

"Garn?" said the professor, "Garn? It's not a swear word is it?"

"No," said the punter in the third row, "Garn."

Time elapsed, the buzzer went and the crowd applauded.

"You've stumped him," said the MC, "How do you use the word, sir?"

"Garn get fucked," said the punter and the show was closed immediately.

It took the network 12 months to get over it. Finally they had the gumption to start it up again with the proviso that they would have to screen the audience in future.

On the opening night they scrutinised each member of the audience as they arrived before asking for the first word.

A man in the third row wearing a vicar's collar and a beard put his hand up. "Smee," he said.

"Smee?" said the professor, "Smee?" The seconds ticked away and he was forced to concede on the very first word.

After the applause had died down the MC asked the punter: "How do you use the word?"

The punter stood up, pulled his false beard off and said: "Smee again. Garn get fucked!"

Z

ZOOS

A KID at the monkey enclosure said: "Hey, Mum. How long does it take to make a baby monkey?"

"About six months," she said.

"Then why are those two in such a hurry?"

* * *

CLEANING out the aviary at a run-down zoo the keeper finds two finches have dropped dead from old age.

In the monkey cage he discovers two of the oldest chimps have also kicked the bucket.

Waste not want not so he puts them in a sack with the finches and later tips them in the lion's cage at feeding time.

"Bloody hell," roars the lion. "Not finch and chimps again."

* * *

TWO zebras were debating. Were they white with black stripes or black with white stripes? The argument went on for hours until they decided to ask the wise old lion.

"Go to the mountain and ask God," said Leo.

The zebras climbed the mountain and after bellowing out the question: "Are we black with white stripes or white with black stripes?" there was a bolt of lightning and a voice roared: "You are what you are!"

The puzzled zebras went back to the lion. "What does it mean?" they asked.

"It means that you are white with black stripes," said the lion immediately, "otherwise He would have said: "Yo is wot yo is!"

* * *

THE city zoo has been showing sex films to a male and female chimpanzee in the hope that it will prompt them to breed. So far it hasn't worked, but the zookeeper and his wife close the zoo early every day.

ZENITH

ZENITH, meaning the highest point, is a ploy to have the author's favourite joke last, The Sex-Crazed Crane Driver:

* * *

CONSTRUCTION of the 50-level city tower was behind schedule and pressure was being applied to finish it on time. Gardeners were moved in to start the landscaping at ground level while carpenters were fitting out at mid-level and the crane was still lifting on the top floor.

One day the crane driver's apprentice drew his boss's attention to the absence of a dunny on the roof and that he was busting for a leak.

Conceding the lack of a loo the crane driver said there would be no problem if the lad hopped into the crane's bucket while he swung it high over the city.

"Look, Son, it's so high that it will disintigrate into fine spray long before it hits the ground. No worries."

So the lad did just that.

By the time the crane driver retrieved the bucket and the lad climbed out the boss himself was strongly inclined to take a leak.

"Well hop in the bucket. I can drive it," said the eager apprentice.

The boss was unsure, but bladder pressure was building.

"Okay," he said with crossed legs. "The green button is for easing the bucket out, the yellow button brings it back.

But whatever you do, don't touch that red button. It opens the bottom of the bucket."

"No worries, boss," said our eager lad.

While the apprentice swung the crane over Collins St with its precious cargo and the boss began to enjoy a well-earned leak a blonde in a mini-skirt swanked by the gardeners on the ground level who gave her an appreciative whistle.

The carpenters way up on the middle level heard it and looked down. They gave her a whistle too.

The crane driver's apprentice on the roof heard it and he leaned over for a look ... and put his elbow fair and square on the red button.

It was only a matter of seconds later when one of the carpenters on the mid level said to his mate: "Those crane drivers are sex crazed."

"What makes you say that?" enquired his mate.

"Well, did you see that blonde walk past down in the street?"

"Yes,"

"Well I just saw one of the crane drivers streak past with his cock in his hand screaming "C

                   u
                    n
                     t!

*   *   *

                   C
                   u
                    n
                     t!"